Praise for *The Abundant Life*

"Aaron Jacobs makes a strong, gimlet-eyed debut with this tale of guns and religion — American culture's two eternal verities — and one cynical young man's improbable attempt to save his family and his own soul through the power of salesmanship."
- Jonathan Dee, author of *The Locals* and Pulitzer-nominated *The Privileges*

"A funny, madcap story that somehow doesn't defy reality."
- Washington Independent Review of Books

". . . uniquely done and definitely reminds me of one of those classic must-reads."
- Manhattan Book Review

". . . an entertaining and edgy rebirth story spun by an unflinchingly honest narrator. Aaron Jacobs has written a novel that is compulsively readable and filled with whip-smart social commentary that is often laugh-out-loud funny. This is one firecracker of a debut."
- Julia Fierro, author of *The Gypsy Moth Summer* and *Cutting Teeth*

"With its delightfully unique, hilarious, and, many times, infuriating characters, *The Abundant Life* introduces us to the Wolf family and we are better for it. I swear my mouth puckered from Jacobs' acerbic wit, just the way I like it."
- Samantha Bee, host of *Full Frontal with Samantha Bee*

". . . a stunning literary debut that will have you laughing from the first page to the last. With an inventive yet utterly believable plot, memorable characters, and sharply crafted sentences, *The Abundant Life* will leave you racing to the end and pleading for more."
- Shulem Deen, author of award-winning *All Who Go Do Not Return*

"It is Salinger-esque in spirit and execution. And you can quote me. Oh, you just did? Well, great then."
- Jason Jones, actor/writer, *The Detour* and *The Daily Show With Jon Stewart*

The

Life

A Novel

Aaron Jacobs

Copyright © Aaron Jacobs, 2018

All rights reserved. No part of this publication may be reproduced, distributed, or transmitted in any form or by any means, including photocopying, recording, or other electronic or mechanical methods, without the prior written permission of the publisher, except in the case of brief quotations embodied in critical reviews and certain other noncommercial uses permitted by copyright law.

Author photo by Shannon Aubourg

ISBN: 978-0-9978256-9-5
Run Amok Books, 2018
First Edition

Printed in the U.S.A.

The Abundant Life

For Katie

From *White Boy Bandito: How a Clever Suburbanite Became Death's Middleman for South American Revolutionaries*, by Dr. Laura Sullivan, PhD. (Verdict Press: 2006, 199-200)

If you were to look up the definition of the word "judge" in Webster's Dictionary, you wouldn't be surprised to see a photograph of United States District Judge Randall Espinoza, and rightfully so. At the age of fifty-three, Espinoza, the "Solomon of the Tenth District," as he was known for his impeccable record of wise rulings, exuded the utmost respect for the law. The bags under his eyes and the stoop in his shoulders told the tale of how mightily this case had weighed upon him. He knew he had a job to do. Justice had to be served and he was her servant.

He brought the court to order with a fiery *Bang!* of his gavel. "Please be seated," he uttered his words, chosen with great care. "Today is sentencing. United States versus Wolf."

This was the moment Alexander Wolf had been waiting for. And dreading. He was about to learn his fate.

Espinoza instructed Alexander to stand. Alexander kept a cool face getting to his feet. Or tried to. He might have been dressed to the nines, but the metal shackles on his wrists and ankles clashed hard with his natty suit. The air in the courtroom was as stuffy as an overheated library, but the mood was electric. The gallery was filled to capacity with journalists, court reporters, sketch artists, law students, and spectators who had devoured every juicy detail in The Case of The White Boy Bandito as if it was the most delicious T-bone steak in the world.

The judge peered over his glasses at the defendant. "Before we get to your sentence I want to say, on a personal note, I know in my heart of hearts that you are guilty of things I cannot prove, things that we don't have laws for. If it were up to me, I would devise a punishment that was truly fitting. I find your crimes, your demeanor, indeed your very character, heinous and cowardly, and made further repellant when the court considers the way you, Mr. Wolf, took advantage of an obviously sick man. Have you anything to say?"

The entire courtroom waited on pins and needles. The hair

on the backs of their necks stood straight up. It was so quiet that when an old man in the back of the gallery coughed, it sounded like a gunshot.

"I guess you could say I took a wrong turn somewhere, somewhere I went the wrong way. I promise to do better in the future," apologized a contrite Mr. Wolf.

"I doubt that very much," countered the judge. "Unlike you, I've dedicated my life to following the laws of our great nation and I must do what is in the best interest of the people of this district. Alexander Wolf you are hereby sentenced to a term of no less than thirty-six but no more than fifty-four months at the federal correctional institution at Otisville."

ONE

All of what follows coincides with my release from Club Fed (to use a ridiculous misnomer) and my thirtieth birthday, in late March, 2008. The events leading up to this point were the subject of a book and a television movie. Not like that should be news to anyone. Thanks to my dickhead luck, my story of exporting the Second Amendment captured the zeitgeist, as they say, and for a minute or two, this book and the movie it spawned were popular in the way lurid pieces of cultural garbage are apt to be. And while I just can't help myself from discrediting these so-called studies and analyses of my life, I'm not going to get obsessed about it. It's important I give my family a respectful showing. I've done enough to them already.

It wasn't even my plan to drag them into this. They're decent people, not without their own failings, and will probably recoil from the notoriety, just as they have any time a spotlight aimed at me went wide of its mark to shine on them. But how do I erase them from a story that's about all of us, about how we were punch-drunk from our troubles and waiting for a breeze strong enough to put us on our asses for good? If my incarceration alone was responsible, I could have done the honorable thing and played scapegoat, but for that to have happened we needed to be blind to my father's gambling, my mother's meliorism, and my sister's greed. Our business flopped, our house crumbled and, like the idiots we were, we refused to admit our problems outmatched our ability to withstand them. Worse, we loved each other. Even that we got wrong. So I was thankful that not long after my release, Jesus Christ saved us. It was a practical and, more importantly, *American* salvation. It freed us from the stickiness of our life together. Except this isn't a story of evangelical yokels or the fevered ramblings of a moral reprobate born again. The fact of the matter is, we weren't even Christians. We were Jews.

To be fair, we were slack Jews—violating the Sabbath, never visiting Israel, covering our heads only when cold. Excluding a taste for Yiddish phrases and pickled herring, the Old World vestiges were barely visible on even my grandparents, who scratched out admirably unexceptional lives in Bronx apartments often redolent of said herring. By the time my parents came of age, all but a few traditions had dissipated like so much of the shitty pot smoke they called their liberal arts education. Suppose we attended temple once a year, I suspect we ate pepperoni on our pizza a dozen times more. Somewhere along the way, my forebears must have been believers, pious guys and gals with a mystical bent no doubt, but over time and continents our faith took on the markers of a loose social identity. Even the scar tissue on my penis pointed not to descendants of Abraham but to a group of people who found the idea of discussing Republican politics over gimlets to be as unsuitable as hunting bears with a paring knife. For that matter, hunting anything with anything.

At any rate, my release, scheduled for midnight, March 22, pushed past two in the morning. I took it in stride. I was used to waiting. Which isn't to say I liked it. I just didn't take it personally. There were people who made decisions and people who had decisions made for them. The border was more porous than I imagined and, having passed through it thirty-nine months earlier, I'd had time to adjust. My endurance had grown into a massive and intricate sandcastle, the kind that wins ribbons on Independence Day. But my mother, father, and sister had driven from their home about sixty miles away and waited for my processing with their patience a sagging and crumbling mess, a July fifth sandcastle.

All because of me. Even Rachel—who, due to our age difference and my limitations, considered me somewhat of a curio and not always a brother—seemed uncharacteristically charitable. They weren't this proud of me at my graduation from college (where I posted a solid, if not quite laudable, 2.8 in every aspect of my life) and this pride, I believe, stemmed from the idea that in many ways I was closer to them than at any other time. I saw them at regular intervals throughout my stay in FCI Otisville, and I received weekly written correspondence from at least one of them, a letter or a card; so that I must now admit that my level of communication with my family was at its all-time highest when I was upstate, doubtless because they knew my whereabouts every moment, a statement they couldn't make during my mid-twenties.

Now they had me to themselves, without bending to the strictures of the visiting room, and could hold me like a real human being, where before we kowtowed to cretinous correctional officers, guards. If I didn't match their enthusiasm it was because I was uneasy about what awaited me on the other side of all those fences topped with endless coils of razor wire. Yes, I was glad to be out, grateful I had somewhere to go, but in the run-up to my scheduled release it became pretty clear to me that I had no agenda: no money, no job, no woman, no friends. The lone bullet point on my customized reentry program was that I was to rely on folks I hadn't lived with since I was a high school senior. The anticipation of taking my first steps as a free man had another component to it. What if I wasn't skipping into the embrace of entirely generous arms, and my arrival, however much desired, would be added weight to an already knee-buckling load?

As the three of them advanced in my direction, my mother hustled ahead, declaring, "Me first," violently throwing her arms around my neck, her body humming against mine. She pulled me down six or eight inches until our foreheads met. It was then I caught her smell and in its familiarity I found the polar opposite of the smell of prison. My father and sister closed in around me.

"Alex, come here," my father said, his hand palming the back of my head. He wrapped his other arm around me, crushing my mother, who gasped, "I can't breathe." Rachel, careful to avoid getting smothered herself, laid a gentle hand on my shoulder. We stayed there a minute outside the Administration Building while the sprawl of the institution swelled around us. Maybe I was the only one who noticed it. I didn't want to be touched anymore.

I stepped back, hands in my pockets, and said, "Where's the car, old man?" I'm not sure what their laughter meant. I had been calling my father "old man" since he was the age I was now and maybe they welcomed the idea that some things hadn't changed.

Heading to the parking lot, I said, "Are there a lot of people out there?"

"Who else are you expecting?" my father said.

"Media? Well wishers?"

This time I knew what their laughter meant. As far as they were concerned, I'd outlived my shelf life as a morbid novelty. How could they know—I definitely didn't—that I would soon renew my membership in the cultural oddities guild?

At breakfast the next morning, the hoopla of the previous night had given way to the reality of our new living arrangement. Rachel sat across from me at the old oak dining room table, her hair snatched back into a ponytail, wearing a pink tank top adorned with a graphic of her high school's mascot, a lion. My father stood over me, refilling my juice glass (I was eye level with his belly softness), and my mother was in the kitchen. The afterglow of my homecoming had not yet worn off, but from what I remembered growing up, we didn't eat breakfast together often, so the meal itself concocted a set of unintended tensions. While I enjoyed the spread my parents were cooking up, I couldn't help but notice the way Rachel sulked over her eggs. This was, after all, a celebration for me, not her. Who the fuck was I to enter her domain anyway? My sister was an achiever, an honor student since she was practically a fetus, so she deserved attention—attention, evidently, she no longer sought but demanded. She had no way of knowing I wasn't there for any birthright; it was hers for the taking.

She buttered a piece of toast for an inordinately long time, reducing the whole world to that meditative act.

"How did it feel to sleep in your old room?" my father said.

I won't go into what it was like that first night except to say I couldn't fall asleep until I double-checked that the door was locked. Besides, it wasn't my room anymore. They redecorated it a den years ago. Though mine to reclaim, the Patrick Ewing poster was long gone, the hole I'd punched in the wall over some girl was patched, all four walls repainted, ceiling fan replaced; and, most crucial, the pint of Jim Beam, along with some low-rent pornography, last seen sharing space on a closet shelf, was MIA. Even my bed, from where I'd hatched my earliest plans of world domination, was nowhere to be found. I'd slept on the fold-out couch, twisted in the sheets, dreaming dreams of underwhelming prospects.

I wasn't up to it, but I dragged my ass downstairs that morning, needing a hot meal to get going. Now I gave my father the answer he deserved. "Really great. Thanks for having me."

"This is your home, too. Always. Judy," he called to my mother in the kitchen, "how're we doing on the coffee." And back to me, "How was the coffee in Otisville? Did you get coffee?"

"Oh my God, of course he did," sighed Rachel.

He jerked his head away from her, as though her voice was a bee.

"What kind of question is that anyway? You think Big Al wants to talk about it? You might as well ask him about the rapes."

"Not as good as the coffee," I answered.

"You've got to understand she's upset about something," he said.

"Way to state the obvious, old man," she said, the use of my nickname for him a sign she wasn't pleased with either of us. She returned to her toast but when her cell phone began buzzing, the butter knife hit the plate. She read the text, looked up from the phone at me, laughed, and then her slim thumbs, with their chipped polish, flitted over the buttons, returning the message. She dropped the phone to the table, picked up the toast, took a bite, and said, "Jelly's coming over, okay?"

"Your friends are always welcome," my dad said.

"You have a friend named Jelly?" I said.

"Jelly Belly, that's my girl. Her real name is Jill."

"Is she fat?"

"Hardly." She rolled her eyes. "She's like obsessed with you."

"How does she know me?"

"Not the *real* you. The you from the movie."

"I told all the neighbors not to watch it," my father said, orange juice container in one hand, grapefruit juice in the other.

"You mean the neighbors who were still talking to us?" Rachel said.

My mother joined us in the dining room. She looked tired through her smile.

"You all right?" I said.

"I'm fine." She smiled again. "I'm glad you're home."

She ate a little and I ate more and my father finally sat down. We all ate in peace and quiet. It was pleasant. Or would have been if I was just visiting, a successful son breaking from his hectic schedule for some brief, but much needed, domestic comfort. Only I wasn't just visiting, though there was little mystery how I ended up here. I'd had an idea for a while and now these scrambled eggs and potatoes and whole wheat toast and coffee and *two* types of juices confirmed my suspicions. I was on the cusp of my thirtieth birthday and living with my parents, not because the sky opened up the day I was born and emptied a karmic colostomy bag over the hospital nursery. The dice hadn't been loaded against me. In fact, one could make the argument that as a white man I belonged to the pantheon of dice loaders (though possibly a provisional member on account of my Semitic extraction). No, in my case, it was an attitude or manner I'd cultivated for much of my life. I was an arrogant prick. Maybe just cocky. Or some other phallic-inspired descriptor. This quirk (a cute way of saying defect) had fooled me into thinking that I was destined for great things, great accomplishments, that I was, in the absence of great things and accomplishments, simply great by myself. It convinced me to scoff at our governing laws because I was, you see, so lovely and thrilling a man that allowances would be made for me. Believe me, there are few lessons harder to take than the slow comprehension of your innate mediocrity.

The front door then burst wide, a girl's voice shrieking into the house, "Hey there, Wolf pack. I smell breakfast." The slap of flip-flops against bare feet echoed down the hall, and here came Jelly, her tits ushering her into the room. Her face was slightly too round, her nose too short; there was an indication she would one day grow heavy in the upper arms. In other words, she wasn't a classical beauty, but from one glance I knew she commanded an unwieldy amount of power over both the boys and girls her age. She was so close a descendant of the girls who held sway over me in my teens that, though separated by more than a dozen years, I had to gather myself when she got close to the table.

"'Sup, slut?" she said to Rachel.

"Nothing, you little hooker."

"I wish you girls wouldn't talk that way," my mother muttered. She turned in her chair to greet our guest. "Are you hungry, Jill?"

"Naw, but I smell coffee. I'd love some of that."

My mother stood but Jelly waved her back down. "I'll help myself."

As she disappeared into the kitchen, I sought relief in my hash browns from her loud, exceedingly comfortable presence.

My mother said, "She and Rachel are like sisters. Jelly practically lives here."

"Just like Raphael," I said, referring to an indigent day laborer my mother once let stay in our house for weeks on end.

"Not like Raphael," Rachel hissed.

Jelly returned with a mug and helped herself to the coffee pot. She sat next to Rachel and began trying not to look at me, but her eyes wandered up from the table. Eye contact in prison is an invitation to conflict. This little game she played put me on edge.

"Mom, Dad, breakfast was great. I'm going to take a shower," I said.

Before I could excuse myself, Jelly extended her hand across the table. "Thanks, Rach, for introducing me. Your sister can be so rude."

I took her limp hand, the first touch of a female who didn't share my DNA in quite a while. I can't exaggerate the effect human contact, or lack thereof, has on a person. My body overreacted, my semi-erection turning overly confident. "Nice to meet you, Jelly."

"You know my name? That's cool. I know your name too. Can I just say I know all about you? *The Wrong Way Son*, what can I say? It's like the best thing that's ever been on TV."

"I wouldn't know."

"Really? I thought you were like a consultant or something."

I shook my head. She said, "Well, anyway, it's amazing. That scene, when you were in South America, you sell that one guy a gun. I was like, 'Don't do it! He killed your best friend.' But then it turns out the bullets are blanks or whatever and when he tries to rob that store the shopkeeper kills him with a bat." She spoke very fast and I didn't know what she was talking about.

"I've never sold a gun in my life," I said. "I've bought plenty, though."

My mother frowned.

"Or what about when you were in the helicopter and the cops are shooting at you and it's going to crash and you jump out, but it's like the jungle or rainforest or somewhere, and you land in this thing that's like an oasis," Jelly said.

"What about when that guy shot at me and I caught the bullet in my teeth?"

"Wait a sec, that didn't happen."

"Look at you, the brightest knife in the drawer. You're right, that didn't happen, but neither did anything else you said."

I was telling the truth. Regardless of what my biographer would like the world to believe, I was never some rogue smuggling weapons across foreign borders. It's not illegal to export a gun. The way I went about it was inventive (if you ask me) and would have made for a more interesting, if less fanciful, story than the one Laura dreamed up. I'll address that later. For now, let me state for the record that I was convicted of and served thirty-nine months for violating title 18, part 1, chapter 44, sections 922 (g) 3,4,5A of the US Code. Without resorting to a ton of legalese here, what this means is that I gave a firearm to someone our government decided shouldn't have one. To be a little more specific than that, I'll add that I was driving with this person beside me when a routine DWI roadblock in southern New Mexico put us, and a rental van full of .50 caliber rifles, in close proximity to state police.

Jelly said, "Come on, really? What about when you were in jail? You were with that lady doctor? The one who wrote the book? That's true, isn't it?"

"Wrong again," I said. This time I was lying. I was furious with Dr. Sullivan, but mostly with myself. The whole thing was a product of my arrogance, and Laura twisted me up, knowing I couldn't go anywhere—outsmarted me, really.

"You should sue them for plagiarism or something," Jelly said.

"Plagiarism is when you steal someone's words or ideas," Rachel said. "It doesn't apply here."

"Whatev, bitch."

"Okay, I hate to break away from this stimulating conversation, but I have to go to the office," my father said.

His announcement was news to me but fazed no one else.

"It's Saturday," I said.

"I go every day."

"Since when?" I said.

"Your dad's a serious breadwinner. Ain't that right, Mr. Wolf?" Jelly said.

"Thank you for the endorsement," he said.

Rachel drummed the tines of her fork against her plate and looked to my mother. I guessed she knew why he was working weekends and didn't like where the conversation was going. I delighted in her discomfort, for then I wasn't experiencing it alone. She grabbed her friend by the arm. "We're going to my room," she said.

Jelly took a last look at me. "Nice to meet you, Alex."

They scampered off upstairs. My parents brought me up to speed. While I don't blame them for hiding things from me when I was away, I was nevertheless shocked to learn that when my father said he was going to the office it was so, in the very likely event that his business folded, he could take solace knowing he'd done everything he could, as if effort had ever trumped luck.

"It's been a tough year," my mother said.

"So, now you know," he said.

What I didn't know, however, was how it happened. My gut told me he gambled Dynamic Business Solutions away, and inwardly I winced as if witnessing a car accident. Outwardly, I gave away nothing, a skill I learned not in prison or in my business dealings. Right here at the old oak dining room table I'd honed my capacity to sop up hostility and disappointment until it was buried within me, somewhere with the acid and bile.

I couldn't ask him what was happening. I wasn't unsympathetic but if I was right about the gambling, it meant humiliating my father, which is a shameful thing for a son of any age to see. "Anything else I should know?"

My mother answered: "Termites."

"What does that mean?"

"In the basement. If we're getting it all out there, you should know. This place could collapse at any minute." She was joking but also seemed resigned to its inevitability.

My father was standing opposite me now, holding his plate. "We've exterminated them, but there's damage."

"Right now we can't afford to fix it," she said.

"What are you going to do?" I asked because I didn't detect a sense of optimism in the way she said "right now," as if in the not too distant future they would have the money for repairs.

What could they do but live with it? Rachel was furious, they said. Ours was an uppity town, and she'd been spoiled vicariously.

"I just hope she understands your mom and I are doing our best, which is what we've always tried to do for you two," my father said.

I believed in his sincerity. But since I also believed his wagering on horse races had caused these problems, I hedged at throwing the weight of my support behind him. This made me feel like an asshole because he never hesitated a second to support me.

The fatigue in my mother's face was still there. The result of a bad night's sleep or wood-eating insects? Of an ungrateful daughter or an irresponsible husband? A convict son? Then I looked at the old man. He wasn't only my father but a man who dealt with the exigencies of life the best he could. That he never gave up might have suggested to some people he was a decent kind of guy. It also might have meant he was too stubborn to know when to pull the plug.

"I've got to go to work for a little bit. Will you be okay?" my mother said. Her going to Franklin Avenue Community Outreach on Saturday was no surprise. My father once offered to relocate their bedroom furniture to her cramped office so they would see each other more often.

"What should I do if the house falls down?"

"Dig."

November, 2004

"I say we go to trial. Tri-al! Tri-al!" I chanted.

Martin Skolnick, legal counsel par affordable, stubbed out a cigarette on the courthouse steps, in Las Cruces, New Mexico. He checked his watch. "Time to go in. Ready?"

"Their case is soft as camembert. Want to know what we're going to do? The golden boy—me—and his furry hedgehog of an attorney— you—are going to serve up that government cheese with some toast points and grapes and an icy pitcher of martinis."

Skolnick glanced up at the entrance. "I think your parents are already inside."

"Focus."

"You've accepted Woods' deal."

"I let her rattle me and that was a mistake. It's not too late. We can dickslap the entire U-S-of-A. I know we can. They have no case. I'm telling the truth about the hunting club."

"Woods is a smart lawyer. That's kind of how you become an assistant U.S. attorney. But even if she was a bad lawyer, she'd still see the absurdity of big game hunting in the mountains of South America."

"Absurd how?"

"Because you don't need a .50 caliber rifle to hunt fucking alpacas and llamas and shit."

"Last time I checked, absurdity has never been illegal. Thank you, Founding Fathers! I bought the guns legally, paid for them with money earned through no criminal enterprise."

Skolnick checked his watch again and decided there was time for another smoke. "They have a witness," he said, shaking out a match.

"I know you don't mean Ernesto. Dude's a paranoid-schizophrenic who smokes a ton of weed to help quiet the voices in his head urging him to hurt himself. If you can't discredit him, what am

I paying you for?"

"Yes, he's a pothead. That's bad news for you. You gave a gun to a drug addict."

"I gave him nothing. He just happened to be with me when I got pulled over. It should've been Ron with me."

"And where's Ron?"

"Not cool."

"I'm just reminding you that you're lucky you didn't disappear with him. Besides, Woods has a sworn deposition from Ernesto saying you promised him one of the guns, that it was a gift for being a 'very, very good boy,' or however that dummy phrased it. Plus he was here on an expired visa and just got off the psych ward."

"Unbelievable," I said.

"Let's go inside."

"Fuck that. Let's fight."

"Woods can make things so ugly for you and your family."

"I need a fighter and I'm stuck with a pussy looking for easy billable hours."

He fired twin jets of smoke out of his nose. It looked like he was smoothing the fabric of my suit jacket but he was really holding me by the shoulders. "You outfitted a guerilla army. Who do you think you're bullshitting?"

"I was helping a friend," I said, but stopped short of saying that I didn't have a lot of friends.

"I know you're nervous, but it will be fine."

"Martin, I don't want to go to jail." What could have been a more natural feeling? And yet it was the first time I admitted it. I wasn't cut out for prison and I was scared, scared I'd be killed, scared I'd be tormented, scared I'd be broken down psychologically and stripped of the posturing that protected me, scared that once my genuine self was on display everyone would see me as I was beginning to see myself, and that wasn't a guy I wanted to hang out with. I couldn't say that though, even at this late hour, not to Skolnick or anyone, couldn't admit how afraid I was standing outside the courthouse. The best I could do was say I didn't *want* to go, as if it didn't suit my preference.

"The deal's in place. You'll get to serve your sentence close to home. Let's go inside and take it."

So I, Alexander Wolf, pleaded guilty to "knowingly transferring a firearm to a person/persons who is the unlawful user or addict of a controlled substance, a person/persons who has been adjudicated as a mental defective or who has been committed to a mental institution, and a person/persons who, being an alien is illegally or unlawfully in the United States." Imagine my luck. I hit the trifecta with Ernesto. I got thirty-six to forty-eight months, medium security.

My parents and Rachel sat in the first row of the gallery. Judge Espinoza closed the courtroom to the media. It was no favor to me, he hated the attention, but I was thankful all the same.

Afterwards, as I shook Skolnick's hand, he assured me I'd be fine. Yes, prison was nasty, but I could handle it. Worst case scenario, I'd be out in four years, leaving me plenty of time for a good life. The crisis was over, he said. He might be right, I thought. I sat down again and even started feeling relieved. Maybe it was all over. Then I turned around and saw my family. It wasn't the first time in my life I'd made them cry, but it was the first time their tears felt commensurate to the moment. It made me want to ask Skolnick what he had asked me: Who do you think you're bullshitting? The crisis wasn't over. Some things that happen, people don't get over. They change and move on, but they aren't the same.

TWO

A few afternoons later, acclimating myself to independent life, I was in the laundry room—the area in the finished basement across the hall from the pantry—waiting for the rinse cycle, and studying the termite damage. I saw it in the exposed ceiling joists and the sill plate of the high window. The wood looked burned in places, gray and flaking and falling apart, the dried mud tubes like miniature versions of coral sold at souvenir shops in beach towns. What was behind the drywall, I wondered, studs reduced to powder? How long had it taken? Months? Years? How many meals had they feasted upon? How long was it before anyone had noticed? That was a better question. Had my parents known early on and watched it get worse, perversely enjoying the bugs' steadfastness? I understood why Rachel was upset that they were living with it, coping. Surrendering was more like it.

The strain of our first breakfast hadn't exactly resolved itself. I would have liked to pretend we placed it under a moratorium but there they were, outside the door.

"The credit card was for emergencies. That was the deal," said my mother. "And I think I've been pretty lenient when it comes to the definition of emergency. Shopping with your rich little friends isn't an emergency. We can't aff—"

"So what if they're rich? That's a reason to be proud. Why should they be ashamed? Their parents aren't broke."

"Don't throw your friends in my face. Especially now. Your father has killed himself so you could be pampered to a disgraceful degree. You should come to where I work for a day."

"Oh my God," Rachel said, "nobody cares about the bums you're in love with. That's going to be us soon. We're going to be the hobos."

"I'll just cancel the card. How's that for embarrassing?"

"I can't talk to you. You have no idea what it's like in this town."

I tried not to get caught up in their turmoil. The best way I could help them was to crawl out of their hair as fast as possible. I had my own worries, like the fact my mother was still shopping for me. She'd bought me a few shirts, a bunch of underwear and socks, a couple of pairs of jeans. True, what she picked out was nicer than the uniform of matching tan pants and shirts I was used to, but the arrangement had the feel of standard issue. How independent was I if mommy was dressing me? On top of that, nothing but the socks fit. I'd come out twelve pounds lighter than I went in.

I sat on the dryer reading a magazine I'd snatched from a bundle of recycling, wavy from previous dampness. *Our County*, distributed by the local Chamber of Commerce, profiled Warren Holden, a prominent, wildly thriving, non-denominational reverend who lived in the area. The photo that ran beside the article presented a sharp and angular face, an upper lip razor thin, hair black as squid ink, and eyes that matched his hair, thin slivers of obsidian. His smile was gigantic, like the guy who could fit three billiard balls in his mouth, and his teeth were abnormally white. He dressed like an obscenely rich real estate developer for whom no amount of money could shake off an unsophisticated, rural upbringing.

The gospel according to Holden went something like this: God wants us to be filthy rich. In the article, he repeatedly said that faith is big business, the next economic boom. Maybe he was right. Religion was hope in a bottle.

"What are you reading?"

I looked up and saw my mother standing in the doorway. I showed her the magazine.

"Who's that? The boy preacher?"

"This guy is in his forties."

"Now he is but when he was barely out of diapers he was the boy preacher."

"It doesn't say that in the article."

"He officiated weddings when he was four or five. I remember hearing about him when I was in high school. His parents took him all over the country healing the sick. Or pretending to. It was a scandal for a while."

I slapped the magazine on my thigh. "Well, he's loaded now."

"That's no surprise. He's a charlatan." She stepped a few feet into the room. "Alex, I've got a proposition."

"Lay it on me."

"How's your Spanish? Still passable?"

"*Más o menos.*"

"Wonderful. I could use you at the soup kitchen."

"Did you hear Doctors Without Borders was soliciting donations and they called a billionaire hedge fund manager? The volunteer said, 'Our records indicate that last year you didn't give to one charity.' The guy said, 'Well, do your records indicate that my mother is dying of cancer and her treatment costs more than she could ever pay? Or that my brother is a disabled veteran, confined to a wheelchair, and can't support his wife and six kids? Or that my brother-in-law was run over by a motorcycle, leaving my sister unable to pay her mortgage?' The volunteer was stricken. She said, 'I'm so sorry. I had no idea.' So the hedge fund guy said, 'And if I don't give any money to *them*, why would I give any to *you*?'"

My mother laughed in spite of herself. "You've always been able to say no without making the other person feel bad. It's charming, but it doesn't solve the problem of your unemployment."

She was a pragmatist, I'll give her that, but ladling out steaming, salty meals to the homeless was an unappealing thought. Truth was I had no truck with poor people. It was just that her work was grueling and when you divided the amount of good achieved by the amount of effort required, you always came up decimals. "It's not my style."

"What's not? Helping people?"

And there it was. Not a job she was offering but a chance to become a better person. If I said no? To her, it would be just one more rejection of her values, her '60s hippie beliefs. I couldn't even tell you what was left of her generation's ideals anyway. Organic foods? The ceaseless Rolling Stones world tour? It was time for the Baby Boomers to step off the stage.

I slid down from the dryer, turned my back on her, and checked the lint catcher.

"You need a job and this looks a hell of a lot better on a résumé than Death's Middleman," she said.

"Where do you come up with this shit?"

"That book. I cried in the store when I read it."
"I told you not to read it."
"Your face was on the cover."
"I never killed anyone."
"Cut it out. You sold guns."
"Bought."
"You contributed to large scale misery."
"Misery is the river of the world."
"Who said that, Nietzsche?"
"Tom Waits."

"Oh." She leaned against the wall. She sighed. "You're a young man. You have to do something positive to balance your life out. I don't feel very articulate right now, but I know you have decent things in you. I've seen it. Your father's seen it. That's why we never gave up on you."

The washing machine shuddered to a stop. A second later the basin began filling with water. "I've got to get this," I said, reaching for the liquid fabric softener on the shelf.

I was unscrewing the bottle when she said, "Who's Glen Holtzclaw?"

"You wouldn't ask if you didn't know."

Glen was my probation officer and a personal reminder that my release from Otisville didn't sever my relationship with the Federal Board of Prisons. I was one of about eighty cases in his workload and, although he is a peripheral figure to this story, I will say he was very concerned about my employment. He was a big guy, balding, a born bureaucrat, which made him both boring and well-suited for his line of work. His job was to see that my transition into society went as smoothly as possible, and he owned the responsibility.

"He called before. He thinks it will be good for you. I happen to agree," my mother said.

"Do I have a choice?"

"Why start out on the wrong foot? He sounds like a tough guy, am I wrong?"

So it was settled. It seemed I hadn't yet hopped the border back to decision-maker status. "When do I start?"

"Glen said sooner was better than later."

I felt defeated and wanted my mother to leave me alone. I asked her a revolting question about Maria Chavez.

"Don't be a creep," she said. "She's married now, you know. Besides, she hasn't worked with me for years."

Maria worked at Franklin Avenue Community Outreach at the beginning. She was probably ten years older than me and, simply put, she ranked among the first entries in my mental Rolodex when I was a rookie masturbator. She was an object of lust at such a pivotal moment in my development that I'm still able to arouse myself thinking about the way the muscles in her arms tensed in a sleeveless dress as she dished out meals to the blighted underclass.

When I was nearly thirteen, compulsory charity was part of the pre-Bar Mitzvah program. The rite of passage itself had something to do with my father's amorphous sense of tradition. Not religious tradition, mind you, but Wolf family tradition, ordeals imposed upon us so that we could look back on them with deranged nostalgia one day, as opposed to the fondness of, say, a tradition of ski trips. As a Bar Mitzvah candidate, I was mandated to volunteer so many hours a week for so many weeks before the big day. Working with my mother was the last way I wanted to fulfill the requirement. I knew she'd give me crummy jobs to teach me humility when all I wanted was to answer phones in a clean office at the local nursing home. Then I saw Maria after school, when I was sitting in the back of my mother's car, in the Franklin Ave. Community parking lot. That was all it took. "Sign me up. Let's feed these poor fucks," I said, profanity an uncontrollable verbal tic I'd developed as my voice changed (a problem when a teacher called on me to give an answer. Example: "That dickhead Eli Whitney invented the cotton gin!")

It was partly because of Maria that I stayed on working there after my Bar Mitzvah. But I now also accept that it wasn't just this gorgeous woman compelling my service as a weak-willed do-gooder—yet the fantasy of escaping into the walk-in refrigerator where she relieved me of my virginity was distraction enough to have me ambling into traffic—it was also a time I grudgingly admired my mother. It might not have been the first time I saw it, but it was the first time I understood that she was a person who, when put under pressure, blossomed. Give her a half dozen schizo vets blurring the line between reality and Saigon because the kitchen was serving rice, on the same afternoon she found out the bakery raised the delivery price of bread, just after two office volunteers quit, and she appeared to grow six inches. No way could I have ever told her she made me proud, but I was impressed, in the same way Mike Tyson then impressed me: They both seemed capable of anything. I felt the simultaneous urge to come to her aid and to stay the hell out of her way lest she trample me underfoot.

Something else I remember from that time: how I resented these dregs for inspiring her in ways that her family, I especially, couldn't. I was the son she loved by the ties of heredity, as opposed to the selection of her passions. I wanted her to spend time with us, not *them*, because we needed her too. Maybe even more than how Maria Chavez's ass looked in jeans, my mother was why I continued helping.

Now, holding the door knob to the laundry room, she said, "If you see your father, tell him I have to stop back at work but I'll be home before dinner. You haven't seen him?"

"Haven't seen him," I said, and I whistled "First Call," the bugled melody played at the start of a horse race.

"Don't be a jerk," she said.

"I don't suppose that has anything to do with what's going on at Dynamic."

"It doesn't."

I couldn't really tell if she believed it, or if her defense of her husband was just so automatic, uttered so many times, it must have felt programmed.

"Why doesn't anyone say anything to him?"

"People have."

"And?"

"If you see someone with a harelip, do you remind him? A guy with no legs? As if there's a chance he forgot. Your father's a good man. He's not perfect. You of all people should be able to relate."

"I'm not judging."

"You are, and I get enough ungratefulness from your sister."

"Wouldn't it be easier if he didn't? That's all I'm saying."

"My life would be easier if he didn't, or if you didn't do what you did, or if the skin on my neck didn't hang like this. What's your point?"

"I guess I don't have one." Where had the firebrand from the soup kitchen gone? The mother of my youth would have single-handedly exterminated the termites and, if not reframed the whole basement herself on the weekends, at least overseen the contractor she hired, beating the poor son of a bitch over the head with blueprints. And if she couldn't have prevented the troubles at Dynamic, she would have jumped at the chance to call customers and creditors and suppliers and lawyers until it looked as if the phone was some kind of growth sprouting from the side of her head. She would have prodded my father until he fixed his business or started a new one, as he would have done anything to keep her off his back. She would have picked up the whole world and shook it until everything fell into place. In the laundry room, she looked worn down in a way that embarrassed me. She'd aged—that was it. She wasn't simply tired. She was old. I hadn't noticed until then.

"Okay, I'm off. You know, honey, I'm looking forward to working with you."

"Thanks."

"You're welcome." She turned and left the room.

January 2003

Pool maintenance wasn't a line of work I felt destined for, but I accepted the Morenos' job offer because I needed a job, because I didn't want to snub their son Ron, my best friend since first grade, because I was twenty-four and bored, having returned from a couple of aimless post-collegiate years in San Diego, where I worked on my tan with greater consistency than I earned a living, believing that the opportunity of a lifetime was ready to fall in my lap at any moment and unable to grasp why it didn't.

I never knew how much English Ron's parents really spoke

or understood. If I could figure out a fourth of what they said, it was as much luck as it was three years of high school Spanish I cheated my way through. This limited communication so that, in the beginning at least, my duties at Crystal Clear Pools consisted of uncomplicated and unimportant office work. But one Saturday a few months after I started the job, Ron took me with him to the Danbury Marriot for a service appointment. I knew nothing about cleaning pools. I only knew it was late January and what hotel had an outdoor pool open in this weather? A pointless question, said Ron, because we were there for the gun show.

"Why would you need me here for a gun show?" I said.

"Why would I need you here to clean a pool?"

We were walking through the lobby. "What's it like? A car show?" I said.

"It's exactly like a car show. Except with guns." He stopped before we paid for admission. "You're an American citizen."

"So are you maybe."

"Who hasn't purchased any firearms in the last ninety days, wiseass."

It was less flashy than a car show, no sexy spokesmodels cavorting around the merchandise. Because my upbringing was decidedly liberal (in the political sense), my parents had instilled in me a deep-seated distrust of firearms. This gave the moment a sense of illicitness. Which, in turn, gave me a thrill. The gun show was crowded with people and I didn't notice where the hell Ron had run off to. Alone, I inspected the goods. I shuffled around the vendors, affecting the nonchalance of a man wholly at home with deadly firepower. I saw guns that cost $200 and guns that looked identical but cost $1,200. I saw collectibles: Civil War era cannonballs, WWI helmets, bayonets, gas masks, canteens, old boots, turn-of-the-twentieth-century military manuals. After cutting a wide berth around a table hawking Nazi memorabilia, I found myself in front of a booth selling DVDs. The vendor was screening a disc in which hunters with high-powered rifles blew up small woodland creatures—now you see them now you don't, except for bits of fur and whatnot. I watched, practically hypnotized.

Vendor said, "If you like *Exploding Varmints I*, you'll love *Exploding Varmints II*."

Next he cued up *Cute Lawyer Tricks*, an informational disc about how scummy lawyers shake down law-abiding gun owners on trumped-up, gun-related, felonies.

"Watch this once and you'll never want to own a gun. It shows what happens when you shoot a guy in your house," he said.

"*When?*" I said.

"It's the civil trial that screws you. O.J., not guilty, then guilty in civil court."

"O.J. didn't use a gun."

And here came Ron, materializing out of the crowd. "There you are," he said and led me away from this oddly-stimulating jurisprudential give-and-take to another booth.

"Check it out." He said Crystal Clear Pools needed me to buy the one called Mac 11/9. Later, I learned this gun was derived from the Mac 11, a .380-caliber machine-pistol, semi-automatic (although there are conversion kits to make it fully automatic—now we're talking!), which itself was a sub-compact version of the Mac 10.

I didn't think Ron was fucking with me because his idea of humor was pulling down your shorts in front of a cute girl. Mind games were more my pace. So before I bought anything, I needed him to explain why a pool cleaning business wanted a gun that belonged in a video game.

"It's for my uncle," Ron said.

"Felix?"

"Another uncle. You don't know him. Enrique's in the army."

"I assume we're not talking about the U.S. army. Is your country even at war?"

"Aren't we always?"

"Better question: Is it legal?"

"You know how American military families send flak jackets to their kids serving in Afghanistan? This is the same thing. My uncle is in an army that's poorly funded because it's a poor country. I see your wheels turning as you try to think up a stupid joke."

It could have been for his uncle or it could have been for his pet goldfish. I was too caught up in the illicit feeling to care, the feeling more like a blessing because there was no flipside to the coin, no guilt to beat back. It was legal. A background check proved it (NICS, National Instant Criminal Background Check System): I had never been convicted of a felony, never hospitalized for psychological complaints. I bought the Mac 11/9 with Ron's money. His money, which effectively made it his problem. We left the Marriott less than an hour after we arrived. A celebration was in order. With the gun in the trunk, we went out and got blind stinking drunk.

Judge Espinoza stopped short of calling me morally bankrupt, preferring to see me as a profiteer, but had he been at work with us on Monday morning, when Ron's parents said, "*Estamos orgullosos de ti*," he might have taken a softer view. Was I that hungry for affirmation? I must have been because I started to suspect (parading around in my arrogance like it was a cape) that this was the beginning of the great life I'd always imagined.

From the screenplay to *The Wrong Way Son* (H.E.L.R. Prod., 2007)

```
INT. CAR - AFTERNOON.

RON and ALEX sit in the front seat of Ron's car
in a HOTEL PARKING LOT. Out the window snow
flurries drift from the leaden sky. The heater
is cranking, the windshield is fogged.

          ALEX
     Tell me why again.
          RON
     They won't stop until they've
     ground us down under their
     boots. We're dying and the rest
     of the world doesn't even give
     a crap!

          ALEX
     What the hell?!
```

                    RON
          I need you to have my back, Alley
          Cat. Don't bitch out.
                    ALEX
          You know me, I love a little
          trouble. What's the worst that
          could happen?
                    RON
          My man!
                    ALEX
          You freakin' owe me.
                    RON
          First round's on me, brother.

Ron opens the glove compartment and palms a wad of bills the size of a baseball, wrapped in rubber bands.

EXT. HOTEL PARKING LOT - CONTINUOUS

Ron and Alex stride toward the hotel conference room.

THREE

I decided to observe a little capitalism, which is an asshole way of saying I went with my father to his job. Knowing that my mother escaped into her work and that my father needed to escape from the wreck of his, I figured he might like the company.

My father's business was copy machines. He started at Dynamic Business Solutions as a salesman when I was a toddler. Dynamic, a third-party broker, represented all the major brands. They sold and leased copiers, fax machines, scanners, all-in-ones, computer networks, telephone systems, in addition to office furniture, to small and midsize businesses throughout the lower Hudson Valley, into northern New Jersey. His great skill lay in sales. He grew Dynamic and became a partner a decade later. When one of the two founding partners retired, he bought in more and eventually became the largest shareholder. The unexamined truth here is that a great salesman doesn't necessarily translate into a great executive officer, but with a staff of only seven, he did well enough to support us, to the point that we weren't dependent on my mother's insufficient salary.

Take note: I wasn't here on a fact-finding mission in a halfhearted attempt to restore Dynamic's solvency. I possessed neither the motivation nor wherewithal for that.

We came through the front door where a man slept in a waiting room chair. My father flipped the light switch and the man woke up.

"Did you enjoy the turn down service?" my father said.

"Christ, did I fall asleep?"

"Lenny, have you met my son?"

The man knuckled his eyes. He reached out a hand. It was stubbed and meaty, coarse-skinned, kind of like the rest of him.

"Howyadoin? Lenny Marino. No relation to Dan." Lenny had brought with him a Daily Racing Form. It was folded in half, on his lap.

"Do you work here?" I said.

"Not in a million years."

"How did you get in?"

He levered himself to his feet. "Your pop's got a real high tech security system." He slapped my father on the back with the Daily Racing Form. "Hope you don't mind, Bob. I didn't want to sit on the stoop like a vagrant. Jesus, this place is desolate. Look out! There goes a fucking tumbleweed."

They left the waiting room, my father snapping on ceiling lights as they went. Boxes, stacks of files, office supplies, and computer components were piled on desks, which was just as well because there were no employees around needing the space. I made presumptions about the nature of their friendship. The shame I felt when I heard about Dynamic's pending demise reappeared. It stood me straight up, as if someone bumped me.

Let's say we're talking about men addicted to women. Each has a type: blonde, Asian, tall, short, hairy, big tits, big ass, big feet, whatever—and that's their thing, that's what animates them. My father was animated by horses, not romantically, unless you considered betting on them romantic. Casinos weren't for him; sports betting was too vast an occupation for him to enjoy; cards required a ruthlessness toward one's fellow man that I believed he lacked. But horses, the ponies . . . My father was what I'd dubbed a "maintenance gambler." I didn't know if that was a diagnosable condition, but I'd heard about alcoholics who didn't go on reckless benders or get sloppy drunk but drank to achieve some normal state of being and then stayed there, not ever really sober and not ever really wasted. Likewise, the old man escaped at the race track, allowed it to consume his thoughts and time, was rooted in self-destruction, but perhaps with him there was a switch he could throw, a safety valve preventing total incineration. What I mean is he never lost the house or cars. None of my birthday presents was in hock a week later. In other words, he always, *always*, got his "nut," no easy trick, though I hesitate to use the gambler's parlance because he never would have said something like that. In fact, he rarely said anything about it. Gambling was his unspoken obsession. But that was my opinion. He might have felt differently.

Or not. Rachel and I were shielded growing up and perhaps I didn't know the full extent of his problem. Maybe there were more than a few very close calls. I imprecisely recalled an irate uncle ringing the doorbell and refusing to leave until my father met him in the driveway. Then there were nights I fell asleep to the not-so-tranquil sounds of a disagreement between my parents, muted by the walls, which grew so loud no walls could dampen them, and I was forced to hold a pillow over my head, squeezing my eyes closed as if the yelling was a bright light into which it hurt to look. There was also a brief encounter so elusive in my mind I couldn't swear it really happened. There was the possibility I saw it on television and claimed it as my own, or dreamt it because it was something I feared. A man stopped me on the street when I was walking to a friend's and said, "He's a real piece of shit, you know that, right?" then went on his way.

Otherwise, I was grateful that news of his finagling and conniving trickled down to me through the tightlipped filter of my mother. You also need to understand that I hadn't lived with them for a dozen years and time had whitewashed the memories so that it seemed I'd blessedly let myself forget the worst parts and all that was left was bereft of its initial power, the stress that resulted from his habit becoming slack, snippets of arguments minus the anger, strained looks on faces dissolving into indistinct pictures as if seen through frosted glass.

The phone rang and my father answered, "Dynamic Business Solutions, good morning." Lenny turned to me and said, "I was watching this show last night about these animals that attack people. You know about this?"

"Guard dogs?"

"Yeah those, but also these zoo animals that lose their minds and go after the trainers and shit like that."

"Was it good?"

"It was hilarious. This couple won a raffle and got a private tour of some conservation center. They were in the chimpanzee habitat and, for no reason, absolutely no reason, I mean one minute the monkeys were doing their thing and the next they went fucking berserk. They attacked this guy."

"Oh, yeah?" I said.

"Kid, they ripped off his nose and his balls."

"Sounds like a laugh riot."

"Thing I've been thinking about is how did they know how to do that? To go right after his balls like that? That's how you know they're intelligent."

"We descended from them."

"Fucking evolution."

My father ended his call. Lenny was only there another minute. He owned a truck and offered to help move out any of the larger pieces of furniture. My father said it wasn't necessary, not yet anyway.

"Just let me know if you need it. I got it in a garage downtown so it's not like I can bring it over on a minute's notice." He said it was nice to meet me and left.

"How do you know that guy?"

"Mad Dog Marino," my father said, as if that explained everything.

"Who is he?"

"Ex-NYPD. Got injured on the job and sued the city. The lawsuit dragged on for the better part of a decade. He won eventually. Huge payday."

"Mad dog?"

"He just wouldn't quit with that lawsuit."

"What does he do now?"

"Part-time security consultant, part-time private investigator. I leased him a copier. He's a nice guy with too much free time on his hands. He always needs to be doing something."

"You guys ever hit the track together?" I asked.

I would be lying if I gave the impression he never got carried away. Or else why would we care if he blew off steam at OTB? The pari-mutuel tickets sometimes found crumpled in the ashtray of his car undid us, so much so that when my sister fell in love with horses as a small girl, as small girls do, there was something tainted about her fascination that made it uncute. The potential was always there, the possibility never far from our thoughts, that one day he'd dig himself a hole and try to climb out of it with one cold exacta that didn't come in. Living with the possibility was worse than any actual win or loss, and since I thought this possibility had come true, that he'd gambled away his livelihood, I couldn't watch him pal around with Lenny Marino and a Daily Racing Form. It didn't help that we were standing in his failing place of business. How the fallout of his compulsion surrounded him and he didn't run screaming from it was an exercise in blind stoicism. Or lunatic defiance.

As usual, he neither confirmed nor denied my suspicion. "Lenny just has more money than he knows what to do with."

"That should be my biggest problem."

"Me too."

I peeked out of his office. "Where's your crack staff?"

"You're looking at it. I'm a one man gang."

"The axe man. Didn't think you had it in you."

"I didn't have to. It's an amazing thing, when you tell people you might not be able to pay them anymore, they don't stay out of the goodness of their hearts. Do me a favor. Don't tell your mom. Not yet. She'll think it's the end of the world."

"It's not?"

"Your mom has a habit of thinking everything's the end of the world." He leaned back in his chair and exhaled, as if we'd just completed an arduous negotiation. Switching conversational gears, he said, "Tell me what you're up to."

"Seems like I'll be venturing into the not-for-profit sector."

"I heard about that. I'm having a hard time picturing it."

"Me too. Of course I had a hard time picturing myself in prison."

"I didn't."

"Thanks."

He sat forward, reassessing his take on me. "You were seven when you asked me what I did for a living and I showed you how to calculate a lease. I thought I was teaching you long division. You were leasing matchbox cars at school inside a week. For usurious rates, if I recall. You remember that?"

I sort of remembered, but I told him I didn't. I was thinking that seven-year-olds now emailed homework assignments to their teachers from their cell phones. Unless that was just something you said about second graders because it sounded plausible.

"Then there was your suspension from middle school for

making book on the Super Bowl," he said.

"People think Buffalo lost because Scott Norwood shanked a field goal at the end of the game. The Bills weren't covering even if he made it." In seventh grade I knew which side of the action to be on. My father, in his late-fifties, still didn't.

"In high school, fake IDs, stolen tests, 'borrowed' cars."

"Harmless mischief."

"Delinquency, to hear your principal tell it. God knows what you got into at college."

"You should have given me a heads-up about prison. I could've used it."

"I didn't say I expected you to end up there. You exhibited some of the same traits as world innovators. You're mad now. I still love you. None of that shit matters to me. I'd love you if you exsanguinated a bunch of humanitarians."

"Strong word."

"I don't sleep a lot. I've been watching the crime channel, history channel, medical channel, hunting channel. You'd be surprised how often that word overlaps."

Stubborn bastard just wouldn't offer up the explanation I wanted.

"So, what happened?

"With what? The business?" he said.

"Yeah. The business."

He threw up his hands as if the answer was beyond his powers of expression. "It's never *one* thing. You can't say 'if I just did one thing differently . . .'"

"Why don't you tell me about the many things?"

"Where to start? I'm to blame for some of it. I wrote deals with people I probably shouldn't have. I was trying to help them but, I'll admit it, I needed money too. I was under duress. And let's face it, these customers were credit risks, so the banks financing the loans would bang them out on the interest rate, over twenty percent, sometimes thirty—talk about usury—and this almost guaranteed the loans would go bad, which got charged back to me. You ever try to repo office equipment? I also hired individuals who turned out to be incompetent, not to mention thieves, which shouldn't have surprised me—they were just like everybody else in the world."

"I get it."

"I'm not done. Okay, so next you've got your day-to-day operating expenses like rent, utilities, phone, premise insurance, advertising, etc. And we haven't even touched on payroll tax, FUTA, Medicare, Social Security, workers' comp., disability, health insurance, 401k contributions, an occasional lawsuit, and inflation . . . it never ends. It's never just one thing."

Why wasn't I relieved to find out he hadn't gambled it away? Maybe it was because I knew this information didn't change the outcome. Or maybe because it illustrated the uncertainty of business, or of life in general. Or maybe because I couldn't shake the idea that thoroughbreds contributed, if not directly. Part of me believed he hadn't been on top of things the way he should have been because, in his mind at least, he was at the track.

Like our afternoon at Yankee stadium when I was eight—or was it nine? End of the summer, right before school started. We were running late as usual. I was worried about missing the first pitch, but he said he had to stop at some store first. Some store I wasn't allowed in. "Keep the doors locked," he said and disappeared. For the better part of an hour I waited alone in his car with the air conditioning cranked, punching the different stations on the radio, looking for the broadcast on the a.m. dial, squirming on the vinyl seat when the clock cruised past 1:00 and the National Anthem was sung. I never knew what they sold at this store because my father came out empty handed. By the time we reached our seats it was the bottom of the second.

Then he kept getting up. He came back with a soda for me, then a pretzel, then he had to use the bathroom, then he went to get popcorn, then a beer. Every time he left, he held what looked like a receipt. This was before cell phones and the Internet—it was before anyone I knew owned a home computer—and what I couldn't put together then was that he was hustling to a pay phone to get the race results. All I knew was that he was acting weird, a suspicion confirmed by the man in the row behind us, with his two sons. On my father's third or fourth trip up the aisle, the man leaned in and said, "Montezuma's Revenge strikes again," and he and his fucking sons started laughing. I kept turning in my seat, looking at them. Worse than their laughter was knowing that I was having a different kind of day from those boys, but not knowing why, exactly. Finally, I told my father, "Don't get up again. You're missing the game." He stayed after that and I didn't speak to him.

"Sorry to hear it," I told him now.

"It's part of life. Just have to adjust. Life's about making adjustments."

"You sound like a chiropractor."

"Today, I have to deal with today. Tomorrow, I'll worry about tomorrow. We could all be dead. Or not. Sometimes you'll see what's horrible today, isn't so bad tomorrow."

"Where did you learn that?"

"I learned that from living as long as I have."

"So that's it? Game over?"

"I didn't say that."

He pointed at a Post-It note stuck to the wall opposite his desk, just above the chair I'd been sitting in. In my father's heavy handwriting: OBESE PEOPLE.

"What does it mean?"

"It means Americans are on average twenty-five pounds heavier than they were in 1965."

"And what, you plan on eating them, burning them for heating fuel?"

"There must be good money in selling products designed for overweight people," he said.

"Reinforced toilets?"

"That's not bad." He jotted it down on a legal pad. His eyes grew luminescent, the strands of gray threaded in his dark hair seemed to shine like the coils of an electric heater. He put his feet on his desk.

"Obese people," he mused.

"I'm pretty sure people don't like being told they're fat."

"Everyone has to deal with reality. You can pretend there is no reality, but at the end of the day you have to wash your ass."

"That's a harsh reality, old man. No one wants to hear it."

"You might be right."

I felt like an asshole watching the glimmer in his eyes dim. And there you have the flip side of things. Were he just a degenerate gambler I wouldn't have felt as conflicted as I did puzzling over a Post-It note on the wall. I wouldn't have been with him, period. There were other memories working on me, of Yankee games where he wasn't running out of his seat every few minutes, of the countless hours we spent at the park, practicing my own ungainly baseball skills, when there was no chance I was going anywhere with that. There were other memories darting back even farther into my childhood, when he indulged my weird obsessions, like when we tried to buy lunch at Burger King with a rock I found and was convinced was a lump of fool's gold.

He was coming back to earth at his desk.

"It's good that you're thinking," I said, in conciliation, "Do you have anything else?"

"Just a few more phone calls to make, then we'll call it a day."

"I mean another idea. Not just fat people?"

He shrugged.

I wanted to say, "You're fighting for your life, old man. Put some heart into it!" I looked out the window instead.

There must have been a moment when the facts settled over him. He'd run out of room and could no longer float the money from one account to satisfy the debt from another. Did he panic when he finally understood? I tried putting myself in his shoes. I'd always thought we were a lot alike, but I couldn't figure out what he felt. There was the moment of realization though, I'm sure, and afterward there was reconciling what a failure of this magnitude meant to a man of his age. Or was the failure a symptom of his age? Was he too sharp five or ten years ago? Never as self-motivated as my mother, he was an extremely bright man who took pride in his ability to juggle so many balls of fire. He might have never loved his work but he found his self-respect in his unorthodox way of conducting it.

I turned back from the window. I was done thinking about it. I was ready to go home and keep a secret from my mother and employer.

Spring, 2003

There were gun shows all the time, if one was willing to travel. The Morenos were eager to have me travel: to Virginia, Tennessee, Texas, Nevada, Montana. Not all of them small affairs like the Marriot, some were in convention centers.

In a short period of time I learned what an AK-47 was and that an American model, semi-automatic, made by Lancaster, cost $729. I learned of periodicals with classified sections and a used AK is even cheaper. I liked that I was an autodidact. It made me think my parents were right to say that if I'd only applied myself I would have been a straight-A student. Of course, they didn't know what I was doing and, as long as I was busy learning, you know, just memorizing information, I didn't have to consider why anyone would want Stinger antiaircraft missiles or Pakistani knockoffs that run about fifteen grand and weigh thirty-five pounds and fit inside a golf bag. It was hypothetical. Besides, they didn't sell missiles at gun shows. Then I learned that, in thirty-two states, a loophole allows an individual to purchase firearms without having a background check. It has to be at a gun show, as opposed to a store, and the seller can't be a licensed dealer, but a hobbyist. There was now no reason to fear purchasing too many guns within a ninety day period, the length of time that background checks are kept on record (not that a background check is any real kind of deterrent; you can buy a gun online with a valid credit card and have it Fed Exed to your house, and there is no check for things like uniforms, Kevlar, night vision scopes, ammunition—even pistol ammunition you only need to be 21. But still the loophole opened up a new world for me.) If everyone at Crystal Clear Pools was proud of me before, they practically adopted me after this. The only thing better than being really good at what you do is being recognized as being really good at what you do, and being appreciated for it. I fed off their recognition and appreciation to an almost literal degree, as if it nourished me the same as sunlight. I was *el chico de oro*, the golden boy, *el amuleto de buena suerte*, the good luck charm.

The Morenos kept me busy. My Spanish improved. I wasn't fluent but I was getting better. Don't forget the money. I wasn't volunteering. As my skill set evolved and expanded, so did my compensation. Ron's parents might not have looked like the kind of people who had a ton of cash lying around. Guess what? They did. And I'll tell you this, while I thrived on their compliments and nicknames, money became the true barometer of my value. I don't mean my value to this new and exciting operation I was involved in, but my worth as a person.

The thing was, even after the excitement wore off, I thought very little about what the guns were for. Still, there were infrequent times when, alone in some American city, when I'd eaten too much and drunk too many, I would look out a hotel window, down on the parking lot or out at the street traffic, and feel dizzyingly remorseful. At once, I saw through my richly hued fantasies of personal greatness to what was true: my participation in this gun enterprise had never been the logical progression of someone so finely tuned that ordinary society seemed bland by comparison. For as much as I wanted to paint the world I had come from as beneath me, and its inhabitants as narrow and lacking imagination, it was I who was creatively deficient. In my inability to find contentment in life, I blamed life. The harshest realization, however, was that I wasn't even chasing greatness but its trappings. I wanted the acclaim that attended those at the tops of their fields, be it fame, money, women—all the lazy markers. Given this mindset, one can see how much safer it was for me to reconfigure a below-average capacity for wonder into unrecognized Genius, rather than digging down and doing the hard work of living.

On those rare nights, I wanted to cry, believing that in my tears I could empty myself of the feeling. Only I was too miswired to cry. I stared numbly out the window, feeling tears rise in my chest; and then I sighed as they one by one disappeared in transport. The guilt faded, as it was nebulous to begin with, because I hadn't done anything to feel bad about, that is, nothing illegal. Not yet. But I was cursed with enough awareness to know that culpability and the law were different matters. If I heard this story involving someone else, I would have thought he either knew the deal or was a patsy. In the crepuscular light of my introspection I knew that saying, "What am I supposed to do if I quit this job, sell copiers for my dad?" amounted to shoddy justification. Even then, I didn't think about the actual guns. They belonged to a part of me that didn't want to know because, once I did, I would have had to judge what that meant in the real world. I would have had to rethink Ron's story about his uncle. What if I didn't like my new conclusion?

FOUR

They were at it again, this time outside my room. Maybe my proximity brought it out of them. I was dressing for my first day of work, inspecting myself in the mirror, noticing that the boy who had lived in this room hadn't taken great care of himself. He looked somewhat soft and gray in his business casual wear.

"You might want to think about starting a summer job early," my mother said.

"For what? Money?" shrieked Rachel.

"I know, it's Draconian."

"You and Dad always say what? That I'm a full-time student? That school is my job?"

"This isn't the same thing."

"And speaking of school, what am I supposed to do about college? I'm a senior in September, in case you forgot. Should I start turning tricks to finance my degree?"

"You dress like you already do. On my tab too."

"This family is a cruel joke."

"I don't have time to argue. You're late for school and I'm late for work."

"That's right. Take your loser son and go run off to the other losers."

Rachel's tantrumming feet stormed off. I emerged from the bedroom. My mother was catching her breath.

"Loser son, reporting for duty," I said.

"I'm sorry you heard that."

"Don't worry about it." Even if what my sister said was needlessly mean, I'd heard worse. Besides, she was right to think that loserdom was contagious.

"Well, you look very nice," my mother said, my appearance a boon to her shitty morning.

"Don't dress for the job you have, dress for the job you want. I want the job of a man who wears wrinkle-free khakis."

"That's very cute, Alex, but I'm afraid you might get dirty."

I'd wanted to wait until we stopped for coffee, enjoying our first aromatic sips, before asking what she had planned for me, but her comment required immediate clarification. "I don't want to have anything to do with the food," I said.

"It's a soup kitchen. That's like saying you're a window washer with a fear of heights."

"I was hoping for office-type work. Stuffing envelopes, soliciting donations. I'm a real charmer on the phone. Paper cuts with a chance of telemarketing. I'd be the luckiest guy in the world."

I took it as a bad sign when she smiled rather than answered.

On the way to Franklin Avenue Community Outreach, my mother and I pretended that she and Rachel hadn't been arguing. This was fine with me. I was having a hard time getting past the idea that I was an $8/hour laborer. Where was I going on that wage? It helped me better understand recidivism. What choice did we cons have? We weren't winning MacArthur grants. Also, if personal responsibility was as important as our rehabilitators would have us believe, didn't it follow that at least some of us—born with an aptitude for mayhem the way others take to real estate sales or forensic accounting—had pursued our hearts' demand? But maybe I was looking at it the wrong way. Were there decent odds I could make a life out of this? My mother couldn't work forever. If over the next few years I learned the trade, I could take over when she retired. Then I could expand the operation.

I pictured my days appearing on cable news networks, modestly proclaiming I was just following the example of my noble mother and continuing in the tradition of her good work, my story of gunrunner-turned-philanthropist the sort of incandescent myth-making that suits our vapid media; afternoons in my office, doors closed, interviewing for the position of my personal assistant nubile college graduates, who came from the heartland via our most liberal of the liberal arts universities, Bowdoin or Bennington perhaps, their desire to help the homeless just slightly less palpable than their awe of working for a man so dedicated to a righteous cause; nights at opulent fundraising galas in which men of impossible wealth opened their checkbooks to me while their wives stood by silently despising them for their free-market ruthlessness and quivering as I took them by the arm and showed them the fleet of vans for my Feed-The-Shut-Ins program, purchased with their scumbag corporate spouses' moolah.

This grand vision began evaporating as soon as my mother turned her car onto the grimy industrial thoroughfare on whose cracked sidewalks stood dozens of cracked souls lining up for her services. I was astonished that this was where she most wanted to be. Inside, vitality-draining fluorescent tubes illumined the whole terrible place. Her office was scarcely large enough for both of us. You had to turn sideways to squeeze between the bank of file cabinets against the wall and her desk, which sat like a block of Stonehenge on the scuffed tile floor. A persistent onion odor drifted up from the kitchen. The one window framed the parking lot that my mom and her staff shared with the children's apparel warehouse next door. If not for the photos of my family or the various philanthropic awards presented to her over the years tilted ever so crookedly on the walls, I could have fooled myself into thinking I was employed at some noirish detective agency run by a down-and-out, alcoholic PI still trying to solve the case that he took too personally and, as a result, got him kicked off the city police force.

Dismal as these surroundings were, I clung to them. As long as I was here, I wasn't in the dining room, where charity meant something different from the bountiful feeling that accompanied the signing of a tax deductible check. The dining room was where those checks came to die. But that wasn't it either. Not entirely. Worse than the true-blues, like my mother, were the sanctimonious assholes who used the downtrodden to boost their own soggy self-worth. These were the shitheads I wanted to avoid because it occurred to me that, given my situation, they might try to recruit me.

My mother (her presence in the building somehow universally known) was paged. I hoped the issue at hand was complicated enough for her to forget me for a few hours, but she returned soon with my first task.

"Sweetie, Delmont didn't show up."

"Tragedy," I said.

"I need you to help Carl in the kitchen."

"But my new clothes . . ."

"I warned you about that. Now let's go, please. I don't have time to sugarcoat it."

And so I was on her heels, down the stairs, through the dining room (which looked like a middle school cafeteria from a movie about an underfunded, inner-city school, whose debate team goes on to win at State, or whose disproportionately Guatemalan eighth graders earn college credit for their free-form poetry, despite investigations of fraud by the slimy Caucasian administrator), into the kitchen (which looked exactly like a restaurant kitchen). At a stainless steel sink, blackened pots and pans abounded. I shook hands with Carl, a short, wiry guy who was either twenty years older or five years younger than me. Behind us, two line cooks were hanging around. Having finished cooking breakfast, they had some time to kill. A woman who looked in charge sat on an upside down bucket, leaning her back against the wall. Her eyes were closed and she drummed a soft rhythm on her checkered pants, her feet tapping a black rubber mat.

"Little Man, you know your way around a sink?" Carl said. I was taller than him by a head.

There was no need to show him the entry on my résumé that had me working food services at Otisville for a six month stretch. I nodded.

"That dude Delmont," he said.

"Yeah," I said. We got to work. We loaded the dirty dishes into plastic bins and slid them into the industrial strength washer. Carl let me know what a terrific mother I had.

"She's like a saint. I've never met anyone like her. And another thing: you being you wasn't her fault. You made your own bed and you slept in it. You pulled some crazy shit, didn't you?"

Another fan, I thought. The hot water was turning my hands red and making my face sweat.

Carl said, "Let me ask the expert: What's the best gun for rhino hunting?"

"Going on safari?"

"What? No. Settling an argument. A buddy of mine thinks an Uzi is best. Full automatic."

Sure enough, grease spots dotted the front of my shirt. "You want something with stopping power. Bolt action. A Weatherby Mark V, or Mauser."

"You're a smart dude, like your mom. Maybe you've got that good instinct in you like she does."

"You never know," I said.

"But I'll tell you something, you don't look dangerous." He released his grip on the overhead nozzle and stepped back from the sink. "Let me show you something." He reached under the sink, into a canvas backpack, and pulled out a bottle of wine. "She gave me this."

"St. Judy compensates you in merlot?"

"It was left over from a benefit dinner. She gave it to me for carrying Delmont's ass all the time. For appreciation. I can't wait to get home, crack it open."

I saw a way out of dishwashing drudgery. "Do you mind?"

Carl handed over the bottle. The woman who ran the kitchen said from her bucket. "I'm not hearing water." She pushed open the back door that led into the alley behind the kitchen, propped it open with a wooden block. A few seconds later I smelled cigarette smoke.

"Carl, I'm going to make you a bet," I said, turning the bottle around in my hands, "and if you win, you can knock off right now and get started on this wine."

"And if you win?"

I pointed to the sink. "You're on your own."

The bet was I could drink from the bottle without opening it.

"You think I'll let you steal my wine, Little Man?" Carl said.

"You're missing my point. Do you think it's possible for anyone to drink from this bottle without altering it in any way?"

"If you smash it you might get a couple of sips."

"You're not hearing me. Without altering the bottle, I said. I'll just drink from it."

The woman who ran the kitchen came back in through the door and kicked out the block of wood. "I still don't hear water running," she observed.

"Hold on, Lorraine. Just hold on a second," Carl said. He was looking at the bottle and then at me. "If I win, I go home now?"

"Paid day of work, my friend."

He seemed to know I had an angle or else why make the bet in the first place. But the offer was too tempting. "All right, you're on."

We shook on it, Carl smiling with the bizarre certainty of a man who believes cobras make charming pets. I reached for the overhead nozzle and sprayed a little water into the punt, the concave depression on the bottom of the bottle. Then I sipped from it. The slow realization that he had not merely been beaten, but made to look like a fool, caused Carl an embarrassment so severe that he lifted a clean pot and sent it crashing down among the dirty pile. "Horseshit! You said you'd drink the wine."

"I never said that. I said I would drink from the bottle."

The line cooks were watching and so was Lorraine. She no longer had much interest in the lack of running water.

"I should beat your ass," Carl said.

I kept an eye on his hands in case he grabbed a pot, or a knife. I held the wine bottle by the neck if I needed a weapon. "Before we go down that road I want to point out two things. One: there was a very good chance you were going to have to wash these dishes by yourself. What if I wasn't here today? That dude Delmont, remember? Two: you can make this bet every time you go to a bar from now on. You'll drink for free, forever. Not a bad lesson, if you ask me."

He looked like he was mulling it over. The threat wasn't behind me yet. We were only going to fight if he couldn't swallow his shame in front of his co-workers. So I added, "When I had this trick pulled on me it was much worse."

"How much worse?"

"A thousand dollars worse."

Carl started laughing, his embarrassment now dwarfed by the story of mine, even if he understood I made it up. He told the cooks and Lorraine, "This is a crazy dude."

I returned his wine to him, before getting out of the kitchen.

My mother caught up with me a couple of hours later. My feet were propped up on her desk, my eyes closed. "Oh, did I disrupt the prince's nap?"

"I'm pacing myself."

"I want you downstairs now," she said.

"So did you hear that Doctors Without Borders was soliciting donations and they called a hedge fund manager—"

"That man works his heart out for me. You're my son. Do you have any idea how that makes me look? You're going to bus tables."

She wasn't asking. Debate was pointless. I kept my mouth shut and got up.

"Jesus, Alex. Any slower and it'll be dinner."

The kitchen staff was putting lunch away, scraping corn kernels into garbage cans, covering trays of sandwiches with plastic wrap and moving them into the walk-in fridge. As I skirted the edge of the kitchen, I caught more than one cagey glance in my direction. Carl and the gang had formed lasting opinions about me. I excused myself meekly through them.

My mother called out, "For the love of god—today." They laughed at my back. "Grab one of those bins and get into the dining room."

"I'm going, I'm going," I said and shoved through the swinging metal doors. On long folding tables sat the detritus of lunch: plastic cups and dishes caked with drink and food, chipped coffee mugs, lusterless, blunt utensils, newspapers and napkins. To complete the middle school cafeteria feel, the diners had arranged themselves in cliques. Those struggling close to the poverty line hung together and seemed to shun the truly impoverished. Maybe they didn't need to be reminded where one more wrong turn would take them. I cleared the tables that had no one eating at them first.

Bin full, I delivered it to Carl. On my second or third trip, I became aware of a man sitting at a table by himself. I wouldn't have given him more than a passing glance if he didn't look like Ron. To be fair, Ron hailed from a South American country where the majority of its citizens were short and shaped like a box, an evolutionary response to the Andes' altitude. Millions of people looked like him, no big deal. What made the likeness unsettling was that Ron was missing, a disingenuous way of saying no one ever found his body. If I had been with him, I would be missing too. He never made his appointment with his uncle, never made his appointment with the general, never made it onto his return flight. For a few days, we clung to the hope that he'd been kidnapped (you know you're playing a losing hand when you look at the prospect of a stolen human as optimistic) and we waited for a ransom demand. When none came, and our inquiries at a few hospitals were unsuccessful, his parents made one cautious request at the embassy. After all, how forthright could they be when Ron's unofficial reason for visiting the country was to overturn the very powers from which his parents now sought relief? It was possible these were the same people who disappeared him. It was now close to four years since the last time I saw Ron, and for a moment, I thought he'd wandered into my mother's soup kitchen.

I hardly needed a second look to realize the guy was someone else. The resemblance wasn't even that strong. It was just at first glance I had a flash of recognition. The flash went away, but I wasn't disappointed. I wasn't hoping this poor man was Ron. I finished busing down the tables. Ron was gone. I preferred to leave it at that, vague as it sounded. When I brought the last of the dishes into the kitchen, my mother had me do some light filing. She said she didn't want to overwhelm me with too much honest work on my first day.

From *White Boy Bandito: How a Clever Suburbanite Became Death's Middleman for South American Revolutionaries*, by Dr. Laura Sullivan, PhD. (Verdict Press: 2006, 236-237)

Some have argued that Alexander Wolf would never have taken up arms if not for loyalty to Ron Moreno, his closest boyhood friend. After all, it is as plain as the hand in front of your face to see that he is an unusual candidate to become a revolutionary. But could it literally be as simple as friendship? Your humble author has a plethora of girlfriends who mean the world to her and so much more, and yet, I would never in a million years engage in felonious and risky behavior on behalf of my supportive sisters. So what drove Alexander Wolf? Was he moved by the people he weaponized? Did he harbor notions of a human utopia paid for by the blood of oppressors? Could the answer be something altogether more personal? Did he have a death wish ultimately?

The answer might be as a complicated as a Rubik's Cube, and at the end of the day as unsolvable as a Buddhist koan. For who can honestly say they know what goes on in another's heart. As a doctor, I worked my fingers to the bone trying to crack the tough nut that is Alexander Wolf. Every time I felt that we were close to a breakthrough, I found out that I was wrong, painfully wrong.

Today's session was tough and tense. I had needed to use each and every tool in my therapist's toolbox to make it through. At every turn, Alexander kept stonewalling me. He sat backwards on the folding chair, with a devil-may-care attitude. He said, proud as a peacock, "You want to know how it happened? I'm a Jewish kid from the suburbs. They never saw me coming."

"You don't believe that," I said skeptically.

"Maybe I do and maybe I don't," he sneered.

At that very moment, I worried that if I lived to be a thousand, I might not ever get him to open up. Nevertheless, his stubbornness strengthened my resolve and inspired me to keep fighting to reach him. If I quit on Alexander, I feared he would be lost forever.

July, 2003

The Barrett .50 caliber rifle. It was a boon for me when it happened. I was tasked that weekend with finding out about bigger firepower and was sent on a research trip to the Tulsa Arms Show, which billed itself as the largest gun show in the world—"Over 4200 tables in one 11 acre airconditioned room!" I wasn't thrilled about being there because it was Oklahoma, no offense to Oklahomans, although who else could you blame for their state being the way it was? If you're looking for guns, however, and want to get them easily, the Sooner State has got you covered. This was a state where you didn't need a permit to own a handgun, shotgun, or rifle. Ordinarily I would have considered my time there a temporary, but necessary, occupational hazard to my sanity, but after five months on the road, maybe I'd hit the wall.

"The *sooner* I get out of there, the better," I told Ron, as he drove me to the airport.

"When did you become a snob?" he said, pulling into the terminal.

"You didn't think that was funny?"

"I just want you to keep your head on straight. You look like shit, you know that?"

He was right. Too much travel, not enough sleep, garbage food and booze, constant interactions with people who weren't my kind of people—I was a mess.

"I'm trying to keep a light vibe before getting on yet another plane for your family," I said.

"There is no light vibe. Fuck! It's scary to watch you do all this stuff and not understand how dangerous it is."

"You're worried about me? That's cute, Ronny Baby, but don't even do that. I'll be fine."

He said he hoped so. A cop motioned for Ron to move his car. I got out with my bag and was soon airborne, on my way to rub elbows with some gun-toting Okies.

Tulsa Arms Show Need-to-Knows
- If all our tables were placed end to end, they would stretch 5.7 miles!
- Like art, antique guns are a good hedge against inflation.

Concealed Carry
- Bring it, but unload it before you get in the building. Guards can hold your ammo at the door so you don't have to walk through the parking lot unarmed.

Open Carry
- Bring it, but unload it before you get in the building.
- Meet Dan Haggerty, star of TV's "Grizzly Adams."

The place was bonkers. Overwhelmed me not five feet beyond the entrance. I forced myself through my paces, wading through an ocean of bodies, chatting up vendors, other customers, and generally getting nowhere. Something was off. The day was taking on an odd shape and I didn't feel like myself. I needed fresh air.

Tulsa in July is damn toasty, but I felt better outside Expo Square. I started eavesdropping on two men smoking, both of them lamenting some "faggoty" senator who was trying to ban so-called big guns. One of the guys mentioned a Barrett, aped firing one.

I sidled up to them. "Afternoon. Did you say something about a Barrett?"

The first one (I later learned his name was Bill, but he said it so it sounded like Biff) said, ".50 caliber. M107. Sniper rifle. You know about it?"

I told him I'd heard about it, but I didn't know about it. The second man (Dexter) said, "We use them to drop Iraqis from a mile away."

I was pretty sure he said "we" meaning Americans, not he and Bill, or Biff, specifically. I whistled, impressed. I asked where I could get one.

"Turn around and walk back inside. You'll find them."

"You can get them just about anywhere. Except California, of course," added Dexter.

"Maybe not for long," said Bill/Biff. "This limp-dick in Congress has a hard-on to ban them."

I offered to take them to lunch, if they weren't busy. I wanted them to tell me more. In the parking lot were several food trucks and we stood around eating hotdogs while I peppered them with questions.

Q: Wouldn't the recoil blow off your shoulder?

A: Oh, it kicks, but the barrel retracts and the muzzle brake vents two-thirds of each shot's energy.

Q: Are they heavy?

A: Around thirty pounds.

Q: What kind of velocity are we talking about?

A: Rounds travel at close to 2,800 feet per second.

Bill/Biff was explaining that some .50 caliber rounds are old and the copper casing gets corroded, thereby increasing the probability of gunking up the barrel and jamming, when his friend interrupted. It was his turn to ask me a few questions.

Q: What do you want to know all this stuff for?

A: It's a hobby.

Q: You don't look like any hobbyist I've ever seen. Where'd you say you're from?

A: New York

Q: *Jew* York?

A: I don't think anyone really calls it that.

Q: Don't mean it's not true. Why'd you come all this way?

A: What the fuck does it matter?

Which I immediately identified as the wrong tone to take with Dexter. And why hadn't I noticed he and Bill/Biff wore belt holsters and we were in the parking lot, meaning I didn't have to ask if those handguns were loaded? Maybe Ron was on to something and I needed to start treating these situations with a higher degree of seriousness?

"Gentleman, I was just making conversation. My apologies if you got the wrong idea. Enjoy the rest of your day," I said and walked away quickly, back toward the gun show, hoping it would be impossible for them to find me inside.

Turned out they were right, though. The .50 cals were sold most everywhere. I made my first purchase two weeks later from a private seller in Pennsylvania.

FIVE

My fold-out bed wasn't folded in to its couch at six in the evening, and I lay on it, rereading the article about Reverend Holden. It was a fluff piece in a countywide circulated magazine and yet I kept going back to it. Its strength came from its subject: his power, his influence, his money, his charisma, his iridescent teeth. There must have been a way to tap into it. I just didn't know how. The more times I read about him, the more it frustrated me that I couldn't find a way in.

For a while, I scanned the words, and then someone knocked at the door. "Come in."

"Can I ask you something, Big Al?" Rachel said, gliding into my room.

"Shoot."

"Are you going to be able to help or what?"

"With what?"

"Because it doesn't look like you are."

"I didn't know I was supposed to."

"When I found out you were coming to live with us I guess I had expectations, you know? From the stories I'd heard about you?"

"For the last time, that movie is made up. You've got to stop hanging out with Jelly."

"Not the movie."

"The book is bullshit too. Laura Sullivan is a vampire. If you had the slightest idea of how manipulative that woman is, you wouldn't believe her if she told you your eyes are brown."

"Then it's not true that you'd be handsome except for comically unkempt hair that makes you resemble a mad scientist, or a suicidal poet."

"Stop right there."

"Page 4," Rachel said. "Right before she wrote, 'He walks like he's attached to marionette strings.'"

"You memorized the book?"

"I just read it. It's not my fault I have an awesome memory."

"Marionette strings. Is that anything to say about someone you were sleeping with?"

"Okay, gross. Look, I didn't come in here to discuss your biographer."

"Then stop quoting her."

Rachel walked to the bedroom door, cracked it a few inches, and peeked into the hallway. "Do you mind if we listen to some music? I don't want Mom to hear us."

"I don't think she's listening."

She rolled her eyes at me as though I was offensively naïve.

"Go ahead," and I pointed to the portable stereo on my dresser.

"Where do you plug in the iPod?"

"You don't."

"Oh, my God, this is so *vintage*, and not in a cool or ironic way." She operated the relic, fiddling with the FM dial. I wasn't familiar with the station she stopped on, nor the artist "singing." I began thinking that I really was old.

"Do you like this song?"

"Yeah, it's good," I said, which was a lie. It wasn't good at all. A girl was rapping about some party, inviting us, the listeners, to this party and she rhymed the words "over here now" with "y'all better hear now" again and again to a synthesized melody that sounded not unlike deaf people laughing.

Rachel sat down on the bed. "You're not listening to me and, hey, that's no surprise, no one listens to me, but I'm not talking about the movie or book or whatever. It's like what Mom and Dad say about you, like how people pay attention to you even if they don't agree with you. So I figured that when you got home, you'd be able to help us. All you do is go to work with Mom and hide in your room. I'm only saying this because you should see how much we need someone."

Help? How? If I could throw them a bone, I would, but I couldn't even help me. I hoped she was just venting.

"I'm so angry all the time. There's going to be no money for me to go to college and all the schools I'm looking at cost like forty grand. A year. And I need a new car."

"What's wrong with your car?"

"It's like six years old."

"Of course it is."

"There's this weight in the house. I feel it so much. The house," she snorted. "It looks like it should be condemned in the basement. Not up to code or whatever they say. And Mom and Dad look ready to die. Have you seen how old they look? I mean, couldn't Dad have a heart attack?"

I knew she was testing me in a way—to say the right thing. I wanted to say the right thing. I did. I just had no answers. Anything I said would have failed her. Why did she think of me as not one of them, an outsider with enough distance to approach the situation with wisdom, or at least a clear head? They were my parents too, it was my childhood home, I was ensnared in our history as much as she was, if not more, because I was older.

"If you ask either of them about it they blow you off, well, maybe not you, but me," she said. "So I want you to open your eyes. You don't know how hard the last year has been. What I mean is, I know your year was hard too, really shitty, but there was a reason for that. Forget it. I sound stupid."

The song ended and the next one began, another invitation to a party that wouldn't end "till the break of for-eva." Rachel was quiet but tense. The fitted sheet had shifted off the corner of the mattress, revealing the manufacturer's tag. At night I felt it scratching against my leg. I leaned over and tore it free.

"Well, you just violated probation," Rachel said.

"How?"

"Removing the tag is a crime . . . you know."

"That's funny," I said, and for the first time since I'd been home, we shared a look free from antipathy or uneasiness.

"Listen, just forget it. Forget I said anything. You got your own shit to deal with. It's just those things Mom and Dad say about you."

I realized she wasn't testing me. She was confiding in me. I didn't know what to do. Despite whatever stories she'd heard, most people didn't trust me enough to share.

"Can I ask you something else?" she said.

"It's not really a violation to rip off the tag."

"Not that. I kind of just wanted to know how you turned out like this."

"Grandpa was pretty tall, so I guess I got the height from him. And people tell me I look like Dad," I said, bobbing and weaving

"I don't mean how you look."

"It wasn't boring."

"That's so lame." A hint of baby fat on her cheeks puffed with disappointment. She spotted the magazine with the reverend on the cover. "Don't tell me you're into him too."

"Who else is into him?"

"You should talk to Jelly."

"It's not an article about the future strippers of America."

"She knows about this stuff, asshole. She's born again."

"*Jelly* is born again? The girl who showed up here practically topless for breakfast? Who you call hooker and skank as terms of endearment?"

"Didn't you see her WWJD bracelet?" Rachel said.

"Her wrists aren't her most prominent features." I should have taken the news of Jelly's spirituality with more tact. I knew how it felt to have people draw conclusions about my moral fiber without getting to know me.

"You're so gross. I really hope you weren't always like this. But, yeah, Jelly is totally conservative in her faith. And this," she said, picking up the magazine and pointing at the face on the cover, "is her reverend."

"Really? He's pretty interesting, this guy. Got me thinking about religious businesses."

"Well she's seriously in love with him. The way she talks about him. 'Oh, Reverend Holden's a great man. One day people all over the world will need him like I do.' It's weird."

"That does sound weird."

"So, you have, like, an idea?"

"It's just something I'm toying with. I only need to find a place in it for a Jew."

"Try looking on a cross," she said, and then stood up, pretended to look out the window but was really checking her reflection in the glass, turned, and fired finger pistols at me.

I pretended to be shot, simulated a death rattle. She wadded the mattress tag and flipped it at me like a dirty tissue, and left my room with her awful dance music still playing.

From the screenplay to *The Wrong Way Son* (H.E.L.R. Prod., 2007)

```
INT. HACIENDA BUENAVISTA - NIGHT

A full-on FIESTA. Reggaeton THUMPS. Lights and
lasers FLASH. A fog machine sprays cool white
mist, hits the lights, turns the air first red,
then blue, then green.

Alex and Ron jump up and down with the crowd.
Sweating. Laughing.

Tuxedoed men wade through the dance floor
offering silver trays of cigars, joints, pills,
powders. Bar girls shower the revelers with
champagne and other liquor.

Enrique pushes partiers out of his way. He is
flanked by two ARMED GUARDS. He finds Ron and
Alex.

          ENRIQUE
     It is time!
Ron and Alex share a look—Seriously?!?! Not now!
          ENRIQUE (CONT'D)
     He is waiting.

INT. HACIENDA BUENAVISTA - MOMENTS LATER

GENERAL FULGENCIO AVILA stands at a window in
his office, arms behind his back. FIREWORKS
explode in the night sky.

A KNOCK at the door.
```

                    GENERAL
          Enter.

Enrique and his guards escort Ron and Alex into
the office. General Avila waves away the guards.
In the staid and brightly lit office, Ron and
Alex look terrible. Blinking. Disoriented.

                    GENERAL (CONT'D)
          Enrique, have you brought me men or
          drowned sewer rats?
                    ENRIQUE
          I'm...I'm sorry. I told them not--
                    GENERAL
          Bravo, gentlemen! Bravo! Enjoying
          my hospitality, are you?
               (to Enrique and Ron)
          Now you must excuse us. I'd like
          to speak to this man alone.

Ron starts to protest but his uncle grabs him
by the neck and drags him away.

                    GENERAL (CONT'D)
          So, they tell me you are the bright
          boy with all the plans.
                    ALEX
          I'm just here to help a great man
          and a great cause.
                    GENERAL
          So you say. Why?
                    ALEX
          For my friend. But for myself too.
                    GENERAL
          You have something to prove then? A
          chip on your shoulder?
                    ALEX
          You could say that.

General Avila opens a display cabinet of guns and
removes a GOLD PLATED PISTOL. He levels it at Alex.

>   GENERAL
>   I could take care of that chip for you.

Alex lurches for a waste paper basket. Pukes. General Avila wads up a handkerchief and flips it at him.

>   GENERAL (CONT'D)
>   I'm not going to kill you
>   in the house where my wife and
>   children sleep. But let me tell you
>   this. I don't trust anyone just
>   because Enrique says so.
>   ALEX (gagging)
>   You can trust me.
>   GENERAL
>   We will certainly see about that.
>   Now tell me your plan and I'll tell
>   YOU if you can really help.

My father was watching TV in the living room. Lit in profile by an end table lamp, the old man looked shabby. He could have used a haircut and the top button on his shirt hung by its last thread. His four-day stubble was no fashion statement and the shadow on his upper lip reminded me that for years he wore a moustache. In many family photos around the house he had one and I couldn't remember when he finally gave it up.

"Let's put on the game," I said.

"I'm watching this."

"Come on. Father and son bonding. The national past time. *The cat's in the cradle and the silver spoon.*"

"Watch it in your room."

"I don't have a TV in my room."

"Tough shit, Kiddo." He turned up the volume to silence me.

Foreign voices rattled out of the speakers, but the image onscreen was iconic American.

"What is this?" I said.

"*Rocky.* Now be quiet. I'm trying to watch."

"You don't speak Spanish."

"It took me a while to figure out something was a little off."

"No one ever accused me of marrying the world's most perceptive man," my mother said, entering into the room, collapsing onto the walnut rocker.

"Wait a minute, that sounds like an insult," he answered, solidly playing the straight man. At times they didn't make a half bad comedic duo. "Now, you two, please, just be quiet."

My mother and I watched him watch the dubbed version of the movie. His interest in it was of real entertainment value and somehow just as poignant as the 1976 Best Picture winner.

Apollo was coming to the ring dressed as George Washington "Creed *en tres*!" the champ sang, as the movie went to commercial.

"What's interesting is how they dub it," my father said, gesturing with the remote control. "They're actors, so they put their own spin on the script. Maybe it's a cultural thing, but this is less gritty. The guy who does Mickey is amazing. Like a gentle grandfather, nothing like Burgess Meredith. Deep voice, calm, full of wisdom. He's like a Spanish James Earl—"

"Holy shit. That's him!" I yelled, literally jumping up from the couch.

"Who?" said my mother, both concerned and bothered by my outburst.

"Him! That's the guy."

Commercial break

A camera tracks along a dirt road where women in worn house dresses wash laundry in a frothy stream of yellow water trickling past huts of corrugated tin. Wild dogs nose into piles of debris with hackles up, ribs showing through patchy fur. Filthy boys in ill-fitting clothes, growth-stunted from malnutrition, sit in a semicircle gouging the dusty earth with sticks and broken toys. A lone girl hugs her mother's thigh and peers around the woman's hip to regard her world with eyes as wide and round as a Japanese cartoon.

A violin weeps over the scene.

Voiceover narration: "These are the neglected, the forgotten, the invisible. Struggling to meet their most basic needs. But they are not without hope."

Over the screen flash the words: *Whoever is generous to the poor lends to the* Lord, *and He will repay him for his deed, Proverbs 19:17*

Enter: a white man in hiking boots, khaki pants so stiff and shiny they look waxed, a belt fitted with no fewer accoutrements than Batman's, an olive drab utility vest over a white linen shirt with two open buttons at the collar. He is middle aged but shows no sag or bloat; neither his hair nor spirit recedes. You would not call him boyish though. If he is anything, he looks to be made entirely of right angles. Among the desolation he walks, visibly troubled by what he sees. As if there remains any doubt he is a savior (maybe not *the* savior, but why split hairs?), he spreads his arms to his sides in a gesture of all-encompassing invitation. The woeful villagers flock to him. He kneels to them but somehow never gets dirty and one-by-one shares water from his canteen. He is out of place completely. He belongs nowhere else.

Voiceover narration: "Why do nothing, when you can do . . . EVERYTHING?"

Cut to: A church, albeit a crude construction but, all things considered, it is the most formidable structure for miles. The violin is joined by a piano and pan flute; no longer funereal, the music sounds like a melody harkening to a former civilization, a tune imbued with ancient knowledge. Inside, the pointy white man and a vibrant woman with yellow hair sit at the head of a massive banquet table with all the villagers. They hold hands, heads bowed in prayer. An abundant meal awaits them.

Cut to: A medical center. White-lab-coated doctors shine lights into chocolate owl-like eyes, wrap blood pressure cuffs around skinny biceps, strike rubber mallets against knobby knees, bandage cuts and scrapes with gauze. The white man inspects the examinations, pleased, satisfied. He finally addresses the camera:

"I am Reverend Warren Holden and, for over fifteen years, the Holden Ministry has been blessed to be a part of these children's lives. Please join us so that we can bring an end to poverty worldwide, once and for all."

The yellow haired woman joins the reverend and the camera pushes in on their faces. Smiles. Fade to black. Over the screen flash the words: *For more information please visit us at holdenministry.org.*

"Dude's a fucking genius," I said.

"Language, Alex," my mother said.

"What are you talking about?" my father said.

"The guy from the article."

"The child preacher, Robert. Forty years ago, marrying people when he was literally in diapers," my mother said.

"Oh, right, him," my father said. He had no idea who she meant.

"I really don't get your fascination with that man," my mother said.

"I just like his style."

"Why am I not surprised?" she said and left the room.

Apollo pounded Rocky in the early rounds.

May, 2005

Dearest Pater, Mater, and Soror:

Greetings from the clink! Sorry I've been remiss in holding up my end of our correspondence, but it's been a whirlwind here. The dressage team has a big meet with our rivals from FCI Rochester and practice has been intense lately. Also I haven't been sleeping well. They keep saying these are 800 thread count sheets, but between us, if this linen is more than 600 thread count, I'll eat my hat. Plus the wagyu ribeye steaks they insist on serving for dinner are starting to upset my stomach. They are tasty though, haha.

Jokes aside, it sucks here. I don't know if you know this but medium security can be more dangerous than max because we have more freedom to move around, which you'd think would be a good thing except there are fewer cameras and guards. It adds up to the potential for real mayhem and even if it never comes, and it hasn't so far (fingers crossed), I'm still constantly nervous. I don't want to depress you with all the depressing details, but this place is making me depressed. I'd rather let a Portuguese man o' war sting my taint than stay another day (Dad, explain to Mom and Rachel what a taint is if they don't know.)

On the upside, I recently got picked to participate in a research group for a doctoral candidate. She's in the process of finishing her dissertation: Experiences of First Time Offenders, with a Concentration on Middle Class Inmates and the Psychological and Cognitive Effects of Institutionalization. A page turner, yes? Funny thing is that Laura (grad student) is only maybe three of four years older than me and she grew up about twenty minutes from our house. I used to play her high school in sports. Small world, huh? Anyway I'm not going to lie, it's been nice to meet someone from a familiar background, and participating in her study gives me something to do besides sit around feeling sorry for myself.

So that's about it for now. Love you, miss you, all that jazz.

Alex

SIX

In the driveway, a police car, lights flashing but siren silent. A Sunday afternoon drive putrefied in my throat. My instincts said the cops were for me and I should slip into a neighboring backyard to begin a fugitive's life before anyone noticed I was home. Those lights were somehow louder, more offensive, than sirens, and they looked the same in my driveway as they had on Highway 10, in southern New Mexico, on the afternoon Ernesto and I were arrested.

I took a quick inventory of my recent activities. I hadn't committed a crime nor otherwise violated probation. Time to ignore my instincts then. I hauled myself past the flashing police lights. Inside, I was greeted by yelling, along with blood on the kitchen counter, bright red marbling the eggshell surface. It wasn't a lot of blood, but when is any good?

The verbal thunder came from the dining room. No screams of anguish or fear, but a continuation of an argument that, from the look of it, preceded the bloodletting. My father, standing behind the chair he normally sat in, held a dishcloth around his left hand, gripping it tight with his right. Both arms were above his head to stanch the bleeding. He looked as if he were trying to grab an apple on a tree branch just out of reach.

My mother, unconcerned with his injury, was shouting, "No employees! He has no employees but somehow he's still in business!" She saw me in the doorway. "Get in here. You had no right to keep this from me."

"You're such a dick," said Rachel, whom I hadn't seen standing behind two officers. The cops looked more like uncomfortable houseguests than protectors of the peace. Each wore on his belt a Glock 22, chambered for the .40 S&W cartridge (Smith & Wesson for the uninitiated), a fifteen-round magazine. I wasn't a handgun guy, but I knew that much. A lot more I could tell you about police rifles—Remington 870 P, four-round tube magazine under the barrel, Mossberg 500 cruiser—if you find those kinds of details sexy in a Tom Clancy sort of way.

"How long did you plan to go on like this? Am I a fool? Is that it?" My mother said, stepping out around the table and toward my father.

The braver cop intercepted her. "Ma'am, please sit down so we can sort this out."

She returned to her seat as though it was her idea. "You know what this means, don't you? Robert?"

"What does what mean?" my father said, as if surprised to find he wasn't alone in the room.

"This situation you've put us in."

"I'll take care of it."

"You'll take care it? He'll take care of it. Children, your father will take care of it. "

"Just like I have for thirty-five years," he said.

"And what's that supposed to mean?"

"It means I'm not asking for your help. It means stay the hell away from me."

Next entered the heavy and lethargic footsteps of two more cops, their radios belching static. The newcomers looked a little bored and aggravated. One brushed passed me and pulled rank.

"Everybody, take a step back."

The other one radioed a dispatcher that they had arrived and were responding. He said to send an ambulance.

The one in charge said, "Sir, are you alright? Why are you bleeding?"

"Get the hell away for me," my father said.

The cop put his hand on my father's shoulder. "Sir?"

"What?"

"Would you like to sit down? I'd like you to sit down."

My father looked at me. "Did you let them in?"

Unlike most people, he would never concede that the police perform a difficult job under demanding conditions. "This is the only thing you need to know about cops," went his typical refrain, "They want that gun so they can shoot someone. You can be a garbage man for the same money. Or a fireman, if you really have a hard-on for saving lives. You only become a cop when you want to make people do what you say. Or else you'll shoot them."

My father reserved his richest contempt for our local police force. As a child of the Bronx, he looked down on suburban cops as the worst kind of power trippers, bullies serving the easily cowed, protecting a province that held little danger. I worried he would give them his opinion now.

The officer in charge said to my mother, "Excuse me, were you the one who made the call?"

"Why would I call you? Bob, do you know what he's talking about?"

After three decades of marriage my parents believed they were entitled to treat each other however they liked and nobody, not even the police, had the right to tell them differently.

"I called," Rachel said, stumbling forward, as if pushed.

"*You?*" my mother said.

"She stabbed him," Rachel whispered. Then, finding her voice, "She stabbed him because we're going to lose everything and it's his fault." She started crying.

A nervous, almost giddy, resolve replaced the cops' boredom. The one in charge walked my sister a few feet away from the table, near the window. Two other cops stationed themselves between my parents. The last one stepped in front of me.

"I see we're playing man-to-man," I said.

"I'm going to ask you to be quiet," he said. He wasn't asking. He was begging me to give him a reason. Maybe he smelled the stink of Otisville on me. I kept my mouth shut.

The one with my sister said, "You saw her stab him?"

It was too late to stop what was going to happen. I, like everyone else, waited for her answer.

"I didn't see her, but . . ."

"But you saw her holding the knife."

"No, it's just that . . ."

"So where is the knife now?"

"I don't know."

"Young lady, I know this isn't easy but we need to know exactly how it happened."

Rachel took a deep breath. "Okay, I can do this. I remember I came home."

"From school?"

"No, it's Sunday."

"That's good. You're doing a good job."

"She's not retarded," I said.

"If you can't restrain yourself I'll do it for you," the cop in front of me said, and although I said nothing, didn't flinch or blink, I was suddenly face down on the dining room floor, a vantage from which I saw the fibrous grain of the hardwood, from which I saw the cops' black boots. I focused on these in case they decided to kick me. Then I stopped looking at the boots because there was a knee in my back. I closed my eyes so I wouldn't make a sound, so I wouldn't let this asshole know he hurt me.

There was shouting to be sure, my family protesting in chorus. A force was gaining power, growing centripetal, and I half expected the objects in the room to fly out the windows.

The cop in charge said, "Let him up."

He hauled me to my feet and said, "Now do you think you can keep your mouth shut?"

Again I didn't answer, flinch, or blink.

Muscles flexed, authority asserted—could we get back to the matter at hand? The cop with Rachel said, "All right, where were we?"

"When I got home, they were arguing and he was bleeding," she said.

The nail in the coffin, I thought. I waited for Officer Ballbuster to throw the cuffs on my mother. But the one with Rachel said, "Back up a minute. Your dad was already bleeding when you got home?"

"Uh-huh."

He walked away and, as an afterthought, turned back to her. "Thank you." He said to me, "You don't look like you know anything."

"I know your boots need polishing."

"Smartass. Okay, back to square one. How did you get hurt?" he asked my father.

"I cut myself doing the dishes." He jutted his chin toward the kitchen.

"How did you manage that?"

"One side of a knife is dull, but don't let that fool you because the other side is a blade."

"Another smartass."

"The sponge slipped. Someone was distracting me." My father dropped his arms and removed the dishtowel. He inspected the wound.

"Could that have been what happened?" the cop asked Rachel.

My mother put herself between the cop and her daughter. "She's a minor. You don't have my permission to speak to her."

"Is every one of you crazy? This isn't an interrogation. I can speak to whoever I want."

"She already told you she wasn't here. My husband is telling you the truth. I don't see what business it is of yours either."

"Whatever was going on here got your daughter so upset that she called us." Again to Rachel, "Do you think that's how it happened?"

My sister stared at him, or through him, emotionless.

"Listen up," the cop said, "does anyone want to make a statement or file a complaint?"

The ten seconds we silently inspected our shoes was enough to reestablish the cops' boredom.

"That's what I thought," he said. He took down our names, made sure he had our address correct.

My father refused medical attention ("I'm not lucky enough to bleed to death," he said, a joke wasted on the cop who seemed ready to commit him for saying it). The officers filed out, taking the air in the room with them, down the hall, and outside. We trailed them, good hosts seeing our guests to the door.

The scene was livelier in the driveway with a newly arrived ambulance and EMT workers waiting for some action. What a spectacle on our quiet street, so early in the day no less, when other families on the block were enjoying mimosa drenched brunches to the strains of Spanish guitar music, or so I pictured. A domestic disturbance. At least I had the decency to get arrested in another state.

Let's face it, when police break up a fight between your parents in your childhood home, it's a clear sign that your life is deteriorating faster than you can conceal it from others. How would the neighbors view this? I was thankful for the ambulance.

Maybe they would think it was a medical emergency. Anything less dysfunctional than the truth.

From *White Boy Bandito: How a Clever Suburbanite Became Death's Middleman for South American Revolutionaries*, by Laura Sullivan, PhD. (Verdict Press: 2006, 59)

In many ways, the Wolfs were your typical happy family, living the American Dream.

Judy Wolf was their lodestar, a can-do woman who could do it all—marriage, motherhood, and fulfilling career helping the less fortunate. With an honest streak a mile long, she taught her family that integrity, along with empathy, compassion, and modesty, was the single most important quality a person could have. Her husband Robert was more laid back, but no less responsible. First a hard-working salesman, and later a dedicated boss, Robert provided financial security for his loved ones. With his easygoing ways, he was a calming force in his children's lives. He was devoted to Alexander and Rachel and was there for them whenever they needed help.

The stability and safety of their home life irked Alexander. It bored him to tears. He liked to shake things up. Always a trickster and show-off, he wanted to ford the peaceful moat he knew so well. A connoisseur of practical jokes, he was known to put beef bouillon cubes inside the showerhead. The unsuspecting victim would bathe in consommé. On one memorable Thanksgiving, he superglued the plates, silverware, and glasses to the dining room table. By high school, he was growing wilder, reckless even. He shoplifted CDs from the mall and then gave them away, without a care in the world. Weekends were spent drinking beer with friends. At fifteen, he was pulled over for driving a car without a license. Guess who was riding with him that fateful night? The answer shouldn't surprise you. It was his best friend, Ron Moreno.

They say hindsight is 20/20 and, looking back in retrospect, one might see the seeds to Alexander Wolf's descent into crime planted in his years of teenage rebellion.

SEVEN

Taking the stairs two at a time, I reached Rachel's room and walked in uninvited, my feet landing on the preposterous pink carpet my parents installed when she was six and princess of the universe.

"Another lazy Sunday, huh?" I said.

Judging by her attitude, she never abdicated. She was at her desk, her posture impeccable in the chair, one hand working the laptop keyboard, the other cradling her phone to her ear. She acknowledged me by sighing loudly and muttering, "Asshole," under her breath. Then into the phone, "No, not you. I'm going to have to call you back. So annoying, I know." She swiveled in her chair and pounded her thigh with her tiny fist. "Get the fuck out of my room!"

Was I the only one aware that we were entering irredeemable territory? No return. What occurred at Dynamic might occur to us, a total liquidation because too many old debts had gone unpaid.

"Okay, I'll go. Wouldn't want you calling 9-1-1 again. Who does that anyway? Talk about a bullshit move."

"You're full of shit," she said, and declaimed a laundry list of my shortcomings that sounded awfully well-rehearsed, mostly personality defects I'd been confronted with for years, but also something new. "How much money do you think Mom and Dad wasted buying you out of a life sentence?"

"Five years max for first timers."

"Whatever."

She was wrong to cast me against type. She was the greedy one, not me. But no one has only one fault and it stood to reason that since we were related, we shared a few. I ponied up the funds for my legal defense, and accepted contributions from Ron's parents. They felt obligated because their nephew was the government's lone witness and they hoped to keep me from implicating them or their missing son, should he have ever resurfaced. When I ran out of money, my parents stepped in to subsidize my bills, multi-page invoices dividing a $350/hour service into every phone call, email, fax, conference, hearing, motion, deposition, etc. (and Martin Skolnick was not what you would call the best money could buy). That I didn't ask where the money came from, surmised Rachel, was evidence that I possessed the same trait with which she was often, rightly or wrongly, tagged.

Before things had the chance to get worse, my father called from downstairs. "Alex, Rachel. Can I see you?"

"How long is it going to take?" Rachel said.

"Just get down here."

We convened in the dining room, the de facto Wolf family town hall. My father brought the meeting to order. "I want to clear the air about a few things: Yes, there is no more Dynamic Business Solutions."

"Yes, we have no bananas," sang my mother. Their argument might have petered out, but that didn't mean she wouldn't take a jab at him.

"I can't keep throwing good money after bad. What does this mean? It means I won't have a job for the time being. But know that I won't be running out on my responsibilities. I'm not about to buy a van and disappear into the American west."

"Why don't you just tell us what you are going to do?" my mother said.

"I'm going to refinance the house. That's my first project. How does that sound?"

It sounded like something he should have done a year ago. I began feeling claustrophobic in a way I never felt in Otisville.

"This will give us a little breathing room until I can think of another, long term, project."

There was some discussion about the risk of borrowing against their only asset of value, which eluded me mostly because I wasn't listening. The fact that actual events had led to this conversation poleaxed me. The takeaway as I saw it was that while things were like this, I could never leave. Glorious autonomy took one look at me and said, "Don't see your name on the list, Chief." Like it or not I was one of them, and if I left before we were fixed, I wouldn't have been able to handle the survivor's guilt.

"I paid the first mortgage and home equity line like clockwork," my father said.

Yes, like it or not, I was a Wolf and, like it or not, it was time that I engaged them with the same dedication that in the past I tried to escape them. I decided to help. I had no idea what that would entail, but that didn't stop me from saying, "I have an announcement."

"I'm right in the middle of this," my father said.

"I know, but I think this will shed a little light on our predicament. Allow me the floor."

"The *floor*? God, Alex. Fine. Make it quick."

As I glanced erratically around the table, I searched their faces for the one thing worth reminding them. If I were to sum up my parents it would be that they treat other people better than what's required, better than what most people deserve. For each dollar my father pissed away at the track, he wasted another trying to help every incompetent that submitted a résumé to Dynamic. My mother volunteered her time and trust and even our home to people I wouldn't save from fire if it meant urinating on them. Rachel, whom I knew least well, had confided in me her concerns for all of us, which proved she didn't think only of herself.

This wasn't what I wanted to tell them. The better truth was that we were stuck with each other. That was the real indignity of Rachel's stunt. She alerted the outside world to what we already knew. You didn't invite outsiders to the show. We had to stick together because we had no choice. Not for better or worse, thick or thin, but just because. We were family. Nothing was going to change that.

"I'm here to help," I said.

My mother laughed in my face.

"I'm sorry," she said, covering her mouth. "That's not what I expected you to say."

"I'm going to make up for the ways I've let you down. You guys have kept me as one of your own, despite everything. And I owe you the same. So, I'm going to help—get involved and fix this fucking family."

I waited to meet their rush of hugs and grateful tears.

"Why couldn't I have bled out?" my father said, deadpan, displaying his wounded hand. He hit his targets. My mother and sister broke up laughing.

I wouldn't be discouraged. "If we band together, I'm sure we'll get through this. Who's with me?" I said.

Rachel had a different idea. "Let's just cut our losses. We have some good memories. Don't we owe it to ourselves to try to keep them? As soon as I finish high school I'll be gone. I'll probably have to deal meth to pay for college, but whatever, that's my problem. Dad, now that you have nothing to do all day you can hang out at the track. You won't have to hide it from us anymore. Mom, by all means, go chill with your bums. We all know that's who you really love. And Alex, as long as we're being honest here, I'm sure it's just a matter of time before you end up back in prison."

How could I deny the merit of her icy pragmatism? I saw in her a natural aptitude for business. It was easy picturing her in a conference room, pant-suited, equivocating about the human element in deciding that torching the careers of several thousand employees and raiding their pensions ultimately served the shareholders. She was also clueless about where she came from. Our clan operated on wobbly intuition, unstable gut feelings, not verdicts rendered in the cold light of facts and reason.

Of course, maybe it wasn't that simple. She was hurting too. My parents' fighting scared her, the blood was a little much and, panicked, she called the cops. Terrified of what my father's unemployment meant for us, she wasn't taking it well. So she chose to explode this town meeting by foisting her worst fears on us.

"You listen to me," my father said to her. "What you did today . . . if I thought you were sorry, or if you even understood what you did, I wouldn't say anything. But I can't take for granted that you do."

"Guys, please, just let me talk. This is what I mean. We need to band together," I said.

"Does anyone know what he's talking about?" my mother said.

"I have an idea. Are you ready? Get ready. It's a great idea."

It was not a great idea. I did not have an idea. I did not have an inkling of an idea. I said the first thing that came to mind. "We're going to start a business."

"Problem solved. Why didn't I think of that?" my father said.

"A religious business." And when I said it, the words sat well on my palate. Surprisingly, the words felt right. "Doesn't that sound good?"

"A few inches higher and I would have nicked my wrist. An artery!" my father said.

"Come on. We need to band together."

"Band together? Why do you keep saying that?" my mother said.

"Because that's what families do. Listen, I read an article about a local reverend who preaches about getting rich."

"Jelly's reverend," Rachel said.

"There's got to be a lot of money to be made by marketing products to this demographic."

"I knew it!" my mother said.

"I just thought of it. How could you know it?" I said.

"The one from that commercial, exploiting the poorest people in the world."

"Actually, I think he's helping those people," I said.

"Oh, please don't tell me you believe that. Do you hear this, Robert? Your son is now modeling himself on that man."

"I'm not modeling myself on anyone."

"You want to sell things to Christians? I'm hearing you correctly? You, my only son, want to sell crosses and rosary beads and—"

"I think only Catholics do the rosary thing," Rachel said.

"—what else, those candles with the saints painted on them?"

"I don't have anything specific in mind," I said.

"That much is obvious."

"We can sell anything. *Anything*," I said.

There was a time I could have sold this idea on the spot. I used to be confident, confidence being a commodity every bit as valuable as expertise and experience. Not only was I confident, I generally believed my own bullshit, a singular talent in and of itself. I was no longer confident. What I was doing in the dining room was faking it, spouting off like I used to but without the conviction behind it, hoping to somehow trigger muscle memory and reactivate self-assurance. So I continued pushing against everything they said, trying to find my poise, because that was what visionaries did. And idiots. "There's a niche that needs filling. That could be us. God's niche fillers."

"It's not our God," my mother said evenly.

"It not like we're going to convert," I said.

"We don't believe in it. That makes it a con. Am I the only one who sees this?"

"It's not a con," I said.

"Why does it have to be Christians? Why does it have to feel so wrong? What about something that will help people? A self-help product. Something like that."

Had she forgotten the cops in this room or did I need to show her their boot prints in the hall? Maybe she was right and we weren't cut out to hawk Jesus' wares, but to think that we should advise others how to improve their lot was at best a wish and at worst insane. Besides, I was sick of self-improvement. I heard enough of that rehabilitation shit in prison. Now was a time for self-acceptance. We needed to accept who we were, with all of our ugliness and juvenile fears. Couldn't she see that? She was going to be a hard sell. I put her on the back burner for a minute, focused my attention on someone who loved attention.

"Darling sister. You're unusually quiet. What do you think?"

"Since when do you care what I think, Señor Lobo?"

"I thought she called you Big Al?" my father said.

"Page 115. 'It was Santa, the General's eldest daughter. She was teasing Alexander by calling him a translation of his last name,'" Rachel said.

"I wish I had a nickname as cool as that," I said.

"Agreed. Call me Señor Lobo anytime," my father said.

"Are we really going to listen to the guy who stared at Dr. Sullivan's 'bosom with a brazen shamelessness.'?"

"Should I bother pointing out the redundancy of brazen and shameless? That's a fucking terrible book," I said.

"Language, Alex," my mother said.

"Rachel. You have an equal say. We're going to need everyone's help."

"I don't know anything about running a business."

"There's plenty you can do. I'll be the first to admit that Mom's right: I don't know much about Christians. Who's better at learning than you? You can teach us what we need to know."

"That's one thing we don't have to argue about. She is an outstanding student," my father said.

Rachel devoured the compliment, shape-shifting under the faintest praise. "I'm sorry about the police, Daddy."

Sorry? Daddy? He was Daddy again. And he smiled at her as if he just remembered why she was so great.

"That's what I'm talking about. Banding together," I said.

"Your heart's in the right place, Alex, but I'm sorry, you don't just start a business. There are going to be expenses. How would we pay for them?" my father said.

"Should we pray on it?" my mother said.

"Does this mean you're in?" I said.

"I have nothing against us going into business, in theory, but let me get this on the record. This idea of yours, morally... it ain't kosher, kid. Does that change anything for you?" she said.

"Probably not," I said.

"I didn't think so."

"So tell me, how do we get it off the ground? That is, until the billions start rolling in," my father said.

They were waiting for me. Money was a problem. If it wasn't, we wouldn't have been having this conversation. But what else could I say? "Don't worry. I have a plan."

August, 2003

I felt fucking great. It *was* a genius plan, as a matter of fact, even if they couldn't get ahold of it—simple and safe and unlikely to draw much attention to us. Best of all, it was legal. But here was Ron's uncle (not Enrique, in the army) acting like *el chico de oro* was oxidizing in their midst.

"Doesn't this asshole know you can't bring guns on a plane?" he said.

"You're a handsome man, Felix Moreno, and possibly the finest pool cleaner this side of the mighty Mississip, and I don't mean to come off rude here, but when you say things like that you sound like a goddamn moron. People have brought guns on planes for as long as there have been planes."

I'd guaranteed the crew at Crystal Clear Pools a genius plan to get the guns out of the country. When I gathered everyone in the office, they were ready to be astonished, mainly because I told them, "Prepare to be astonished." Was it my fault that properly filed paperwork didn't astonish them? I never said it would be glitzy.

"I'll try it one more time. The Sportsman and Conservationist Club USA. We're now an official entity, registered with the New York Secretary of State. We're also on file with the Department of State," I said, nodding vigorously to Ron and his father and his mother and his uncle and everyone else in the room.

"On file for what?" Ron Moreno Sr. asked his son in Spanish, who then asked me in English, even though I understood what I was being asked.

I explained the process. Yet again. Not at all agitated because, like I said, I felt fucking great. If there was a problem, it wasn't with my plan. My plan approached perfection. The problem was liable to be a communication breakdown. First time I presented it was in an uneven mix of English and Spanish, and since my *Español* was still *no bueno*, I'm sure something was lost in translation. This time I stuck to my native tongue and explained how it was a good idea not to fly into or out of New York airports. "Too many laws, too many lawyers." I explained about storing the guns in a lockable hard case, unloaded of course—"Unloaded," I repeated, "And make sure the chamber is empty."—and locking the case with padlocks. Dealing with ammo was another story altogether and I would get to that later. I explained to them how to fill out a CBP Form-4457, including make, model, caliber, and serial number of the weapon, and how to declare the firearms at check-in, when you meet the ticketing agent. "You can't do curbside check in," I explained filling out the orange declaration card, and about waiting for a TSA agent to show up, and about keeping your padlock keys in your pocket or your carry-on bag. "If you need to open the case for the TSA agent and your keys are in a bag that's already been checked, the agent will be more than happy to cut the locks off, in which case you'll be shit out of luck because you need to relock the case."

"And our reason for traveling with guns is?" Ron Sr. said.

"We're going to be a hunting club. Hunting *amigos, sí?* And we'll be taking international hunting trips. Are you getting it now? Is it sinking in? In a post-9/11 world, we'll fly commercial flights out of major international airports and will never have a problem because everything is going to be above board."

This time they got what I was trying to say. They just didn't believe me.

"And what happens when we don't come back with the guns?" Felix said. "That's not suspicious at all, no?"

"Is that supposed to be a serious question? Are you a serious person? Return flights can't be directly to the U.S. We put a country or two between us. It will be harder to track what we declare and when we do it. Besides, guns break, get stolen, lost. Maybe we have to doctor up a police report or something. The key is we don't come back empty handed. We'll always return with a pistol or hunting rifle."

"It can't be that easy," Ron said, but said it like he really, really wanted it to be true.

They all really, really wanted it to be true.

"Fucking-A, right, *es muy fácil,*" I said. I could have been Magna Cum Laude at the University of Smug Dickheads' School of Shit Eating Grins. It didn't go unnoticed.

"Look at this asshole," said Ron's uncle. "So happy with himself."

"You got that right, Felix Moreno, I am an asshole. The smartest asshole you've ever met," I said.

"You go first. See if they don't arrest you on the spot."

"Gladly. I need a vacation. I'll hit up the southern hemisphere, handle my business, work on my tan, and then take a run at a few of your *primas*. Going to come home with a new *novia*, or three."

I might have overstepped my bounds with that one. Luz Moreno, Ron's mother, elbowed Ron in the shoulder. "Pump the brakes, okay?" he said.

"Why would I do that? You're coming with me. We're rolling together," I said, triumphantly air-humping my immediate vicinity. My crass egotism was only one-third genuine. A large part of me liked to think of it as a kind of performance art, or at the least I expected them to find me somewhat funny and charming.

"You're lucky you're my brother," Ron said.

"That's right, *Yo soy tu hermano.*"

EIGHT

Like an adulterous spouse, I made the cardinal mistake of forgetting to delete the web browser. My mother confronted me with what she deemed noncompliance.

"Just so we're clear, I have grounds to dismiss you," she said from her desk, perusing the evidence of my insubordination, the various Christian-oriented sites I frequented.

Hat-in-hand contrition, I fumbled, "Mom . . ."

"Don't *mom* me. I'm your boss. And right now your boss has to decide whether she wants to report this to Glen Holtzclaw."

"Let's not go overboard. You don't even know it was me. You keep your office unlocked. Anyone could have come in."

Though true—anyone could have come in—it was I who harnessed the power of the Internet to put a glowing red X on my back so Inspiration would see it. A simple Google search turned up over nineteen million hits containing the word Evangelical. His word was being spread like California wild fires in August. While supposedly doing my job, I often disappeared into my mother's office (she was overworked and I went easily unnoticed) and pored over articles and message boards, joined organizations for their literature, trying to pinpoint a spiritual cramp, however miniscule, that I could massage. And here was where my mother's indignation rankled: What did she expect? After that breakthrough day when we agreed (if not enthusiastically) to band together and form a business, things settled down, but nothing really changed. We were still broke, still suffering each other, still saw nothing on the horizon to signal improvement. So far, their support for the biz was in name only. Whatever contributions they were going to make had to come from time chiseled out of existing schedules. A religious upstart lagged in priority to school, work, and lining up a second mortgage. Leaving everything to me. Which would have been fine if I knew what the hell I was doing.

My research was an attempt to solve a significant glitch in my plan. My mother had been right. I didn't know squat about what made Christians tick. Perhaps they were motivated by the same things as Jews, that they sought answers to the big questions about life and death like us. Then I remembered that there was no such thing as Jewish Crusades or Jewish rock music. Bottom line: I needed information. Reading and studying gave the illusion I was making headway and that was at least somewhat encouraging, I guess, seeing as how hard it was to stay positive otherwise. Given the direness of our situation, was it not obvious that results, and nothing else, counted? Research wasn't fixing the basement. And that opened the door to the power of negative thinking, against which I struggled unsuccessfully to resist looking up how many new businesses fail in their first year. What made me believe *we* were the exception? What would happen if, after uniting as a family, we bombed anyway? Which then brought me to recriminations. With half a lifetime in sales, there was surely something out there for my father, an outfit that might have benefited from his experience. It was his family to lead. Why waste my prime? Hear that, Old Man! Dust off the résumé and get back in the game!

I stuck with it and learned a thing or two. Quoting Scripture was a common method of proving one's point—Matthew and Mark were popular fellows—and I noted that on message boards there was a lot of talk about witnessing. "I once *witnessed* to an Atheist," they might write, or "Esmeralda first *witnessed* to me when I was four."

Part of the problem was that I had no faith of my own to fall back on; another part of the problem was that my brain had let itself go in prison. Mentally flabby as I was, the information was staggering. According to a Harris poll, two-thirds of Americans believed the Nativity story was historically accurate. About seven in ten believed in angels and miracles. Eighty-three percent considered the story of the virgin birth too improbable to be false. That anyone viewed the Bible as reportage should have roused my hibernating intellect. If you believed that, you'd believe anything and, by extension, you'd buy anything. The statistics should have encouraged me. Instead, I felt estranged from these people. I didn't understand them and had no way of guessing what they wanted. Eighty-three percent! Could that be true? Their logic was alarming. Too improbable to be false.

I could say the same about the survey.

Among this dizzying slew of information, I found a website selling Christian-themed bumper stickers. I copy-and-pasted many of them into a Word doc with the idea that, in these slogans, I could distill an entire dogma to its essence and locate my muse. Or not. Some were just funny.

After stumbling upon my search history, my mother did a little investigating of her documents folder. She threw the file in my face.

"jesusjunk.doc. What is this garbage? *Jesus: Legal in all fifty states . . . Pray is a four letter word that you can say anywhere (except in a public school) . . . God grades on a cross, not on a curve.*"

"Bumper stickers."

"*This car is prayer-conditioned . . . In case of Rapture, this car will be driverless . . . 1 cross + 3 nails = 4 given.*"

"That's my favorite."

"*What if Mary and Joseph had been pro-choice? Abortion doesn't make you unpregnant, it makes you the mother of a dead child!*" She looked up from her computer. "These make me queasy."

"Let's not act like I'm betting on Saudi camel races, or—"

"I'm acting like I have an employee who isn't doing his job. I'm not paying you for this."

"I thought we were working together. Isn't that what we agreed?"

"One day, if you have your own family, you'll learn that sometimes you have to bend. That afternoon, I bent."

"I think what's bothering you, Mom, is that Christians are strange to you and that makes you unsure about our business."

"You patronizing little shit. If you'd bother to do your job you'd know what goes on around here. I'm contacted by churches every week. I know very well who Christians are. They're *everybody*. The problem is that I don't think we should make money by exploiting their beliefs."

"That's not what we're doing."

"That's exactly what you want to do and what I don't understand about you. You don't believe in anything."

If it wasn't obvious that I was doing this for them, or us, then I was doing it for nothing. "I'm trying to help. Would I be doing that if I didn't believe in it?"

"You love your family. That's wonderful, but it's not the same as standing for something. That's what I never accepted about you selling guns."

"I bought guns."

"We both know what you did. I don't think it would have broken my heart as much if I felt you had the tiniest interest in the cause. If the ideology inspired you, maybe I could have understood why. But you did it for no reason. Like you were just passing the time. And now you're ready to do it again."

"If I was born again you'd be all for it?"

"At least I'd know your heart was in it. It's my job to support your passions. I don't know what your passions are. Do you?"

I would have preferred she fired me. As much as she was upset with me, her disappointment grew from an intrinsic need to share the blame. It was an attitude I could no longer stand. Here I was doing something, *trying* (which is all you can ask), and what did she do? Shoot it down. I was ready to let her have it once and for all, tell her to give it a fucking rest already. *I'll think more of you if you stop shouldering guilt for things that have nothing to do with you.* This was what I was going to tell her. The world's problems weren't hers to fix.

Except on the eve of the town youth fishing tournament when I was eight, with my father away at Fax Con '86 (an annual office supplies convention in Sandusky, Ohio, the roller coaster capital of the United States), my only rod broke. My mother stayed up that night fashioning a rod for me, a cockamamie contraption made of a broomstick. She'd rummaged around in the cluttered utility drawer and found three hook-and-eye latches, from which she screwed the eyes into the underside of the broomstick and ran my fishing line through. More ingenious than the homemade rod was that she somehow convinced me I wouldn't look ridiculous using it at the tournament. I don't remember if I caught any fish the next day, but I remember that she helped me bait my hook with live worms. Why did she do that? Impaling live worms for me to dunk in the Long Island Sound? She had a visceral aversion to animal cruelty of even the smallest kind!

So I couldn't cut her down that way. This was my mother, my mom, and it was a beastly irony that of all her crusades, of all her wrongs to right, I was the only one she had a deliberate hand in making. If she had sole legitimate claim to fix one problem in this world, it was me.

"I don't believe in Jesus Christ any more than I do Ronald McDonald, though they both have large followings and unconventional taste in footwear," I said.

She laughed. "Have you ever thought that the reason you can't come up with an idea is because you shouldn't be doing it in the first place?"

"I'm not sure that's what's wrong."

"When something's right, even when you're on the brink of disaster, you find a way to get by. Even when it seems hopeless there's another part of you that knows there's a reason to keep going." She was no longer speaking about me, I didn't think, or about us forming a business. It could have been a declaration for her life, or at least an explanation as to why she didn't fire me.

February, 2005

Dear Alex

You were in second grade the last time I had a prison pen pal. My friends Sheila and Wayne were amazing peace activists. I'm sure I've told you stories about their work with the Nevada Desert Experience. Do you remember? Who can be sure of what you remember? My friends helped organize the first vigils at a desert nuclear testing site. They were much more political than I ever was. They walked the walk. Very brave souls both of them. No one was surprised when the government labeled them anarchists . . . like that's a bad thing. When they were serving their sentences I wrote to them with messages of prayers and encouragement.

This won't be that kind of letter, I'm afraid. I never imagined my next prison pen pal would be my son. I'm still having such difficulty wrapping my head around what you did. I go around all day saying to myself, how can this be the same boy I gave birth to? How does something like this even happen? When I was pregnant with you, I had the Tay-Sachs test. Thank God you didn't have the horrible disease, but what I think about now is, did you inherit some odd genes anyway? Did your father and I pass down this mentality of yours to you? What did we do to make you think your actions were ok? I know it was nothing we taught you. You weren't raised this way.

When you were an infant, all I wanted was for you to grow up healthy. That was my one wish. Afterwards though, we saw that you were intelligent, and curious, and funny. You were so funny. You made everyone laugh. I thought, Ok, well maybe he has potential, maybe he might make his mark on the world. I started having hopes for you. I'm sorry you're going through a hard time, but you're not the only one. You've hurt all of us. Disappointment isn't even the word. You have devastated this family. I'm sorry, but that's how I feel. It would be easier if I didn't love you so fiercely. I love you so much. Do you even know? I just can't understand any of this.

I don't want to end on a harsh note, let me add this. It's not too late for you to redirect your energy into something constructive, not just to validate your self-approval. You can still contribute in a positive way to help other people. You have it within you. I believe in you.

I love you.
Mom

NINE

In an act of obstinacy and/or optimism (both misguided), my father prepaid six months office rent in January. It was his way of challenging his despondent staff, which already saw the writing on the wall. "Does it look like I'm going anywhere?" he'd boasted. This meant that though he now had no business to conduct, he had a place not to conduct it in until the end of June. When I met him that afternoon, he was behind his desk exuding an attitude slightly less delusional than a homeless woman I saw at Franklin Ave. Community who was convinced the doll she pushed in a stroller was her daughter.

"Okay, I've given it some thought and, you know, you're right. Religion is big time. Bigger, even, than obese people. Pardon the pun. Now have you talked to Jelly about meeting this Reverend Holden?" he said, in an animated way I found infectious despite the empty office.

"Was that part of the plan?"

"Like I said, I've given it some thought." He looked like he was about to reveal the secret of a magic trick. "Holden is the key. And we have a direct link to him."

"Shouldn't Rachel do that?"

"Things aren't easy for your sister right now. Jelly's her friend. I don't want to confuse things between them."

"But I'm another story?"

"You're another story. What I mean is, this is your idea. I'd like to see you set up a meeting with the reverend and pick his brain."

"He has no reason to meet me, you know."

"Other than being famous? Plus, you're famous in a way these bible thumpers really get off on. They want to save the corrupted. Not that I think you're corrupt. But he probably does."

It wasn't the first time I'd been asked to play bait. Not long ago, I was the ethically malleable gringo with sterling citizenship. Now I was being asked to use my intriguing back story to manipulate a man of God. As much as things had changed, they hadn't.

He brought out several sheets of paper, stapled together, from a desk drawer. "I've been working too. Take a look at this."

He'd printed out a series of pages from www.strongfaith.net, a forum dedicated to religious topics as varied as the role of God in the twenty-first century (integral, as many commenters referred to End Times and quoted Revelations at length) to debates about the piety of professional athletes (it was generally held that their sinful actions off the field spoke louder than their game-time bravery, with few exceptions). Through my own research, I was familiar with the website.

"I use the handle *prayerguy*," he said.

"You're kidding."

"I was trying to blend in. I thought it was a good name. I found out later that people go by regular names, like George or Julie, but there's a *BibleBill*, and a *Soldier4JC*. If you have a few minutes later I'd like you to read this. Tell me what you think."

www.strongfaith.net: Testimonies (Posting by *seeker*)

i used to be everything under the sun. i shoplifted each and everyday even if i had money in my pocket i cheated in school i never did homework only if i copeed off a boy or a girl in class. i smoked cigarettes and took the LORDS name in vane 2. that wasnt even the worse thing i did. i lied everyday to everyone even my sister my mom even my grandma. one day i killed a bird cause i felt like it.

i was so bad my mom cried everyday she prayed cause she didnt want me to be dead or to get to jail but she knew id be dead very soon so she begged me to do YOUTH BRIGADE. i did that in 9th grade thats where i met my first witness DWAYNE i even lied to him because i told him i was a CHRISTIAN but i didnt take JESUS into my heart.

and in summer DWAYNE and me go to YOUTH BRIGADE retreat thats in pensecola. we got to retreat the first thing that happened was so weird i got hiccups worse than anything you ever saw it was funny but got scary cause it was all day i COULD NOT STOP. one of the kids JASPER hes my best friend now but back in the day he called me Froggy cause my hiccups sounded like a FROG thats still my name but i dont hiccup. so for three days i keep hiccupping i can not stop and one day BROTHER ANDREW tol me dont worry its just GOD fightin real bad with the DEVIL for my soul. DWAYNE tol me same thing and i knew it was true.

   then sunday at retreat i was still hiccupping i thought it must be some battle going on i couldnt believe after all these days JESUS just didnt give up tryna win my soul then i went to service to help him cause the DEVIL is week in the HOUSE OF THE LORD. the hole time i was tryna hide my hiccups everyone could hear them anyway and probly thought i was a rude kid. they didnt know there was a fight for my soul going on. at the end of the service BROTHER ANDREW said anyone that wants me to pray for you raise your hand. i will never forget he said this. i felt all lite like i could fly away i never felt like that before i knew what was happening. so i raised my hand i couldnt believe i was doing it cause i was worse person you ever saw. as soon as i did my hiccups went away GOD had won my soul my life is amazing since that day. im still with youth brigade to help kids like me. that was 2 years ago im still a CHRISTIAN and i will be 2 the day i DIE.

   Your cookie cutter redemption story, I thought. Although, for its lack of surprise, *seeker* was putting himself out there, exposing his inner terrain, and the stupid sincerity of his confession, the incredible artlessness of it, made me uncomfortable. I felt embarrassed on his behalf, and I looked to counterbalance my chagrin the only way I knew how: by mocking him. It was an absurd story and the kid was simple, saved or not. But since I was reading alone in my room and there was no one around to impress with my cruel wit, I attempted, I really fucking tried, to understand why someone else might find it inspirational. Broad consensus among the commenters was that it was awesome. No one questioned the story's veracity, nor did they attack *seeker's* barely literate telling of it. He did come across as a person who wanted to be good, and I had to admit he'd persevered and struggled over some obstacles at a young age. Only I found it too difficult to shelve my smugness, my superiority. I formed a picture of *seeker* that was unadulterated white trash. Lanky with bad posture, in need of five grand worth of orthodontic work, a gold-plated crucifix on a gold plated link chain around his scrawny neck, sporting pajama bottoms and a knock-off NBA jersey, facial hair soft and blond and making him look younger, not older. Now I saw his whole family: his older sister addicted to her son's Ritalin and trying to look sexy for *seeker's* friends; his mother cruising through a Wendy's drive-thru on a rascal scooter; grandma calling black guys "colored" and thinking she's progressive. Then it occurred to me *seeker* was roughly Rachel's age. They weren't peers. They lived on different planets. He probably thought SAT stood for Some Ass Thumpin'!

Some Ass Thumpin'. I caught myself laughing at that one, LOLing alone in my room as I mentally tore down some kid I'd never met. What kind of shitheel was I? And who was I to talk? I was so fucking precious I'd spent my late twenties in prison. I hated myself right then, and maybe saying "right then" was just more cowardice in that I couldn't come clean that this feeling wasn't fleeting or newly arrived. I couldn't remember a time when I wasn't ashamed of the way I willfully confused my narrowness, my biases, my ugly bullshit with singular talent. Want to know why I hadn't been able think up just one idea for a business? Well, you didn't have to survey too deep into my core to find the reason. *seeker* was a retarded hillbilly, a *Floridian*, fine, but if I was sizing people up at least let me render an honest self-portrait. I was the grown man who lived with his parents, the adult with the cathedral-sized ego wholly disconnected from his second-rate life, the lazy guy who understood it was easier to lie to himself than change. That guy crumpled *seeker's* testimony and threw it across the room. He got up and went downstairs to watch television, hoping the last few innings of the game could help him forget who he was.

TEN

Having redoubled my efforts at Franklin Avenue Community Outreach, trying to get back into my mother's good graces, I dispatched everything she put before me, including a dozen phone calls to perennial donors at whose feet I groveled for more contributions. By early afternoon there was nothing left for me to do. In an attempt to prove that she was a hard, but fair, boss she let me knock off early. At home I cruised the websites as *prayerguy*, memorizing a little chapter and verse, as they say— John 3:16—which I considered important if for no reason other than its odd relationship to rabid sports fans cheering their heroes into battle. "For God so loved the world, that he gave his only begotten Son, that whosoever believeth in him should not perish, but have everlasting life." That brought an end to the studying. What did that have to do with the Jets beating the Dolphins?

I was in the kitchen eating a turkey sandwich with a can of ginger ale, chewing over the kitchen sink to avoid using, and then having to wash, a plate when Jelly snuck up behind me and goosed me under the arm. She was in jeans that looked airbrushed onto her legs and a pink and lime-green striped Polo shirt that was just long enough. Or short enough, depending.

"Alex, Alex, Alex," she said, eyeing my sandwich. "Save me any?"

"Knock yourself out."

She took a dainty bite. "Mustard? Yuck. Don't they have mayo in jail?"

"As a matter of fact they do, but the warden made us cage fight for it."

"Can I just say that you have a weird sense of humor?"

"Where's Rachel?"

"That ho's getting boned in a parking lot."

"Really?"

"Oh my God, no! Rachel? Are you serious? Where else, studying. Or maybe tutoring some dumb kid. We didn't get into details, you know what I mean? She wanted me to give you this."

She handed me an envelope of my sister's stationary. The note inside was one line: *Sorry, Big Al. Dad made me.*

She stepped back, rested her weight on one leg, ran a hand through her hair, shifted her weight to the other leg, inspected her fingernails. Her every move had the fluency of premeditation, rehearsal. "So . . . I'm waiting."

"For what?"

"I didn't come all the way over here for my health. I have a life, you know."

"You live ten minutes away on foot and I'm sure you drove."

"Word on the street is you want to talk to me, which is cool, my door's always open. But if you're going to stand there playing the shy guy, I'm going to get moving."

I was the *prayerguy*, not the shy guy, but I saw no reason to dwell on the difference. "Rachel told you I wanted to speak with you?"

"Hey, it's flattering, but you don't have to be so invertebrated."

"I think you mean introverted."

"Slutever."

She had a capricious and unreliable energy, as if the unfocused curiosity of a toddler and the strength of a grizzly were contained within the five-foot frame of her overdeveloped body. God help the high school boys who contended with her daily!

"Maybe Rachel exaggerated," I said.

"Maybe, maybe not. The point is, I'm here, you're here. What's on your mind?" She stood there, shifting from foot to foot.

What the hell! Might as well put it out there. "I understand you're pretty religious."

"I've been born again according to John 3:3 . . . 'Except a man be born again, he cannot see the Kingdom of God.' Man can mean girl. I'm no dude."

"I know a little John." I recited the verse I just learned.

"You don't know how happy it makes me to hear you say that. You're good people and it totally sucks that because you deny God's only Son, who died for our sins, you'll never enter the Kingdom of God."

"Yeah that's a real bummer, Jill. Want anything to drink?"

"Nah, I'm good."

I took a sip of soda, buying time. How was I to have this conversation while ducking the issue of my family's problems? It wasn't her business. Maybe she already knew from my sister, but Rachel should have learned to keep her mouth shut after she invited the cops over.

"I was wondering if you could . . ." But what I really wanted to say was, *Just tell me about some piece of crap that will drive you Christians crazy and make me a mint. What is it? Tell me!*

"It's okay," she said. She placed the sandwich on the countertop and closed her fingers around my hand. "Whatever you have to say is safe with me." Sure enough, on her wrist was a narrow yellow band with blue letters: WWJD. She saw me looking. "I wove it at camp last summer. I was a counselor."

"What Would Jelly Do?"

"Want one? Might be a good reminder. Not that I'm judging because I'm so not."

I'd killed a lot of time in Otisville dreaming about what it was going to be like when I got out. Not even my most outlandish fantasies approached this. Because it seemed such an obvious manipulation on my part, I was nervous asking, "Would you mind telling me something about your personal relationship with God so I can have one too?"

It was misplaced concern, for my sister's friend had faith enough for us both and that made her unable to see my question as anything but guileless. She lit up. Her gray eyes fluttered, sort of rolled back in her head for a second, as if she were a robot rebooting her mainframe. She hugged me.

"Can I just say that I love Jesus? Not a day goes by that I don't talk to him. No offense to Rach or anything but He's like my real best friend." She released me and stepped away. The skin on her neck had flushed.

"You talk? To Jesus?"

"That's what I just said."

"How do you know you're not just talking to yourself?"

"The shepherd listens to his sheep," she sang, her body language suggesting she was horny for good ol' JC more than anything. "He always gives me a sign. Sometimes the sign is no. Man, it's like sweltering in here. I'll have that drink now."

"What can I get you?"

"I'll help myself, if you don't mind," she said and rummaged through the refrigerator. She cracked open the can, and gulped a large sip. She burped, did nothing to muffle it. "Excuse *me*! Where did that come from? You know, I used to burp the alphabet."

"Me too."

She hopped up onto the counter next to the fridge, her legs hanging. She crossed one over the other, a flip-flop dangling from her toes. "We're like peas in a pod, Alex. Can you feel it?" She started laughing, a dizzying, porpoise-like laugh. "Gosh, you're so serious. Loosen up! You act like my grandfather and he passed away years ago. Aw, I miss my grandpa."

Jelly was a character all right. What I liked about her was that she was hard to pin down, either smarter than she looked or more naive than she acted, and she used this to her advantage. It made her unflappable. "You're pretty excited, I don't think I can match you."

"You could if you had the Spirit in you." She slid down from the countertop. "I wake up like this every day because I know that Jesus is taking care of me. It's awesome to feel this way. You can feel this way too. It's good that you came to me. I've witnessed before."

And there you have it. Like Dwayne and Brother Andrew to poor hiccupping *seeker*, Jelly was going to witness to me. Maybe she already was.

"I want to introduce you to someone. Can you guess who? It's Reverend Holden."

I didn't even have to ask. You're welcome, Dad.

"He's a great man."

"I'm sure," I said.

"If it wasn't for Reverend Holden, I don't know where I'd be today. In a lot of trouble, let's leave it at that."

Okay, Jill, let's have it, deliver the goods, give me that conversion story, your tale of hiccupping before being saved. "I doubt that," I said.

"You're kidding me, right?" She raised her hand in front of my face to display a silver band on her third finger. "Do you have any idea what this means?"

"Congratulations. When was the wedding?"

"It's a purity ring, silly. And you know who gave it to me?"

"A great man?"

"He definitely ministers to teens everywhere about the blessing it is to wait until marriage."

She informed me that not only is abstinence God's law, but the only way not to get pregnant, or AIDS, or diseases less fatal than AIDS but that will nevertheless make your genitals resemble boiled lobster tails, not to mention whip your mind into a psychotic frappe. And what worthy suitor would want you after you've been permanently tarnished?

"Condoms work, at best, like twenty percent of the time," she said. "That's a fact. It's science. Reverend Holden tells us to choose ourselves and we can't lose."

Not wanting to argue her ridiculous statistic or tell her that her beloved reverend (a great man, remember?) might be a dangerous zealot, I said nothing.

"How awesome is my wedding night going to be? I mean, what better gift could I give my husband?" asked chaste Jelly. "And I know what you're thinking: what guy will wait until he's married to bone?"

I believe it's important to note for the record that this wasn't the conversation I had in mind.

"I wasn't thinking that." I was thinking that.

"Don't worry, he'll be satisfied," she said with enough confidence that it seemed reasonable to believe she was a twenty-five-year-old undercover cop working a sting operation. She leaned close to me, as if there were others around who shouldn't hear her. "I give blow jobs," she whispered.

It was good she was leaning into my ear because I didn't want her to see what I imagined was a look of acute terror on my face.

"You don't say?"

"Like a champ," she said, with too much self-possession for any real girl of any age. In two seconds, a SWAT team would repel off the roof and crash through the windows to subdue me with rubber bullets. "But it has to be with a boy I really like."

As a person with flexible character, even I marveled at how she reconciled her cute hypocrisy. Unless it wasn't hypocrisy but an advanced way of thinking. It was the Internet generation, hers. They'd seen it all. There wasn't a whole lot left to the imagination when you'd viewed the copulation of an elderly Dutch couple, a young Filipina, and a butternut squash. My formative years were pre-modem. We had to hustle for our smut. Reports show that American students lag behind their European and Asian counterparts in science and math, but I remembered working like an electrical engineer to descramble pay-per-view channels late at night.

These were reflections after the fact. That afternoon, intellectually, okay, I accepted I had to get out of the kitchen. I needed the dining room table as a buffer. A few feet of solid oak between Jelly and me would do the trick. On a baser level—masculine, genetic, maybe even institutional—I hadn't seen any action since Laura threw me over right before her book was released. Jelly was a babe, *practically* legal, who understood condoms to be the devil's work and talked about giving head as though it were a competitive sport. There was the saying: Hate the sin, love the sinner, if sin was even the right word, age of consent a manmade demarcation, varying on what part of the world one visited. Better yet, my Bar Mitzvah made a man of me at thirteen, the same eternal age as Romeo, making Jelly a woman by Hebrew law, and whatever a man and a woman choose to do in that man's parents' kitchen is nobody's business.

She was still leaning into me when I felt her hand between my legs. I looked to the ceiling, as if I could literally look the other way, somehow not be complicit. And then down came my fly and her hand searched out the opening in my underwear and I thought she'd better find it soon because I was about to tear through my jeans, and then she had me in her hand and she slid down and true to her word, she was proficient. Now I wasn't thinking anything (there were primitive drums beating in my head, the percussion of a sacrificial rite), and if she was a cop, she deserved to make detective or whatever pay grade she was gunning for. I heard what sounded like an explosion, and I thought it was an aneurysm, or the shattering of my grinding teeth, but Jelly was now standing and looked scared to death.

"I'm sorry. It was a mistake. Don't tell Rachel," I said.

"Didn't you hear that? What was it?"

It happened again. A loud crashing sound. I thought of a gas leak, but I didn't smell gas. The hot water heater, maybe. Could that blow up? I grabbed Jelly by the wrist and started leading her away.

"Um, shouldn't you do something about that thing?" she said.

"Oh, right," and I zipped myself back into my jeans and pulled her through the house, to the front yard, where we ran to the sidewalk.

"Call 9-1-1?" she said.

Had I not been me, had the police not just visited this address to break up a potential knife fight—in other words, if I were a normal citizen—I would have told her, yes, please summon the authorities.

"I don't know, do you see smoke in the basement windows? What about an earthquake? A sink hole? How are the other houses?"

As I enumerated these possible disasters, she hugged me, not seductively, but like a child who had awakened from a nightmare and needed reassurance.

"I'm freaking out like really bad," she said.

I felt a complexity of emotions myself: embarrassment that she was touching me in public, where anyone could see us, fear that my house was about to explode, and insecurity over my inability to prevent it.

"This is totally a sign. Didn't I tell you sometimes He says no?" she said.

If to deny me a beej God would destroy my family's home, then He wasn't a deity I wanted to mess with, nor was He in tune with the messier and, therefore, worthwhile nuances of human life. "Fine, let me see your phone." I located the three numbers that brought on the cars and trucks with their sirens, and this time it was the firemen flying into the house, living out heroic fantasies. Jelly and I stayed on the sidewalk. Owing to my height, I had an unobstructed view down her shirt. I saw a gold cross pendant around her neck. On the vertical part of the cross was what looked like a broken toothpick.

"What's that?" I said.

She was more than happy to model it. "It's a piece of the cross. The real crucifix. I got it for my sweet sixteen."

"How do you know it's real?" I said.

"A certificate says so."

Jelly was right: He does give signs. It came to me right then that another token with similar Holy Land vogue was what I was after. The Wolf family fortune lay in dressing up ancient sacredness in twenty-first century packaging. I was about to ask if she could show me the certificate when one of the firemen interrupted.

"All clear," he said.

"Are you sure? I heard an explosion."

"You didn't hear an explosion because there was none. And if there was, you wouldn't have heard it because you'd be dead."

"So, what was it?"

"Part of the ceiling collapsed. And then a wall came down. The one separating the laundry room from, what do you got down there, a pantry?"

"Yeah."

"Yeah, well, that's what fell. You know you got termites?"

"They've been exterminated."

"Anyway, you and your girlfriend can go back inside," the fireman said, and left.

"Thank God," she said, crossing herself. "I was afraid we were being punished for what I did to you." She hugged me again.

Her arms around me, mine around her, this was the pose in which Rachel and my mother found us.

"What happened? Is everyone alright?" my mother asked.

As I tried to tell her that we were fine but the house, on the other hand, not so much, Rachel demanded to know, "What are you two *doing*?"

October, 2003

Another day, another international flight with a Remington R-15 VTR Predator. I wound my way through the line to the ticketing agent, gave him an oversized smile, a hearty hello, and placed my license and boarding pass on the counter.

"Good morning. I have a bag to check and a firearm to declare today."

The first time I said this I felt as if I was confessing to a crime. Even though I had yet to encounter any problems, I was still nervous checking in. I just tried to present myself as God's most innocuous and polite creation.

"I need you to fill this out," he said and gave me the customary form. It stated that by signing and dating it, you agreed to the terms of the airline's (in this case Delta's) firearm policy. There was a portion for the agent to fill out and on the back, in bold, was the declaration that the weapon was UNLOADED.

"Is this your firearm?" he asked, indicating the hard plastic case.

"Yes, sir."

"Is it unloaded?"

"Yes, sir, it certainly is. Would you like to see it?" I said.

They always wanted to see it. I unlocked the case and displayed the rifle for the agent, pointing it at the floor, which is the safest direction to point it, and I locked the action to the rear to show it was clear.

"Hunting?" he said.

"You know it. Llama."

This piqued his interest. "For trophy?"

"For meat."

"What's that taste like? Got to imagine it's pretty gamey."

"Not the way I cook it. I make a sausage and put it in a stew. That's some good eats. Smelling it will bring tears to your eyes." Did it matter that I'd never seen a llama outside the Bronx Zoo and wasn't positive people even ate them?

"Man, you're making my mouth water. Well, good luck." He

nodded at the rifle. "You can lock it back up," he said. After I closed the action and locked the case, he taped on the card I filled out, then checked the rifle and my other luggage. "Please wait over there," he said, pointing to an area nearby. This was where TSA would meet me if they had a question or wanted to see my firearm.

"Thank you very much," I said.

"You have a nice day," he said.

"I will. You too."

It was really as easy as that. Today no TSA agent came. After fifteen minutes, I went through security and straight to the bar nearest my gate. Two double bourbons later, and I was ready for a nap.

From the screenplay to *The Wrong Way Son* (H.E.L.R. Prod., 2007)

```
EXT. AMAZON JUNGLE - DAY

A HELICOPTER maneuvers over the roof of the
rainforest, zigzagging recklessly, its propeller
beating the bright sky. Bullets WHIZ through the
air, PING against the metal body.

INT. HELICOPTER - CONTINUOUS

              ENRIQUE
        Freakin' policia.
              ALEX
        I can't get arrested.

A rocket grenade comes humming out of the
overgrowth, just misses the cockpit.

              RON
        They're not trying to arrest us.
              ALEX
          (To PILOT)
        Get us the hell out of here.

Just as he says this, a bullet cracks the wind-
shield glass, rips through the PILOT'S head,
kills him instantly.
```

                    RON
          Shit.
                    ENRIQUE
          Our Father, who art in Heaven,
          hallowed be Thy name.

The Helicopter loses altitude, starts spinning.

                    ENRIQUE (CONT'D)
          Thy Kingdom come, Thy will be
          Done.

Tree tops rush up at the helicopter, a green blur from all the spinning. Alex unfastens his seatbelt, yanks open the door.

                    ALEX
          Come on!

The helicopter CRASHES through the trees, flinging Alex and Ron and Enrique out the door, right as the helicopter EXPLODES.

EXT. AMAZON JUNGLE - CONTINUOUS

Their bodies break tree limbs as they fall. Flaming wreckage rains down on them. It looks as if they will die when they hit the ground. From the corner of Alex's eye, he sees:

A PRISTINE SILVER LAGOON.

The three splash safely into the water.

ELEVEN

My mother, Rachel, and I watched on television a biography of a former child sitcom star who, on the heels of his fifth rehab stint, was optimistic about his chances in Hollywood. Outside fell a thin, cold rain that for all its stinginess seemed as if it would never stop.

In the basement, my father and a contractor surveyed the damage. I'd already done my own walk-through. To use professional terminology: shit was fucked up. As the fireman said, the ceiling in the laundry room came down. Chunks of drywall and plaster were on the floor, dust everywhere. The wall separating the laundry room from the pantry hadn't collapsed but buckled at the bottom where the studs gave out from a wall too heavy to support.

The show went to commercial, an ad for a German sedan doing 120 down the Great Wall of China. From the exterior, the car thudded up and down on the uneven bricks; inside, in the backseat, a black baby slept in heavenly peace, for the ride was so smooth he felt neither the speed nor bumps. The crossroads of commerce and multiculturalism.

If I were a man of faith, I might have said that Jelly's cross was the answer to my prayers. I needed a symbol, that much was clear. The contractor's boots and my father's shoes banged up the stairs. The basement door opened and they came out. Together they walked to the front door. They shook hands. The contractor left.

My father called to my mother, "Judy, come with me and I'll show you what he's talking about." She followed him downstairs.

"This is so humiliating," Rachel said. "We're the people all the neighbors wish would move away because we drag down property values or something." She changed channels to a show where amateur costume designers vied for a position on an off-Broadway revival of *Starlight Express*. "What do you think is going to happen?"

We hadn't spoken since I failed to convince her that Jelly and I had been just hugging, nothing more. An innocent hug—innocent, the opposite of guilty—brought on by the trauma of our near-death. It was a poor excuse. Weak, Rachel had called it.

"Hellooo?" she said.

"I'm sorry, were you talking to me? I assumed you were complaining to the world at large."

"God, you're no help. I'll tell you what's going to happen. We're going to have to sell the house for, I don't know, nothing, and move into one of those motels poor people live in. You and I will get bunk beds."

"Sounds like you've got it figured out."

"Wait. You think I'm right? I was only complaining." She flipped around on the TV some more. Every channel she alighted on, no matter how briefly, was celebrity gossip-oriented.

I returned to thoughts of religious symbols. Lambs? Fish?

"This is the worst thing that's ever happened," Rachel said.

"Will you please stop? I'm trying to think."

"Daydreaming about Jelly?"

"For the last time . . ." but how vehemently could I deny it? If they really were best friends, Jelly would confess (or brag about) the pathetic details of our oral coitus-interruptus. And then Rachel would take up against me. At any rate, my mother, back upstairs now, broke up my latest weak excuse.

"Have you seen my car keys? Every day I leave them on the table by the door, and every day they're never there."

"Ghosts," I said.

"At this point, I wouldn't be surprised if we were haunted." She patted down the pockets of her windbreaker.

"What did that guy say to Dad?" Rachel said.

She rummaged through her purse. "Who? The contractor? Please, you two, help me look."

From her purse, she pulled out her wallet, tissues, Chapstick, bottle of ibuprofen, paperback book. "I have to get back to work. If I don't restructure the second quarter budget we're going to run out of food before the end of June."

"What about running out of food here? This is child neglect," Rachel said.

"Neither of you are children, regardless of your behavior."

Something jingled. "Okay, got them. How did they get all the way down there? Alex, a word, please."

I followed her to the door. She said, "The contractor said eighteen thousand."

"Yikes."

"Might as well be a million."

"What about home owners' insurance?"

"I don't know if they'll put our claim through. They're calling it a maintenance problem right now. Or a maintenance issue? Something to do with maintenance. We're trying to get them to change the classification."

"And the hits just keep on coming."

"I could kill him right now."

"The contractor?"

"Your father." Her hand was on the door knob. She lowered her voice. "Don't tell Rachel. We can't refinance the house."

"Why not?"

"Our application was rejected. Poor income to debt ratio. Basically, they don't think we can pay it back."

"They might not be wrong."

"Thank you for telling me what I already know."

Once she left, I went downstairs and watched my father watch the damage, sort of the way I watched him watch Spanish *Rocky*. Staring at where the ceiling used to be, he resembled a man awed by an art exhibit he only dimly understood. "Some mess, huh?" he said.

I agreed with his assessment of the situation in both the specific and general sense.

"Mom said eighteen grand." I left out the part about the bank declining his loan application. I wasn't sure if it was even true or a hyper-advanced marital warfare tactic he used to upset her and that would make him look like a savior when he pulled off the refinance in spite of it, one more miraculous flourish by Robert Wolf.

"This could've been bad news if someone was down here when it fell." He pointed to one of the larger hunks of fallen ceiling.

"What about your friend Lenny?"

"Why would Lenny have been down here?"

"You said he has more money than he knows what to do with. Eighteen grand is no joke."

"That's one estimate."

"Would Mad Dog help?"

"I'm not asking him," he said.

"Where are you going to get the money?"

"I don't need money. I need a stove of butter."

"The American dream."

"You don't know that story? From when my father emigrated from Russia?"

I told him it didn't ring a bell.

"Shame on you. This is your history. When my father landed here, he had to take a psychological exam."

"Why?"

"Didn't you learn anything in school? I guess some countries liked to open the doors to the asylums and send their loonies our way. At least that was how our government justified quotas. Anyway, your grandfather was with the examiners and they were asking questions. He was barely a teenager and these were intimidating men."

"Sure," I said.

He paused, grinned. "They asked him 'Can you make a stove out of butter?' Which is such a stupid question if you think about it because you're dealing with someone who speaks a foreign language. But your grandfather said, 'Of course!' Very confident, you know. 'Would you mind repeating yourself?' they said. 'Certainly. You can make a stove out of butter.' The examiners consulted each other, they talked it over a minute, and they turned back to my dad and asked him to explain himself. He said, 'You sell the butter and you buy a stove with the money.' They let him right in after that. Talk about an American attitude. So, I don't need $18,000. I just need a stove of butter."

"Should be simple enough."

He put his hand on my shoulder. "I've got to run an errand. Can you keep an eye on Rachel? Try to be there for her. You're her big brother."

Perhaps weak excuses ran in the family. I didn't press him

for a better one. He just turned from me and I let him go, knowing what his errand was and that the word errand, even as a euphemism, shouldn't have gutted me like this. I finally understood that gambling had nothing to do with money. That was just how he kept score. What he needed was the action, to feel the release, on this day especially. But this was a day he just found out he was $18,000 worse off than when he got out of bed, and he was in a hole when he woke up. How depressing it was to watch him disregard his best interest, maddeningly blind to what everyone else saw, though I suspected he saw more than he let on.

I gave him a minute to clear out of the house and then I came upstairs. Hanging on the wall in the hallway was a framed certificate from the Jewish National Fund, the people responsible for planting trees in Israel. For $18, you buy a tree that gets planted in the desert. You get a certificate. Jews buy trees to memorialize their dead or honor a birth or wedding. The framed certificate in our house was for four trees purchased by my grandmother, one for each of us. I don't know why she bought them, but since she lived on a fixed income I imagined it was an occasion of some significance.

The Trees for Israel certificate was another decoration in the house. I either glanced at it in passing or ignored it altogether. *With love for Robert, Judy, Alexander, and Rachel.* Four trees. Thanks, Bubbe. I wondered if the trees flourished or withered in drought or were destroyed in civil unrest. I wondered if they were ever planted in the first place or was it a scam to raise money from American Jews who felt good helping a homeland they never visited? And it was while I was balancing my curiosity about the Trees for Israel certificate with the story about my grandfather's butter stove, along with the numb disappointment I felt for my father, that I remembered Jelly's cross pendent. I looked at the certificate. I thought about the pendent. Then I rushed upstairs to Rachel's computer.

Who knows why this was the afternoon the certificate caught my eye? It had been there for years. Rachel wasn't in her room but so monomaniacal was my focus that she could have been using the computer and I would have sat on her lap, never asking why the chair felt lumpy. The answer was obvious. The value of a meaningless symbol is that it can mean anything. I only needed to find the right plant. Frankincense? Myrrh? No and no.

Bingo! There it was on the monitor: *Paliurus spina-christi*, or a related plant: *Ziziphus spina-christi*. In laymen's terms, Christ's thorn. Of the Rhamnaceae family. Notably resistant to honey fungus. In flower from July to August. Can grow in alkaline soil. Just look at that unimpressive photo. A bush, green leaves, some kind of yellow-greenish round blossom lacking the superficial beauty of other flowers. Of course it lacked. Jesus was humble. You'd expect nothing else.

I was going to sell the spiny shrub commonly assumed to have been used for Jesus' crown of thorns. A thin wreath pressed in Lucite? In a ceramic pot? Have the whole thing authenticated by some clergy, maybe Holden, saying it was harvested in Bethlehem, or Jerusalem—somewhere in the Holy Land—and a portion of the proceeds was going to such and such charity or ministry? This was it. This was the answer. *Paliurus spina-christi* was a plant you would kill with poison if it grew in your garden, but call it another name and it was transformed into something bespeaking faith and sacrifice. Hell yes, sacrifice! They were going to sacrifice $19.95, no, $29.95 (standard shipping and handling rates applicable).

Even in my excitement I perceived hurdles lining up in my way. Where did the plant grow and how could I get one? And then what? Did I need a license to sell it? What type of clergyman would be open to a partnership? And yet I saw the pitfalls of proprietorship fall away. I was undaunted by these obstacles, convinced I would trounce them. In saving my family from bankruptcy—fuck that, in saving them, us, *period*—I was motivated by what my mother called the Great Good of the world. For once I was traveling the moral high road. From up here, I could barely make out the filthy landscape below.

February, 2004

I walked out into the courtyard, hoping to find Ron or Enrique or anyone who could get me some gentle fare for my sensitive stomach but found a girl of about ten or eleven, kicking a soccer ball against the wall of the compound. Two days earlier, Ron and I had passed through customs, each toting a .50 cal with our luggage. At least once a month for six months, I'd flown into this country with guns and Enrique said the time had come for me to meet the General, a logistical nightmare in any case made completely hellish due to a thigh-quaking bout of diarrhea that had left me dangerously dehydrated, in addition to being a stinky travel partner. My North American gut was outmatched by a shaved ice I ate the afternoon we'd set out for Hacienda Buenavista. Where I'd been vigilant on all my trips south to drink nothing but bottled water, and eschewed salads altogether, I somehow forgot the advanced economic principal of raw materials, as related to profit margin, which posited street vendors most definitely use tap water, or worse, to make ice. My lips were still stained pink from the strawberry syrup in the *raspado* when the bacterial pathogens entered my intestines, liquefied my bowels, and propelled them from my body at sound-barrier-shattering velocity.

"I need a hospital," I moaned through the bathroom door, when Ron's uncle came to pick us up at the apartment we were staying in.

Ron weighed in with his medical opinion. "Like Willy Wonka's chocolate river but, you know, with shit."

Enrique said we were soldiers and soldiers followed orders no matter what.

"I'm an army contractor, at best," I said.

"The general say you go, so you go."

So I went. Enrique gave me a couple of bottles of water to rehydrate. They didn't help. The ride to Hacienda Buenavista was eleven hours by direct route, but given our cargo, and the fact that our host was a paramilitary enemy of the state, we took a circuitous route to throw off anyone who might have followed us, stopping to change vehicles three times. When we switched to the Jeep, our handlers gave me a tea made out of *guayaba* flowers, a folk remedy to tamp down the flow of sewage pouring out of me. I was too sick to tell if it worked. By the time we reached the compound, I was hugging the side of the Jeep's roll bar, shivering, mouth caked with a white paste, a savage headache thumping my brain. Ron and Enrique carried me out of the vehicle and helped me inside the house. I was given a shower and anti-diarrheal medicine, and served aguapanela, a drink used to treat colds, then shown to my bedroom. It was agreed I was in no condition to meet anyone, let alone General Avila. Then I slept. And slept. And when I woke it was morning and, aside from what felt like a hangover, minus the fun memories to go along with it, I knew the worst was over.

Here in the courtyard, still weak, I watched this girl smash a soccer ball over and over against the wall of the compound. I could tell this wasn't a game for her. She was practicing, ten kicks with her right foot, ten with her left, her head down, her plant foot landing in the same spot every time. She had an impressive single-minded concentration. I didn't think anything could distract her, not even the man who walked out into the courtyard and stood beside me.

I'd seen photos of General Fulgencio Avila, so I knew this short, boll weevil of a man was him. But even if I had no idea what he looked like, I wouldn't have been mistaken. He moved with military discipline, the calm comportment in the face of death that always intimidated me. I straightened up and tried smoothing down my bed head.

"That's my daughter, Santa," he said.

"Quite the athlete," I said.

"She is why I do this."

He had that good politician voice, the steady and resolute timber, reassuring and strong. It sounded the same in any language.

"The government does the opposite of what its citizens need." He used the phrase *a contramano*, meaning *going against the traffic*. "How can I let her grow up like this? Behind walls? We have to make a change *a como de lugar* . . . no matter what."

It could have been my depleted state, but I believed him. A parent's wish for a better world for his children was an honest enough desire, even if he was taking it to a violent extreme. That he put himself at the center of the conflict, however, pointed to less self-sacrificing needs, his willingness to force himself down the throat of the world proof of selfish, wild ambition.

"Is your father alive?" he said.

"The last I checked."

"I hope he's proud of what you're doing."

"He doesn't know."

"He wouldn't like it?"

I shook my head. My father avoided Vietnam through deferments. He wasn't a die-for-a-cause kind of guy. This wasn't a criticism. I respected him for it.

"Do you think you're feeling well enough to eat?" General Avila said.

"That would great," I said.

"Wonderful. Let's have coffee and breakfast."

TWELVE

Inmates suffer the loss of phone privileges for infractions as insignificant as participating in a three-way conversation. This is my way of explaining why I called Jerry Handley, owner of Cragg's Hill Nursery, from my father's office. Calls like this were unauthorized at Franklin Avenue Community Outreach, and I was done bucking the system. Tension thrived well enough among my family without assistance.

When I called Jerry, he explained that while the *Paliurus spina-christi* was indeed a beautiful plant, capable of showering joy and tranquility on whoever beheld it (he had a real boner for things that grew in the ground), unless I was planning a garden, chances were it would prove unmanageable. "It's a full bush. Eight feet in diameter. It's not what you're looking for, I don't think," he said.

He suggested the Crown of Thorns. "Now *this* is a lovely little houseplant. The stems have the sharp thorns, which is what you want, right? I carry a variety called the Helena. I hope this next part isn't a deal breaker. Many people think the plant is religiously significant, but I can tell you it wasn't used at the Crucifixion."

"How do you know?"

He coughed. "Excuse me. *Euphorbia milli* is native to Madagascar. Wrong country. But hey, just the same, it's really delightful."

"How much do these delights cost?" A better question from where I was sitting.

"Four-fifty each."

I pressed Jerry to get the upper hand. "I'm worried it isn't the real deal. I think I'll need to see it first."

"I can email you a photo."

"I'm a hands-on guy, Jerry, always have been. If I'm going to pursue this venture," I said, as if selling religious plants was just one of several burgeoning enterprises on my plate, "I'll need to see it, hold it, really get up close and personal. If all goes well, and I'd be willing to commit this to paper, I'd clear out every single one you have, every single one you can get."

"Be my guest, but it's not like I'll be retiring to the south of France either way," he said.

My father, who couldn't break the habit of going to the office every day, was staring at one of his legal pads as if in his notes was the true meaning of life.

"He has *a* plant, not *the* plant," I said, when I got off the phone.

"Sounds encouraging."

"I don't know about that."

He tapped the edge of the legal pad distractedly against his head. "I'm sorry, what's the problem?"

"It's not the plant used at the Crucifixion."

"Nobody knows for sure if Jesus even lived and you're worried about a two-thousand-year-old plant? Let me tell you something. No one's asking for a religious plant to keep in their home. You are creating the market and that means it doesn't matter what goddamn plant you sell because you're not selling a plant. You're selling what the plant represents."

"You might be right," I said.

"You're goddamn right, I'm right." He never missed an opportunity to pass on the wisdom accrued over thirty years in an unforgiving business. "You should know at the outset that some people, no matter what you say or do, aren't going to buy your plant. They just won't. But if you can find what most of them need, and find a way to make what you've got fit their need, there is money to be made. So don't get discouraged. A lot of times salesmen spin their wheels. It doesn't mean they aren't making progress. Hang in there. It's the only way."

That weekend I made the peace offering without having considered the ramifications of actually spending time with Rachel. "I could use the company," I said.

"Just don't talk about your girlfriend," she said, rolling her eyes. She grabbed her purse and walked out the front door ahead of me.

Jerry Handley walked with stiff knees, a possible symptom of years spent digging in the dirt on all fours. He led us to a bench in a greenhouse where rested ten or so plants in plastic pots.

He lifted one and held it as though it were Yorick's skull. "*Euphorbia milli.* Crown of Thorns. This is it," he said.

His had been an honest bill of sale. The plant stood about eight inches high, grew in four branches, with inch-long thorns. One flower was beginning to sprout white petals from the oval green leaves.

It wasn't what I wanted. I knew it right away, though I couldn't nail down what was wrong with it, except that it made me feel as if I wasn't up to the job. In this plant, I saw the newest entry on a compendium of lifetime blunders. Without thinking, I asked Jerry what the fuck I was supposed to do with it.

"It's very simple to care for. Does just fine on table tops and windowsills. Mealybugs and stem rot can damage it. Oh, you should know that the sap is poisonous, not deadly, but be careful trimming it, and wash your hands afterwards. You shouldn't let little kids or pets get their hands on it. Or paws, I mean."

"Jerry—J-Bone—the mistake is mine. Even I don't have the balls to pass this off as important." I turned to Rachel for a final verdict. "So, waste of time or what?"

"Wrongo, Broski Alexi. It looks kind of lucky or something. Can I get one?"

"You sure?" My sister's tastes ran to the trendy, not to mention pricey. If she wanted a five dollar plant there must have been something to it. "You really think I should buy it?"

"Not for relig but, you know, just to have."

A woman browsing her way through the greenhouse saw it and remarked, "She's right, I like it too. It's simple and pretty."

Which forced me to reconsider this fourth-class flora. How could I reject a plant with broad enough appeal to interest both my sister and a middle-aged woman? And why had I expected it to blow me away when its simplicity was its hook? Not beautiful or flamboyant, this was no peacock. Maybe it had originated in Madagascar, but it *looked* like something Roman guards tore out of the earth and twisted into a torturous tiara. I took the plant in my hands, warming up to it. I ran my fingers over the thorns, over the smooth green leaves, a father holding his newborn for the first time and seeing the future in his face. What a fresh and powerful vision! Me, an honored guest at a convention, not for guns this time—Evangel-Expo '08—the attendees casting down their eyes in deference to the plant's understated presence, their cash-laden fists thrust into the air. I saw my family with me. Handley was there too. We had never been happier. "I'll take this one and another for my sister. And I'll take however many else you have. You can ship those. And I'm going to need more soon. As soon as you can get them."

"I know we just met but you look like very nice people," Handley said. He might have been counting his money but I took him at his word.

In the car, Rachel guarded the Crown of Thorns in her lap, taking her eyes off it only to reapply lip gloss in the visor mirror, the whole time talking a manic rush, dumbfounded that I pulled it off.

"It's not like I doubted you, because I didn't, but I mean, seriously, nobody would have thought that, you know, just from hearing about it, that a plant was any kind of idea. Know what I mean? But, just look at it. Do you really think it's going to work, that people will like it and then we can fix the house and I can get this dress for junior prom that I absolutely love? Oh, and I sincerely hope you don't think Jelly's going to ask you to go with her because, you know what, we're having fun and all right now, but my convict brother, no offense, who's in his thirties—"

"Who's only thirty—"

"—isn't tagging along."

My own prom was a blur of binge drinking and finger banging. It seemed quaint now. Who could have imagined that fewer than fifteen years later we'd look back on the Clinton administration and see an age of innocence? Rachel was running out of breath she was talking so much. I was pleased for my own reasons, not the least being the unmatchable satisfaction of succeeding. An unassuming success by any measure, it shone brighter against the frustration of long defeat. As I drove, I was semi-distracted by my ever-evolving fantasy. The phones at Dynamic Office Supplies rang with the type of urgency reserved for national crises. Overwhelmed with orders, we could do nothing but chortle at our need for rapid expansion. There were logistics, of course, getting the plants and releasing them into the marketplace. Those were concerns for another day. Now was the time to celebrate. We stopped at a diner for lunch, crossing the parking lot like warriors returning triumphant from battle.

That the hostess/waitress found our good mood more irritating than infectious eluded Rachel altogether, as she texted a lengthy document of indeterminate importance to Jelly, while continuing to expound on her overall amazement at my basic social proficiency. I brushed it aside with the confidence of a man who knows he is living at precisely the right time. Rachel's request of chocolate chip pancakes with whipped cream brought our waitress to life. She complained that my sister was too old to order off the children's menu. They bickered awhile. I knew to stay out of Rachel's way when she wanted something.

"Why don't you bring me the pancakes I want and I'll pay for blueberry pancakes, which are right here on the adult side of the page?" she said, stabbing at the menu with a not so subtle middle finger.

The waitress conceded it was a reasonable compromise, but was loath to give in. She yielded finally with an exasperated, "Fine," and turned her attention to me. I ordered a cheeseburger deluxe with onion rings. After she left, Rachel and I mocked her slavery to menu protocol.

"I mean, who really gives a shit? How sad is your life to get an attitude about breakfast?" Rachel said.

"Not everyone is as forward thinking as us." We toasted our progressiveness over coffee.

Such camaraderie was nearly our undoing. While killing time waiting for the food to arrive, I took another peek at the menu. The establishment served an assortment of adult refreshments. I might have vaguely alighted on the fact that Rachel was short of the legal drinking age when I thought to order a bottle of sparkling wine and, if so, I dismissed it out of hand, as it was a Puritanical dictate and I wouldn't suffer for it. The lengthy interval separating our births wasn't our fault. Not to mention, I needed a drink, needed to cool my overheated imagination that now placed me behind a dais as the keynote speaker at this religious conference and, later, mediating a round table discussion whose topic was listed on conference literature as

TBD. "At $17.50 a pop, how can we lose?" I said.

The prospect of mischief brought high color to her cheeks. "You seriously think we should?"

It was conspiratorial, the two of us doing what other brothers and sisters do, sneaking drinks on the weekend. Sure, I was a decade too old for the scenario if you wanted to be a stickler for details, but we'd never had the opportunity before. "Let's do it," I said.

I asked the waitress if hers was an acceptable vintage. It was downright silly, my asking, though she took me as pompous and, given her hostile pancake tête-à-tête with Rachel, seized the chance to restore her clout.

"I'm going to need to see ID," she said.

I produced my restricted license, which she scrutinized with undue zeal before passing it back to me.

"You too," she said to Rachel.

"I'm sure she takes it as a compliment, believe me," I said, interceding. "Can you tell she's my older sister? Okay, I'm kidding, she's younger than me by a couple of years. So I vouch for her."

"I'm not getting fined because you want to drink at lunch," said the waitress.

Rachel took her cue. "Here," she said, nonchalantly flipping an ID onto the table. Our waitress needn't have worked for the FBI to determine its authenticity. While it was probably a true state-issued driver's license, it belonged to a woman who resembled my sister less precisely than she did a trout with hair.

The waitress couldn't have studied it harder with a jeweler's loupe. She rubbed the letters of the woman's name, her address; she flipped it over to see if the woman was an organ donor. Something was no doubt amiss. She held it in front of Rachel's face, trying to close the gap between the photo and the genuine article. "Thought you said she was your sister. Why does she have a different name?"

"Our mother remarried. We're half related," I said. I'd run across too many diligent TSA agents to be stumped by someone working the lunch shift.

"I don't know. I should ask my manager."

I was buying alcohol for a teenager. The moment would lose its nuance on a police report and Glen, my probation officer, was a black-and-white kind of guy. I slid a folded ten dollar bill to the edge of the table. "Too many cooks spoil the pot, isn't that what they say? I'm sure we can live with your decision, however you decide."

She dropped Rachel's ID onto the table and palmed the bill in one motion. She bent to our level and said, "I'll be right back." And she was, carrying a tray with our wine and two glasses, chocolate chip pancakes and cheeseburger. The celebration was back on.

"I can't believe you bribed her," Rachel said.

"That's just one of the tricks in my bag."

From across the Formica, Rachel seemed to be reevaluating me, weighing today's events against visiting days at Otisville. If I was lucky, I had achieved permanent status in her world.

"Where did you get that ID?" I asked.

"It's a friend's older cousin. I needed it to get into a club one night. I forgot I even had it."

We ate our food and drank the very sugary and scarcely bubbly wine, getting louder, gesturing bigger. I proved our gratitude to our waitress on the tip, leaving her fifty percent on the bill. I could afford the generosity even if I really couldn't, for soon my financial problems would seem like the history of another man, with another sister, from another family.

July, 2004

"What's his fucking deal?" I asked Felix Moreno of my new partner, Ernesto.

"No deal. He's one of our cousins."

He definitely had a deal. If eyes are the windows to the soul, this house had no tenant. A flat, voided look hung on his face. Plus he was standing right next to Felix with no idea we were talking about him. "He smells like cat piss."

"Go easy on him."

"You'll give it to me for being a good boy," Ernesto mumbled.

"Is he talking to you or me?" I said.

"Hard to tell."

"Give it to me for being a very good boy," Ernesto said to someone or no one.

"Have a heart, Alex, he just got out of the hospital."

"What's he got?" I said.

"Homeboy's touched by the hand of God. Angels speak to him," Felix said, absent any sarcasm.

"What do they say?"

"To cut himself mostly. It's nothing to worry about. Really. Let him smoke a bowl. It chills him right out."

"I'm not worried. I don't give a shit. Ernie, let's hit it."

"For being a very, very good boy," he said, with sudden insistence.

Under normal circumstances, I'd never work with this mental defective. These were not normal circumstances. At this point Ron was missing ten days, long enough to realize what that meant, and I'd lost my capacity for shit-giving. Ron Moreno Sr. was sequestered in his heartbreak, and Luz, fiery broad that she was, was making unilateral decisions as if nothing was amiss. Already I'd sworn this was my last buy. I was retiring. I said it in English and since Luz was hurting too, tough as she was, she understood my attitude if not my words. She never asked why. I guessed she thought it was obvious—I wanted to live. Which was true in the sense that my survival instinct sought to maintain the status quo, existence-wise. What really drove my decision though was a craving for nothing. I don't mean that I was without desire. I had an actual hunger to feel not anything, to feel the way Ernesto's face looked. Vacant, checked-out. You needn't be Carl Jung, Albert Ellis, or even Laura Sullivan to figure out I was unwell from grief.

THIRTEEN

Weekends, April through October, rain or shine, Sid and Shelly Rosencrantz managed the Hudson Valley Flea Market from an office in an American Legion on whose parking lot gathered between thirty and forty vendors pushing "fine" jewelry, baseball cards, LPs, VHSs, DVDs, cell phone accessories, knives (kitchen, hunting, and commemorative), make up, paperbacks, vintage magazines, forgotten artistic masterpieces, knickknacks and bric-a-brac, tchotchkes and trinkets. This particular Saturday, in lot 37, four individuals, doing their best to look the part of experienced flea marketers, lined a folding table with twenty-two Crown of Thorn plants. As newcomers, we were assigned a location in the back, not far from a wooden enclosure housing the dumpsters. I'd petitioned for a spot with greater foot traffic and saw no relief from the Rosencrantz's.

"Sid," I said to the husband in his office, "what about this spot here, by the entrance? Number 4?" We were examining a layout map of the flea market, its numbered lots.

"First off, boychik, I'm Shelly. Short for Sheldon. Second," he said, tapping his finger on the envy-making lot in question, "you've got to have seniority to get here. Or here," and he drew a tantalizing circle with his finger around the choicest locations. Then he twisted his chubby finger onto my spot as if he was crushing out a cigarette. "Lot 37. Pay your dues," he said. "Aw, don't go away glum. You got Pete's Pups next door. Hotdogs. People smell them from all over. That'll bring them your way. Right, Sid?"

"Pete's a darling," said Mrs. Rosencrantz from her seat on the office couch, looking up from a book of word jumbles, a pair of reading glasses dangling from a string of plastic pearls.

At Lot 37 we were bookended by Pete the hotdog man and Les, an old hippie who sold model WWI airplanes made from flattened soda cans. While we displayed our wares and hung our sign—CROWN OF THORNS, *The Holy Houseplant*—my father delivered a homily known to the rest of us as his *Isn't This Great?* speech, a recital of which never failed to compliment a family outing at its onset, before anything capable of derailing our good time had opportunity to do so. In fact, it seemed it was a sort of prayer, a warding off of bad juju, that my father felt compelled to point out his appreciation lest some dark force take it from him.

"This is what it's all about. Isn't this great? I mean, look at us. We're moving, we're shaking, we're rocking and rolling. I'll tell you what, it's nice when the family gets together like this. Really, you think about that. Come on, admit it, isn't this great?"

I was too busy sizing up the competition to take pleasure in his well-worn oration. Vendors who knew one another partook in friendly banter. A rookie to the flea market, I knew no one. Each lot between the entrance and me was a station on an obstacle course designed to grab the customer's cash before I had my chance. This game was zero sum. At $29.95, *The Holy Houseplant* wasn't a penny ante trinket. It was a mid-list product, not as expensive as those Oriental rugs or antique armoires, but not something one would buy on a whim. The first wave of bargain hunters made their way through the bazaar at an excruciating pace. I wanted to throw up a detour, reroute them.

I turned to Pete and said, "This blows."

"I'm not too worried about it," replied the hotdog vendor.

I redirected my complaint to those with incentive to agree.

My mother, reading a book, said, "You're a little intense."

"Just take it easy," my father said.

Rachel was doing something on her laptop and I left her alone. When the first customers turned the corner to our aisle, I ordered everyone to be on high alert—smiles, solicitude, service.

"It's go time, people," I said.

The first to reach us was a teenage couple, possibly undergraduates, a few years older than Rachel. She was mortified to be seen by anyone in her peer group because, according to her, this was one step away from working as a carnie.

"Oh, shit," she said and hid behind her computer screen. The couple didn't stop (I don't blame them) and Rachel relaxed when they were past us, fondling a nearby pyramid of irregular socks.

A few more people drifted by, pretending to be deep in

conversation and unaware of my very desperate staring. Soon, however, a lone shopper came to our table. She read our sign, silently mouthing the words.

She picked up one of the plants. "What's the story? Does it have powers or something?"

"It doesn't *not* have powers," I said.

"What makes it so holy?"

"The Crown of Thorns, or in Latin, *Euphorbia milli*, with origins in Madagascar, is reportedly, allegedly, apparently the plant used to make Jesus' thorny crown. Watch out for Mealybugs."

"It's infested?"

My father nudged me aside. "Ma'am, I want you to think of it as a reminder."

"A reminder," she repeated.

"Of sacrifice." His voice couldn't have had more gravity if it orbited the sun.

She lowered the plant to the table, but it was only to get her wallet from the large bag slung over her shoulder. "This is wonderful," she said, foisting two twenties on him. "I've been looking for something just like this."

He made change out of our cash box. "Bless you then," he said.

After she'd gone, he wagged his eyebrows at me. "Looks like we're in business."

"How did you do that? *A reminder*? What does that even mean?"

"Sometimes less is more."

"That's all?"

"What do you mean, 'That's all?'"

I hadn't realized until then that, in his eyes, there was a limit to the help I could offer. However near or far my apple fell from his tree, I was low hanging fruit to begin with.

By noon, we had moved four Crown of Thorns to six of Les' soda can airplanes. Pete was well into double digits and with lunchtime approaching, looked primed to hit his stride. Some shoppers zipped by us wearing blinders, our plant not worth slowing down for. Some stopped, gave the goods a once over, but shunned our sales pitches, our small talk, our simple hellos, slipping away to buy those damned irregular socks. Our closing rate was pitiable. I waited for my father to break out the crafty veteran maneuvers. When he didn't (it happened that doing nothing was a veteran move; the ups and downs of sales taught him to be expert at waiting; we were a long way from the end of the day and then we had to get up and do it again tomorrow) my mother resumed her three decade power struggle with him, marching off into the flea market with a plant cradled in her arm, vanishing into the throng of noontime shoppers.

"Where are you going?" he called after her. "Where is she going?" he asked me and Rachel.

We sent Rachel to trail her.

"Gladly," she said. "Anything to get out of here. It's like being put in the stocks in the village square so the whole town can ridicule you."

"All right, just get going. See what Mom's doing."

She returned a little while later, fingering a narrow leather bracelet she had picked up in her travels.

"What's your mother up to?" my father said.

"Sitting on a bench."

"Doing what?" I said.

"Talking to people."

"What's she saying?" my father said.

Rachel shrugged. Before we could unravel her cryptic answers, I spotted my mother, headed back to us, leading a small group of old folks. They were at least in their seventies and looked like the kind of people who attended flea markets to fill the hours not spent worrying about home invasions.

My mother was talking to them. "It's like I was telling you, I was out minding my own business when I came across this family business." She addressed me as if I was just anybody. "I met these nice people and they'd like to hear about your gorgeous plant. Tell them about it like you told me."

"It's a reminder of sacrifice," I said.

"Excuse me, I don't understand what you're saying," said a man standing next to my mother. He seemed morose, as if he'd been tricked. He was wearing a VFW cap. I saw an angle.

"What I mean is, no one has ever lived a long and full life

without making sacrifices. Sacrifices for our country, for our freedom, for the things that matter most. That's the name of the game, right? The Crown of Thorns symbolizes that."

My mother's crony was unconvinced. "I don't know. If I can get one with a greeting card, I could always give it as a gift."

"One time a friend of mine was opening a business so I sent flowers to his office. He called me up and said, 'What kind of sick joke is this? The card says Rest in Peace.' I told him it was a mistake. He wasn't buying it, so I said, 'Hey, I'm really sorry but think about it: at a funeral somewhere there are flowers with a note saying 'Congrats on your new location!'"

"Ha!" the old timer barked. "I love it."

So my father wasn't the only closer in the family. And with my mother working as a ringer, a mole, a *plant*, roping in customers, my father and I unloaded six more Crown of Thorns. Taken in summary form, our afternoon was breezy and productive. Summarization also glosses over an incident, an accusation actually, leveled against us by an epicene man who mistook the Wolf family for the true believers he himself was. Our interaction began pleasantly enough. He approached us in a slow and unsteady waddle, waving from three vendors away. "You there," he called.

"Good afternoon, brothers," he said when he reached us. He noticed Rachel behind her laptop. "And sister, a good afternoon to you, too." He shook my hand, or rather held my fingertips with his fingertips. "Peace to you."

"Right back at you," I said.

He tickled the leaves of the plant. "'And the soldiers platted a crown of thorns, and put it on his head, and they put on him a purple robe.' Who knows the quote?"

"Guy Fieri?"

"No. John 19:2."

"That was my next guess."

"I see." He fixed his pink-lidded eyes at me. "I'm going to tell you what I think."

"Please do."

"I have a feeling you're not really washed in the blood."

"Ew, gross," Rachel said, confirming his suspicion.

"Sorry," I said.

"I'm not mad. I just don't get it. You could sell anything. Why do this?"

He trundled away and Rachel said, "Washed in the blood? What a psycho!"

I was glad my mother was somewhere else. She would have agreed with him.

When there were half as many plants as we began the day with, my father started packing up all but two. "Hey, guys, make a wall with your bodies while I put these away. We're going to create a little supply and demand imbalance," he said.

He boxed the merchandise and took it back to the car. Rachel and I were instructed to take orders from anyone who wanted a plant.

"On what, Pete's napkins?" I said, as he schlepped the boxes out of sight.

What happened next was notable because here was when Rachel stepped up, meaning we all contributed on our first day of business. Without being told, she shelved her embarrassment, somehow found a Wi-Fi connection in the American Legion parking lot, downloaded an invoice template, tracked down Shelly Rosencrantz in the office and made use of the printer, and returned to lot 37 waving a stack of blank invoices just as I was referring a woman, who wanted to pay by C.O.D., to our unbendable return policy for damaged or lost plants that I invented on the spot. My parents came back, my mother with another bushel of elderly birds on her heels. By the end of the day we had sold or taken orders on our entire stock.

At closing, Sid and Shelly took a glacial loop of the parking lot, checking in with the vendors, judging the day a success. Sid winked at me. "I see you got some nice receipts. Lot 37 is not looking so bad, eh?" she said.

I conceded it was a fine lot, a rare feeling of pride for my family branching throughout my chest. My mother and Rachel tallied the cash in the box. And there was my father with Shelly.

Shelly said, "I've hired plenty of guys in my day, various businesses I've owned, some work out and you wish you had ten more just like them. But a lot turn out to be thieving bastards, corrupt sons of bitches. Pardon my language. I can tell you, sir, that it's people like you've got here," he waved at me, my mother, Rachel, "that's who you can trust. You've got a nice little organization here. Sid and I hope to see you again."

"I've been in business a long time too, and you're absolutely right. I was just telling them pretty much the same thing. I mean, this is what it's all about. Who else can you trust? I mean, isn't this great?"

July, 2004

It was while nursing this need for oblivion that Ernesto and I flew to New Mexico, where I made the purchase of two .50 cals and a few police rifles. Then we were back in the rental van, driving on Highway 10, on our way to hand the guns off to an associate who would do whatever he was supposed to do with them.

"Do you know what scrapple is?" I said, giving Ernesto a polite interval to say nothing in rejoinder. "It's a breakfast meat, tiny parts of the pig that fall on the slaughterhouse floor, mixed up with flour and spices and crammed into a gray loaf. Your face reminds me of it."

He peered into the back of the van to our weapons. "You're going to give me a gun for being a very good boy."

"I can see why you might take it the wrong way. Human scrapple is faint praise."

He packed his pipe with a fat bowl and smoked himself into a near-catatonic state.

"I'm only bringing it up, your face, because I was hoping you could tell me how you do it, that empty thing you do. I'd love to be able to. Not just make my face like that, but to feel the way it looks."

Ernesto was no help.

Half an hour later, our van passed through a DWI roadblock. The two troopers conducting the stop were justifiably ill-tempered that day, owing to the insane heat. Nevertheless, they went about their job with sadistic aplomb. Ernesto was still unresponsively high so that, had he spoken more than a variation of his one sentence—"For being a very good boy,"—I'm not sure he would have been able to answer any of the officers' questions. This didn't bother the patrolmen as much as I imagined it would, as one remarked to his partner that Ernesto was, "Another drunk Mexican."

I chose not to correct him, though he'd mistaken the substance abused, and the nationality of the abuser. Instead, I complied with his request that I unlock the rear doors. Ernesto's condition had also opened the door, the one of probable cause, and the police were interested to see where we were hiding our liquor. Now my purchases were exposed for them to see. I don't remember them ordering us out of the van, but in no time, we were on our knees on the debris ridden, scorching hot pavement. Maybe it was the juxtaposition of Ernesto beside me—we didn't look like hunting buddies—that did us in. Or maybe it was just that touching Ernesto turned out to be a bad idea because when the cops moved to handcuff him, he freaked the fuck out and was quite frankly lucky he was only Tasered into submission. Eventually I proved legal ownership of the guns, but the authorities were astute not to uncuff us and let us go.

Of course there are enough laws on the books for the government to jam you up if they so desire. Once I was arraigned, Skolnick struck the deal that let me escape a max sentence and do my bid closer to my family, actions that made him feel like a hero because, as he often told me, it could have been so much worse for me. I never mentioned to him that life metes out its own punishments, and no sentence I got could have rivaled my suffering at this time.

FOURTEEN

Monday morning, I answered a phone call that put our nice sales receipts into perspective. Vicki, on behalf of Visa, wanted to speak to Mr. Wolf.

"Which Mr. Wolf?" I said.

"How many of you are there?" she inquired in a sweet, yet not innocent, voice.

"Didn't say I was one of them."

"I'm looking for the Mr. Wolf whose Visa account ending in 9544 is sixty-three days past due. Now you wouldn't happen to be him, would you?"

"Sorry, not me. Like to leave a message?"

"When would be a good time to reach the real Mr. Wolf, since you said you're not him and you wouldn't dream of lying to me?"

"Gosh, Vicki—you said your name was Vicki, right? Or is it Valerie? Either way, those Bio Dome projects are pretty damn demanding. To be on the safe side, try back in fourteen months. Better yet, make it an even year-and-a-half."

"Look here, Robert Wolf," she said, her voice now sharp as snake fangs, "I know for a fact it's you. I know everything there is to know about you."

"That doesn't sound right."

"This is a serious matter," she shrieked, and I moved the phone away from my ear.

"I'm not trying to sell you short, Vick, but guys in Mumbai with mechanical engineering degrees do your job for five grand a year. This is what you get for dropping out of community college."

"I bet you enjoy all those things you bought with the credit card. All those cash advances I'm looking at. Why don't you be a man and pay for them? 'Cause all you've done in my book is steal. You're a thief is what I think. I want to know how much you're sending in today. I want to see a payment today or else I'm turning this matter over to the city marshal. He'll come down there and bring the police with him."

"Are you reading from a script because you sound like a troubled individual," I said. "Now, before I lose my patience and contact a consumer advocate, I'm going to tell you one last time that I'm not Robert Wolf. I don't know when he'll be available to speak with you." I hung up the phone.

As composed as I'd been with Visa's viperous debt collector, I was shaking with adrenaline when I returned the phone to the charger. At least Vicki was rude enough that I could transfer the blame to her, as if my parents were the victims of identity theft, wrongfully badgered by uncompassionate, oily, creditors. I jotted on the notepad on the wall: *Vicki, from Visa. 8:40.*

I picked the phone back up. I wanted to see if Jelly had any luck arranging a meeting with Holden for me. I wasn't so completely unrealistic to think I was above his help. Holden had resources and credibility. Pin his name to my plant and no longer would anyone doubt I was washed in the blood. Whatever that meant. I made a mental note for *prayerguy* to look it up. I started to call Jelly but instead my fingertip danced over the buttons 4-1-1 and heard myself asking for the number of my father's former customer and occasional gambling buddy, an ex-cop who took on New York City in court and won. Lenny Marino. The Mad Dog. We needed breathing room. We needed to buy time from Visa and contractor's estimates and other debts I didn't know about but most certainly existed. If my father refused to ask Lenny for help (which wouldn't be help at this point, but an investment) I would do it for us.

"Bob, that you?" Lenny said.

"No, it's Alex,"

"Don't play games. I've been meaning to call you."

"You've got it wrong, Mr. Marino," I said.

"So enlighten me, but do it quickly. I've got a slice of pizza in the toaster oven."

I told him I wasn't Robert Wolf, but his son, Alex, whom he'd met at Dynamic Business Solutions.

"I have a business opportunity I'd like to discuss, over lunch, any time, preferably soon, my treat, of course."

He hemmed and hawed before agreeing to meet me the next

day at a restaurant called Cactus Jack's, a Tex-Mex place that made "the best freakin' margaritas in the world. Hey, you know that your pop and I go way back? Bring him along," he said.

> ### Certificate of Authenticity
> Personally signed and sealed by Reverend (name goes here), this Certificate of Authenticity confers all the blessings of the holy Crown of Thorns onto (purchaser name goes here). The Crown of Thorns is a reminder of the sacrifices made on our behalf by our Lord, Jesus Christ. It is a symbol of our shared faith. Rejoice in His message of love and redemption and know that, through charity, His word is spread.

Armed with the unfounded confidence that only the truly green possess, I devised elaborate scenarios of how My Lunch With Lenny would unfold. In one, I astonished him with my inventiveness and self-possession and he rewarded me with enough money to fix the basement and take the business to the next level, even paying for lunch he was so impressed. In another, he was ice and I melted him with my persistence, swaying him with the Certificate of Authenticity I'd drawn up. The end result was him forking over a large check right there in the restaurant. Every imagined version of lunch culminated in success, my sales pitch indomitable. It wasn't until I showed up fifteen minutes late the next day that it occurred to me Lenny might not be as gung-ho as his fantasy counterpart. I circled the block looking for parking, thinking: he's an ex-cop; I'm an ex-con. Where, outside of zany comedies, did we partner up? Walking into the restaurant, I realized this was very different from soliciting donations for my mother. I was sick with presumption.

Cactus Jack's was fashioned in horrific southwestern kitsch, the booths upholstered with what looked and felt like real cow skin, long white and black hairs tickling your neck whenever you leaned back. The walls supposedly gave the impression of eating inside an adobe and on them hung the heads of animals wearing oversized sunglasses and cowboy hats. Over the bar was a longhorn from which hung articles of lingerie. Lenny was seated at a booth, a half empty margarita before him. He picked gingerly through the basket of tortilla chips on the table, plunging them into a clay bowl of salsa. I waved from the hostess stand to get his attention but he didn't see me. I walked over and joined him.

"I took the liberty of ordering a drink. I get antsy sitting around."

"I understand, Mr. Marino. It's my fault. I couldn't find parking."

"Don't mention it. Where's your dad?"

"He couldn't make it."

"How's he doing?"

"Doing well, I guess," I said.

"Your pop is a real fucking stoic, you know that? Most guys would've put their heads in an oven if they had to deal with half the shit he did these last couple of years. It's good to hear he's holding up. Where's he working now?" He ran his tongue along the salt-trimmed glass, then drained its contents.

"He's not. I think he's still waiting it out, but that's why I wanted to meet with you."

A waiter slid up to the table.

"Can we have a minute please?" I said.

"Kid, I'm starving," Lenny said. "Pick anything, you can't go wrong. Everything here is the best."

So I ordered, then he did, including another margarita. I took it to be a good sign that he had a few drinks in him. We ate the chips and salsa and waited for our meals.

"You've got to be pretty psyched to be out of . . . where were you upstate?" he said.

"Otisville."

"That's not so bad," he said, scanning something just over the top of my head.

"Thank you for telling me what it was like in prison."

"Don't get pissy. I'm just saying."

He glanced at the door of the restaurant as if expecting someone to join us. For a cop, he was pretty scattered. When the food came, I pushed my chimichanga around on the plate, too nervous to eat. I wondered if it was better not to bring up money. I could just pay for lunch and return to work, no harm done. Of course, that begged the question of why I invited him in the first place.

"What'd I tell you? Fantastic, right?" he said.

"It's very good, yes," I said, taking a mouthful of rice and beans.

"Sometimes I think I should retire to Albuquerque. Maybe Santa Fe. Someplace like that."

"Why don't you?"

"My wife's mother lives with us." He flagged down the waiter and ordered another margarita. At nine bucks each this was turning into an expensive lunch not to get anything in return.

"If you'll excuse me, nature calls," he said. He stood. "Whoa, I'm a little lightheaded. I told you nobody makes a margarita like this joint."

I decided to take a shot. If nothing else, I needed to tell him about the plant. Then if I didn't ask for money outright, I could drop hints and hope he picked them up. His new drink was waiting for him when he returned. Out came his tongue again, lapping at the salt rim. "You sure you don't want one?" he said.

"Can I ask you about your investments, Lenny?"

Now he looked at me with his wet, droopy eyes, really seeing me for the first time. He cocked his head and sniffed, a canine-looking expression. "What would you like know, Alex?"

One question about his investments and I had his attention.

"I have an idea for a business I think you might be interested in."

He wiped his mouth with a napkin. "Don't jerk me off. What's this about?"

I thought I did a fine job presenting my idea, but at the end of my speech he looked confused.

"Let me see if I get this. There's this plant, the euro something . . ."

"*Euphorbia milli*, but that's unimportant. They call it the Crown of Thorns."

"Who calls it that?"

"Plant people. Botanists. It's what Jesus' crown of thorns was made out of—maybe or maybe not, but that's another conversation—and, to make a long story short, I want to sell it."

"Who the hell would want to buy thorns?

"It's a symbol. Like a cross. Evangelicals are a powerful religious group. And they spend money like you and me. This is a product that caters to them."

He thought about it. "Aren't you a Jew?"

I don't believe any gentile can ask this question without it sounding, at least in part, critical. "Yes," I said.

"Why do you want to sell thorns to Christians? It's like you're playing for the wrong team."

"Personally, I see no difference between this and selling copy machines. There's a need and there's a person to fill the need. That person should get paid for it." There's nothing worse than a Jew admitting he's doing something for money. It's always taken the wrong way. I tried to soften the implication. "You know we've hit hard times with my dad's business going under. I'm trying to take on some of the responsibility."

"God knows your pop deserves a break. Why don't you just get a job like a real person? Leave the Jesus stuff to the priests."

"It's a good idea. I know it could work. We had a small inventory of plants and sold out of them at the flea market."

"Who's we?"

"My family and me."

"You've got everyone wrapped up in this?"

Wrapped up in this sounded shady, criminal even, cheapened what took place at the flea market. I said my family and I supported each other and we were working hard together.

"I'm a lapsed Catholic, so I don't think much about Evangelicals. I don't know, it sounds funny coming from you. Like you're fucking with people?"

We were off the topic of my religion and onto the one of my morality. This was comfortable ground. I was used to dealing with it. "The people who buy this, they will feel closer to their faith, feel better about life in general. How is that a bad thing?"

Lenny sipped his margarita. He cocked his head again. "Are you shitting me?"

"Absolutely not. Let me tell you a little more about it." I told him about how I wanted a reverend to authenticate the plant or say a prayer over it, and then I told him about the profile of Reverend Holden in the magazine that started me thinking. That Lenny didn't interrupt, and even nodded from time to time, I considered making progress.

He gulped the rest of his drink. "Where, exactly, do I come in? Wait, don't tell me. I'm the wallet."

"I prefer to call you the financial arm of the enterprise."

"You've got a smooth touch. I can see how you talked your way into that lady doctor's pants. Yeah, I read the book. Your pop told me it's trash. Is it?"

Another fan. "He was telling you the truth."

"They don't call you the White Boy Bandito?"

"Nobody calls me that," I said. "Lenny, what do you think about my idea?"

"All right, all right, I'll quit busting your balls. You want to talk for real about this billion dollar idea? Okay, show me your prospectus."

I had a vague idea what a prospectus was. "Well, I've already told you about the product. I would have brought one for you to see but we sold out this weekend. Very good sales receipts. Excellent receipts, in fact. Nice return on investment. R.O.I., I believe it's called. Healthy profit margin, too," I said, dropping business-esque terms. "I can describe what the certificate's going to look like."

"I have a guy, David Weinstock, he's my investment guy. When Davey calls he doesn't say, 'You want me to describe it?' He sends me a prospectus. Now since you don't have one, I'd say you're not ready to start a business, but I could be wrong. Answer me this," and he wiped his mouth with the palm of his hand, "What do you estimate your first-year expenses to be? How many fiscal quarters do you anticipate posting a loss before your first gain? What rate of growth can I expect for my investment? How many shares of stock do you plan to sell? How many other investors are you contacting? Et cetera, et cetera, blah, blah, you get my drift?"

I got his drift in a big way and because I didn't have an answer to any of his questions, I scraped together a few loose grains of rice with my fork and took a huge sip of water. "Maybe I gave you the wrong impression. I was thinking more along the lines of a loan."

"Oh, a loan. That's different. You should have said so. What are the terms of this loan?"

Funny, in my daydreams he never came at me like this. I underestimated him. Or, to be honest, overestimated me. "Excuse me?"

His elbows were on the table. "When are you going to pay me back?" said captain of industry Lenny Marino.

"As soon as possible."

He clapped his hands, lifting his face to the ceiling. "What month is ASAP? Forget it, don't answer. Here's a better question: What rate are you prepared to pay? I'd need at least three points over prime to make it worth my while."

His business acumen had me wondering which one of us was the Jew. "How about interest-free?" I suggested.

He scratched his head playfully, as though considering it. "That sounds like a gift. You just want me to give you money?"

"I don't want a gift. I'm going to pay you back."

"I'll grant you it's not an entirely retarded idea. I've heard worse. But for all I know, the money is going to buy guns or some shit and you'll see me on the news financing a revolution. No, thanks."

"Then don't give it to me. Give it to my dad. He'll make sure I use it right."

Lenny reclined against the booth. He shook his head slowly like he was debating something. "Do you know your pop is into me for four grand?"

I really didn't want to know, but I said, "Since when?"

"He was already into me for $1,500 but that was just a couple hundred here, a couple hundred there. This last time was $2,500. I assume you didn't know that."

Right then I wanted to leave the restaurant without having the conversation I knew we were going to have.

"I'm not telling you this because I want you to think your father is an asshole, because he isn't. I'm telling you because I think you have an unrealistic view of the situation and, if I decline your offer, I don't want you to get the wrong idea why."

"I get it," I said, hoping to end the lecture and lunch.

"No, you don't. Do you know what kind of sweetheart your dad is? I don't know one man who's got a bigger heart. Do you know about the guy who used to work for him? He couldn't afford to bring his mother over here from some Eastern European nightmare of a county, so your father stepped up and paid for her flight, co-signed a lease on an apartment for her. That wasn't a loan either. Another time, he bought a guy hair."

"Hair?"

"This was another winner he hired. Guy looked like he'd been scalped. Old Bob outfitted him with a brand new 'do. You could barely tell it was a piece. Bet you didn't know that."

"So you gave him money because he's a nice guy but you don't want to give any more until he pays you back."

"Not even close. I knew I was never getting it back when I gave it to him. See, as much as I'd like to help, I can't give you anything because of who you are, and it doesn't matter if I give him one dollar or a million because we both know where it's going to end up."

I always wanted to believe that my father's gambling wasn't a real problem because it didn't outwardly affect the quality of my life. It was a lie I told myself but one that was easy to believe because, as I've mentioned, he supported us; and since he kept his habit a secret (and we looked the other way too) it was easy to ignore. What was most painful about listening to Lenny Marino was that I could no longer ignore it and I could no longer believe the lie. I didn't give a shit about the people my father helped. For the first time in my life, I felt like it wasn't his family anymore. In telling me about this owed money, Lenny stripped my father of his place at the head of our house. Without a leader, we were doomed. Making a last and desperate effort (which is what last efforts usually are), I said, "You could give the money to my sister. She hates gambling and she's not too thrilled with me."

"I hear she's a good kid. How old is she now?"

"Seventeen."

"You're serious about this plant thing?"

"It's crazy because I never thought it was something I'd have to do. Help out, I mean. Hell, you could give it to her and my mom. My mom's responsible."

"I think your dad is a real sweetheart but maybe he did you a disservice by not teaching you how the world works. Boy, I need a nap. Too much tequila. Tell me something, there's a scene in the book, when you first go upstate. You're scared that you're going to get your ass kicked and you're talking about it with the doc and you say that you're thinking of joining the Aryan Brotherhood, for protection. She says, 'You're Jewish.' And you say, 'It beats being a dead Jew.' Did that happen?"

"Something like that."

"I loved that. That was hilarious. I was a cop a long time and I could've sworn when you called that you were trying to hustle me. I'm thinking you might be a straight shooter after all. Anyway, kid, thanks for lunch." He stood up, and said, "Here, let me get the tip." He dropped a ten onto the table and left.

And because I was so off kilter by everything that had preceded his leaving, I hardly realized I was alone in the booth, empty plates and margarita glasses around me, a puddle of spilled salsa on the table. Then the waiter showed up and handed over a bill that I could barely afford but couldn't ignore.

January, 2008

Hello there, Old Man,

Great seeing you guys New Year's Day. I've gotten used to visits on the weekend so it was a pretty nice break in routine to see you on a Tuesday. How was the traffic heading home? That's right, I'm giving you an opening to bitch about holiday travel.

Go ahead and let me have it. Unload the gruesome details. Was it bumper-to-bumper? How long did it take to get home—four hours? Five? Ten-car pileup? Disabled trucks in the middle lane? Oh, the humanity!

Ok, I'm being a bit of a jerk. I really didn't mean for that to happen. My plan was to offer a quid pro quo. I listen to you grumble about traffic, and you do me a favor. Not actually a favor, but just give me some advice, father to son. If everything goes as it's supposed to, I'm getting out in a few months. I realize I don't have shit lined up for the outside. I always sort of assumed I'd go back to living my life, but I now see I have zero chance of pulling it off. I can't afford an apartment. I have no job interviews lined up. What kind of job could I even apply for? I don't have what you would call appreciable skills. And that fucking book and movie have turned me into a national joke. Don't worry, I'm not asking for money. I was just hoping you could tell me what the hell I'm supposed to do. You've taught me plenty of things like how to ride a bike, how to throw a curve ball, how to throw a punch, how to change a flat tire, how to snake a clogged drain, how to flip an omelet with just the pan (it's all in the wrist, right?), how to parallel park, how to tie a tie, how to solve for x in algebra, etc., and it's all been very useful stuff (well, maybe not the algebra, but the punch and omelet definitely), but now I need you to show me how to live like a normal person. How do people do it? How do you do it? How do you wake up and go to work every day? How do you live with the same woman forever? How do you not end up in prison? I feel like if you nudged me in the right direction I could build up momentum on my own.

Don't feel any pressure to answer right away. You've got a couple of months lead time to organize your words of wisdom. Thanks.

Love ya,
Your Sonny Boy

FIFTEEN

"You want to tell me about this message?" my father said, waving the note I'd left him about Vicki, Visa's collection agent.

"Isn't it self-explanatory?"

"Did you get her number?"

"I did not."

"How am I supposed to call her back?"

"I don't know."

"When did she call?"

He was the last person I wanted to see, so of course he chose now to bother me with his bullshit. I took the note. "I wrote it right here. 8:40."

"Thanks for clearing it up. 8:40 on Friday the 13th, 1992. Or was it July 4th, 1976, the bicentennial? Or wait," he lowered his voice to a whisper, "Was she calling from the future?" then bellowing, "Start up my time machine!"

"There's an easy way to avoid these calls so you won't have to rely on my message taking."

"Is there?" he challenged.

"There is." If he was really going to argue this tedious point then I had no problem telling him my sketchy note was the least of his problems.

"This is how you take a message," he said. He showed me another scrap of paper. "Jelly called you. Today. See, I put the date right here. At 4:45. Here's her number. Gee, what a genius I am."

It wasn't what I expected him to say. It caught me off guard. "What did she want?"

"She wants you to call her back. See, I wrote it down. Call her back, it says. What I didn't write down, because I wanted to tell you personally, is that Reverend Holden is eager to meet you." His attitude had changed to one of cautious giddiness. "*Eager*," he repeated.

The guy had agreed to meet me, for what reason I had no idea.

"If it were me, here's what I would do: I wouldn't wait too long to call her back," he said. "We don't want to lose the roll we're on from this weekend. If we could go back to the flea market with his endorsement, that would be ideal. Or maybe he has ideas of his own, who knows?"

"You're not me," I said, but what I really hoped was that I wasn't him.

And to think I was in a great mood when I woke up. Now I was tired and stressed out, unprepared for Holden. Of course, Jelly—like Vicki, Lenny, and my father—wouldn't hear me.

"This isn't something he does every day," she said. "He just got back from Russia and he's crazy jet-lagged, but he wants to meet you. It's like a slap in the face if you don't show."

"What was he doing in Russia?"

"He ministers to people all over the world, silly. You don't think we're selfish enough to keep him all to ourselves."

"Tell him I'm sick."

"You're going to make me look like a douche if you don't go. Don't you realize who he is?"

"Fine."

"Yay," she trilled. "Promise you'll call as soon as you're done. I want to hear everything."

From *White Boy Bandito: How a Clever Suburbanite Became Death's Middleman for South American Revolutionaries*, by Dr. Laura Sullivan, PhD. (Verdict Press: 2006, 114-115)

It happened fast as lightning. Two klicks south of the General's compound, their Jeep was ambushed by a band of armed men without warning. Men bedecked in befouled fatigues. Men who shouted at the travelers as if they hated them in mind, body, and soul. Men pointing the remorseless lethal steel of their weaponry through the open top of the Jeep. Upon seeing these men up close, Alexander had a revelation: these terrifying men were no more than boys, not yet old enough to grow a thin dark downy mustache over their boyish upper lips. He was already nervous about meeting General Avila for the first time and this ambush made him think his heart would explode. What did these boys want? Were Alexander, Ron, and Enrique about to be kidnapped? Murdered? A fate worse than murdered?

Ron's hand went to his ankle holster. "I'm not going down without a fight."

"Shut your fool mouth, you mother lover," snapped Enrique. "These soldiers are part of the movement. They will give us safe passage the rest of the way."

When Alexander heard this, he stopped believing he was about to suffer a massive heart attack.

Enrique's words proved true. The soldiers marched beside the Jeep until they reached the walled compound at the top of the hill. They waited for what seemed like an eternity for the gates to swing wide and admit them to the inner sanctum. Finally, Alexander thought, I've made it all the way to Hacienda Buenavista.

On the flight from the U.S., Ron had revealed the importance of this meeting. Not just anyone got to meet Fulgencio Avila. Only the most trusted individuals could see him face-to-face. It was a testament to how much the People's Army valued Alexander's work that he was being introduced to the great man.

In the courtyard skinny chickens scratched and pecked at the dirt. The three visitors stretched their weary bodies. A courier for the general greeted them. Just when he was about to take them inside Alexander became distracted by a young woman hanging laundry on a clothesline.

"Good morning, Señor Lobo," she called over to Alexander, her voice the sweetest and saddest song he'd ever heard.

It was Santa, the General's eldest daughter. She was teasing Alexander with a translation of his last name. No man alive was immune to her. Every man she met instantly fell in love. She possessed almandine eyes and lips as soft as the pillows at a 5-star hotel in Paris. Her complexion was the color of apple blossom honey and her long black hair flowed to her waist like silk. Her body was the reason God created Eve.

"Well, good morning to you," he replied saucily.

"Don't even think about it," cautioned Ron, pulling him away.

General Avila's office was on the first floor. The currier explained that his office used to be on the top floor, but enemies of the people attempted to assassinate the leader by shooting through the windows. The new office was concealed behind the walls of the compound. Its furnishings were minimalist, to say the least, but the general himself was a magnificent specimen, a powerhouse, a paragon of action and ideology. Alexander had never met anyone as impressive. All at once, he adopted a respectful tone, as if his usual joking manner was a pair of ill-fitting pants, not suited for the occasion.

"I'm honored to meet you, sir," he said.

They ventured back to the courtyard so General Avila could inspect the shipment of weapons they brought with them. Alexander unlocked the first hard plastic case, unearthing a .50 caliber rifle. The general just nodded, and Alexander could not tell if the man was pleased or disappointed.

"When Enrique first told me we had help coming from America, I thought *el burro sabe más que él*—the donkey knows more than him. But you men have shown me that our *hermanos en el norte* don't forget where they come from."

He shook hands with Ron and Enrique, but he dropped his hand to his side when he came to Alexander.

"They tell me that you are the crazy one with the plans, that you are loyal to the People's cause. Is this the truth?"

"Yes, sir," Alexander answered proudly.

The general reached out and grasped Alexander by the shoulders and pulled him in for the most masculine of embraces.

"My people, my family, and me personally, from the bottom of our hearts, we thank you, you White Boy Bandito."

Reverend Warren Holden's home office was one of eighteen rooms in a gated mini-mansion on the bank of a manmade lake about thirty minutes over the Tappan Zee Bridge, on the outskirts of Orange County. I buzzed the intercom and waited for the wrought iron gate to swing open. This dude had not taken a vow of poverty. I parked beside a garage roughly the size of my parent's house.

Safely ensconced on his tremendous property, I concentrated on not fucking up this meeting like I had my lunch with Lenny. Mad Dog Marino upended me because I was rusty and took for granted his friendship with my father, assumin it softened my reputation and made me at least a little trustworthy.

Incandescent gravel crunched beneath my feet as I crossed the gleaming white path to the front door. I decided that lunch had been rehearsal for now. It was good to have gotten it out of my system. Holden I could sway, I figured, because it was his job, his calling, to take a charitable view of a man's limitations. His belief system expected it of him. I could squirm through the gap opened by the smallest benefit of the doubt.

The person who answered the door was the same yellow-coiffed woman from the rescue-the-poor-kids commercial. Up close she was blonder and tanner, and everything about her looked taut, except for the skin just south of her saucer-sized brown eyes, though there was plenty about her face suggesting augmentation. She proffered a hand shimmering with gold rings, pointy jewels catching the entrance light and scattering it. Her eyes grew increasingly vacant the longer she smiled, as though she disappeared from her body. She snapped out of it and introduced herself as Isabella, the reverend's wife, and continued holding my hand after she invited me in, her rings digging into my skin.

"Warren's very excited you could make it. Sometimes he forgets that people all around the world would literally kill to have an audience with him." She smiled and did that disappearing act behind her eyes again. "I shouldn't have said *literally*. He just cannot fathom how many people love him. That's part of what makes him a great man."

Isabella and Jelly agreed: Holden was great. We stood in the foyer beneath a massive cut-glass chandelier, impressive in terms of its audacity. She smiled toothlessly and hugged her elbows and I grinned back, not knowing what to do but wait, and it was at the point when I was about to ask if Holden was coming soon that five children raced into the room and aligned themselves in height order, three blond like their mother, two dark haired. They launched into a song that, given their age, was surprisingly good. Even the youngest, a child in diapers who didn't look strong enough to shake her tambourine, kept the time. The eldest boy led them on guitar while two of his sisters accompanied him on flute. One of the other boys balanced a violin on his collar. A halfway decent harmony escaped the boys' mouths as they sang, *Welcome to our home where we hope you'll stay/ We'll be so sad when you go away/ What's ours is yours, please get cozy / From our hands to God's is ever so rosy.*

They bowed when they finished. I clapped out of more than courtesy.

Isabella said, "They have the Spirit in them. They all do. I couldn't stop them if I wanted to. But why would I want to?"

"I can't think of a reason," I said and, looking back at the children, was startled to see a man now standing with them. I hadn't heard him come into the room. It seemed as though he'd risen from a crack in the hardwood.

He put two of his fingers to his temple and closed his eyes. "You're Alex," he said. He opened his eyes and smiled, pleased with the accuracy of his clairvoyance. "Warren Holden," he said and laughed, as if somewhat startled by his own identity. "What do you say we go to my office?"

I followed him to a dimly lit enclave near the back of the house on the first floor, furnished, it appeared, by the set director of *Caligula*. The room was ornate to the point of stifling. The curtains were gold in color, and probably in material, and looked like they weighed two hundred pounds each. His desk was a glacial expanse of deeply burnished wood and the chair behind it was more throne than conventional office furniture. The wallpaper was heavy with gold arabesques and the brown carpet was two inches high. For all its oppressiveness, the office was as chilly as an operating room. I sank into one of two overstuffed leather chairs that were in front of his desk. He sat in his throne. On the wall behind him was a diploma from Western Interstate Bible College. On its frame, a lamp illuminated his scholastic achievement.

Holden watched me and said nothing. This went on longer than worth mentioning. Finally he said, "You're like me, you prefer to listen. That's a strong quality for a man to have."

"I defer to my host. Jelly, excuse me, Jill, told me you just returned from a trip."

"Is that all you've heard?"

I decided now wasn't the time to bring up his condemnation of devil-produced prophylactics and the oral-sex-virginity loophole. I also left out the rumor I'd heard from my mother that he was the same Warren Holden who, at the learned age of four, wedded couples upstate. "She said you're a great man."

He closed his eyes and rested his fingers against his temple. "'Be sure of this, O young ambition, all mortal greatness is but disease.'"

"Sorry to say I don't know much scripture."

"That's Melville. From a secular bible of sorts. The Whale. Have you read it?"

"I saw the movie."

"Gregory Peck. Great actor, but miscast as Ahab," he said.

"Loved *Guns of Navarone*."

He jumped up like he suddenly remembered he left a pie in the oven and rushed to a standing wooden globe next to a brass telescope aimed out the window. He rolled open the globe, revealing a subterranean liquor cabinet out of which he excavated a bottle and two rocks glasses.

"I've never been a huge fan of vodka, but I stumbled upon this tiny distillery on my latest trip to Russia. It's buried deep in the woods. The roads leading to it aren't paved. It's far, far away from most modern amenities you and I take for granted. Outsiders are normally forbidden from visiting, though the area is so secluded that few people even know it's there. Yet there it is, operating for hundreds of years just under their noses! It was a great honor that locals entrusted me with their secret. Smirnoff probably spills more in a day than they produce in a year." He held up the bottle. "This is simply fantastic. Join me?"

Who was he kidding with that far, far away nonsense? But I remembered where sobriety got me at lunch. If I was going to hit him up for cash, I needed some lubrication. "Why not?"

"Magnificent," he said, and poured two drinks. He corked the bottle and rejoined me at his desk.

"What were you doing in Russia?" I said.

"I've long had a fruitful relationship with that region. In the late '80s I smuggled Russian-language bibles into Godless Soviet Union. Ingenious plan, if I say so myself. We brought them legally to Finland, and then sent them over the border carried on balloons. Thousands of them drifting down in small towns all around the Kremlin. Satan never knew what hit him." He inhaled the vapor of his liquor and shifted gears. "How old are you?"

"Thirty."

"I hope you don't mind me saying but you don't have a lot to show for it."

"I don't mind you saying."

"Any children?"

"Sometimes I wish I did. Then I could blame them for the death of my dreams."

"It wasn't my intention to offend you."

"No worries. I'm only joking."

"Okay then, let's drink to the two most well-known men in town."

"Do I know them?"

"I hope so." He gulped his drink, nodded that I do the same.

I thought he was going for another round, but he crossed to a bookcase against the wall, another baroque piece of furniture, drawing out a hardcover edition that he displayed at arm's length. There I was, scowling, cigar stub clenched in my teeth, helming a .50 caliber rifle, the bipod resting on a hood of a pickup truck. It was a cartoonish pose, taken as a joke (the gun wasn't even loaded), so of course it made a great jacket photo.

"I should stop you before you get started," I said, "Whatever ideas that book gave you, whatever you think you know about me, you're probably wrong. It's a book of lies."

"I wanted to reserve judgment until we met. That doesn't mean I haven't followed your case. You and I are the two most well-known men in the area. It only makes sense that we become acquainted." He returned the book to the shelf. "What did you think of the vodka? I'd love to hear your opinion."

"It's good." I swirled the remaining drop around in the

bottom of the glass before finishing it. "Thanks for the drink but now that we're acquainted—"

"It's my turn to cut you off." He had a severe look on his face. "Jill might not have told you much about me, but I'm a fan of the book . . . even if it is lies, like you say. I followed your story from the very beginning. When you were arrested in New Mexico. The local coverage here was spectacular. Did you know your high school yearbook photo ran in the paper? Your family, the scrutiny they endured. I can't imagine what that was like for them. Perhaps I shouldn't admit it, but I was rooting for you to beat the charges. Imagine how I felt when I learned that one of my congregants was a close family friend of yours. But I recently heard some disturbing things about you and I decided I couldn't wait any longer to meet you."

Was he talking about the blow job? That's what this was about. Fan or no fan, Holden wasn't about to have one of his young Christian soldiers defiled by a gun-smuggling Jew who resided in a house structurally compromised by termites. "I have an idea what she told you, but you should know she's very persuasive."

Out came his glowing white teeth. "My misunderstanding. I was under the impression that you sought her out with questions about her faith."

I should have known. Jelly wanted me saved. That could never happen if she confessed everything. But what disturbing things had he heard? It didn't matter. I saw my opening. A chance to be his prized heathen. Here I was, thirty years old with little to show for it besides notoriety. If he converted me, well, that was a home run for his ministry. Sure he'd witnessed before, but he'd never run across the likes of the White Boy Bandito.

"I'm the mistaken one. I did ask her about it," I said.

"That's good. You're a listener and inquisitive. What specifically did you want to know?"

"I was asking abstractly."

"She explained that your family is Jewish."

"In theory."

"And in practice?"

"I don't really believe in God."

Holden didn't appear concerned. "You might not believe in Him, but He believes in you. You were created in His image, after all."

"He must have lousy self-esteem."

"Care for another?" He poured a shot into his glass and did the same for me. He sat down at his desk and sipped his drink contemplatively. I downed mine.

"I guess you don't get to be where you are without racking up some big conversion numbers," I said.

"I'm not soliciting you, Alex. Contrary to what you must think about my calling, I can't make a person convert. I don't have any special powers. The Lord has the power, I am simply his servant. When a person is saved, it means he saved himself through the power of the Lord. I'd like to tell you about my ministry. Would you stay a minute more?"

He had a way of looking at you with those eerie black eyes that made you feel wooed without ever getting the impression he necessarily needed you around. And that was a charismatic quality, to make someone feel wanted if not needed. So, I, one of the two most well-known men in the area, comfortable in Holden's chilly office with two belts of vodka in me, said it would be my pleasure to learn about his ministry.

"You won't hear fire and brimstone at my services. People have real problems and they don't need to be cursed to Hell. What kind of message is that anyway? Scaring a person to behave a certain way produces inauthentic results. God is a comforting agent in our lives. He's not the boogeyman. I preach prosperity. To the youth that includes scholastic, social, athletic, and civic prosperity. With adults, I preach those same values, but I also express a strong belief in economic prosperity."

He sounded like a politician enumerating the hallmarks of his administration. "God wants us to be rich?"

"Of course he does! He invented the American Dream. I tell my congregants," he said, getting more animated as he spoke, "to invest in God. To go into business with Jesus. And once you have, you will be rewarded with the abundant life."

When he talked, he took over the room. If he could modulate

his temperament it seemed he turned the knob in only one direction, ever livelier.

Then he dropped the subject. There was more vodka, a few more words about Gregory Peck's lesser roles, a brief rundown of his courtship to Isabella. He had a deep and well-informed interest in bass fishing (hence the lake in the backyard), albeit an academic one, as he rarely had the opportunity to enjoy any angling. At some point he turned the discussion back on me.

"Aside from that book of lies, as you call it," and he pointed with his drink hand at the bookcase, "I do know you. I know your probation officer's name is Glen. I know that you work part time at Franklin Avenue Community Outreach, where your mother has served as Director of Operations since it opened in 1987. I also know, and I don't mean to be indelicate, that your father's business recently closed and that your home is in need of repairs."

There were ways for him to have gotten this information and Jelly could have told him most of it. Worse than his knowing, however, and the way his knowing made me feel exposed, was that he had the upper hand. He'd already bested me before I met him, another Lenny Marino hiding his top intelligence and letting me dangle the whole time. "Is that what you were talking about when you said you heard disturbing things about me?"

He began growing manic, his arms gesturing as he spoke. "No, no. I was talking about The Holy Houseplant."

"*Euphorbia milli?*"

"You ask Jill about her faith. You sell a Christian plant. You admit to me you're a Jewish atheist."

"When you put it that way, it does sound unusual."

"I'm just summarizing. It's a memory device. Now, it's come to my attention that one of my congregants quizzed you on Scripture and you looked like a deer in headlights. His words."

"Was he a womanly man?"

"What are you doing at a flea market?"

"It's a jumping off point."

"You have something and you're squandering it."

"What?"

"Name recognition."

"I'm testing the market. We had very nice receipts last weekend."

"Last year Holden Ministry averaged over four million a month in gross revenue. We're on pace for a better year. I have a new book in prepublication that will be in every major retail chain in the country by Thanksgiving called *The Spiritual Road to Easy Street*. It will debut on the bestseller's list just like my last book. The video podcasts of my sermons on holdenministry.org are so popular that twice in the last month the site crashed. We've had to double our capabilities, technologically speaking."

His increasingly spirited face frightened me. He seemed self-possessed and possessed by an exterior force and both these possessions operated in concert upon him; rather than wearing him down, the conflict made him stronger.

He reached into his pocket and tossed a plastic packet in my lap. It looked not unlike a packet of duck sauce from a Chinese takeout, except it was filled with a clear liquid.

"This is what I was doing in Russia," he said.

"What is it?

"What is it? What is it? It's water. *Miracle* water. Its source is a spring near Chernobyl."

I tossed the packet back onto his desk like it was a hot potato.

Holden was vibrating as he retrieved his meltdown water. He had come ungrounded, without warning. His thin splinter of an upper lip quivered. "After the accident at the power plant, locals testified that this spring protected those who drank from it. It has healing powers!"

Was he for real? Was he a con man? Or was he something more sinister: a true believer who had misread the lessons of the bible to validate his own demented worldview? At four million a month gross revenue did it matter?

He leapt to his feet, unable to restrain himself. His hands gesticulated in front of his body before he regained control of them and shoved them into his pockets. He opened his eyes as wide as he could and I still saw none of their whites. Did he have entirely black eyes?

"I want to give you a job," he announced.

"What?"

"In order to spread His word, I rely on the best people in their respective fields. As much as I'd like them all to be devout, the reality of the marketplace doesn't allow it. You are intelligent and you can ingratiate yourself with disparate people to achieve your goals. Above all, you are resourceful."

Lucky for me, Holden hadn't seen me fail at lunch. Still, his sales pitch was similar to the one with which I'd dreamed of dazzling Lenny. Part of me delighted in his selecting me and it drew me toward him, this being the shallowest type of love—affection for a person because of how he makes you feel about yourself. Another part of me—one I presently ignored—found him as slick as the country bible salesman whose own antics were antecedent to Holden's.

"Right now I'm involved in my Crown of Thorns venture," I said.

"I don't mean to stop you. You have my blessing."

"Blessings are fine and good, but I was hoping you might want to go in as a partner."

"I'd have to ask my other partner first," he said, and contemplated a cross on the wall.

"Professional curiosity, what are you charging for that water?"

"You can't charge for a miracle," he said. "I'm giving it away. But this plant, sure, we could sell it. Sure. Now that I think about, we could debut it at the same time as the miracle water. We'll hit them over the head with it. They won't know what hit them. So tomorrow you get on this."

"How would it work, money-wise?"

"Name it."

I worked a fast calculation of the basement estimate, the Visa bill, Lenny Marino's loan, a little more for living expenses. With a nauseating thickness in my throat, I quoted him a mid-five figure retainer.

Holden wasted not a second considering my request. "Fuck off. Tomorrow morning I want you at my office." He said we would talk money then.

"Fine."

At home, my family took the news of our merger with the Holden Ministry with that unique Wolf-ness of ours—a mulligan stew of flummoxation and reticence and gratefulness and excitement. And though I expected to know how they would each react, as usual I was nevertheless surprised by one of them, my mother this time, whom I'd figured would put up a final splendid protest, dissenting for dissension sake. Instead, her sole contribution to our conversation was, "I'm going to miss working with you, Alex. But this is for the best."

As for the rest of the talk, I won't bother recreating it. It occurs to me that maybe my family only ever had one conversation, just one long ongoing talk we were born to have, forever turning the words over, a double helical pattern of words that over the years unspooled and piled up around us like souvenirs and garbage alike, and that bound us as well as our blood, one long conversation we couldn't end no matter how sore our throats or dry our lips.

From the screenplay to *The Wrong Way Son* (H.E.L.R. Prod., 2007)

```
EXT. STASH HOUSE - LORDSBURG, NM - DAWN

A SWAT ASSAULT VEHICLE tears onto the dirt lawn
in front of a sagging MOBILE HOME.

TEN SWAT OFFICERS file out of the vehicle in
combat gear, rifles in hand.

The CAPTAIN gives the signal. Officers break
down the front door of the house with a BATTER-
ING RAM. One officer throws in a FLASH GRENADE.

INT. STASH HOUSE - LORDSBURG, NM - CONTINUOUS

Grenade EXPLODES. Officers rush through the
smoke, shouting.

A group of LATINO men stagger around disorient-
ed.

                OFFICER #1
            Down! Get down!
```

                    OFFICER #2
              On your faces! Down now!

Officer #2 slams LATINO #1 on the floor.

More officers push through the mayhem, down a
narrow hallway.

LATINO #2 jumps out of the bathroom. He slices
Officer #1 with a MACHETE. BLOOD SPRAY arcs
like a rainbow on the wall.

AN AFRICAN AMERICAN OFFICER fires a round into
Latino #2's chest, dropping him. He kicks the
machete out of his dead hand.

In the first bedroom, two officers find LATINO
#3 climbing out the window. They yank him back
inside.

Latino #3 punches OFFICER #3, tackles him,
grabs him around the throat.

OFFICER #4 jabs a Taser into Latino #3's stomach. He rolls over and starts convulsing.

                    OFFICER #4
              Ride the lightning, bitch.

Officer #4 helps up Officer #3.

                    OFFICER #4 (CONT'D)
              You okay, buddy?
                    OFFICER #3
              Just my pride is bruised, is all.

Meanwhile the rest of the officers, led by the
Captain, file into the back bedroom, where they
find:

Alexander Wolf, the White Boy Bandito, calmly
playing XBOX.

All the officers have rifles trained on him, red dots from their laser scopes wiggling over his face.

          CAPTAIN
Hands, Bandit! Let me see your hands!

          ALEX
Hang on, I'm saving my game.

          CAPTAIN
I'm not playing with you. I will blow your goddamn brains all over that goddamn wall!

          ALEX
Dramatic much?

Alex slowly raises his hands. The officers rush to him, jerk him to his feet, throw him up against the wall, handcuff him.

          CAPTAIN
I hope you like prison food, Bandit.

          ALEX
I love it.

          CAPTAIN
Good, 'cause where you're going they got plenty of it.

SIXTEEN

Along with office space, Holden Ministry headquarters contained a parking garage, a call center, a warehouse for his products, an employee day care, a production studio and, in a rumor I was disappointed to learn was untrue, a helipad on the roof. The reverend ran his organization out of a business complex a mile from his house and little about it when walking the halls conveyed the brain center of a religious juggernaut. Sure, a cross hung on a wall here or there, and the waiting room shared the same garish style of furnishings Holden preferred for his home, which struck me more as horrible taste than the emblems of a spiritual higher calling. Maybe it was because I didn't know what to expect that I expected something else, something ethereal, heavenly; or maybe it wasn't in the décor but in the employees that I anticipated more. The type of person who chose this as a career couldn't treat it as a job—punch in and punch out, collect a check. Working here, I assumed, required fierce dedication and discipline because the nature of the business was to trade in ideas essential to the meaning of life for those who believed it. In that way, Holden's clientele (again, I assumed) was owed matchless customer service.

My arrival was met with slight confusion and then efficient disinterest. Holden hadn't informed them of a new addition. The receptionist escorted me to the tastelessly appointed waiting room, where I was sequestered until it could get sorted out. She was nice enough to ply me with coffee while I waited. I sipped my beverage and perused the reading materials. Holden's face was ubiquitous, on magazine covers, flyers, pamphlets, books. It was addressing a crowd of thousands on a wall-mounted TV. It was on the Holden Ministry coffee mug in my hand. That made me laugh. His mug, on a mug.

A young man entered the waiting room and said, "Who's up for a little tour?"

He was ruddy and blond and appeared to be in the process of transforming his teeth into the same extraterrestrial shade of white as the man whose face was everywhere. I pegged him to be in his early twenties.

"I know there's been some confusion, but I'm not a visitor. Mr. Holden—"

"*Reverend* Holden," he said.

"Yeah, sure, Reverend—"

He interrupted me again. "Reverend Holden has entrusted you to me."

That the order came from on high wasn't as impressive as I initially thought. Holden didn't delegate authority. His wasn't a chain of command but a web, and from its center, he issued instruction in all directions.

"Let me give you the lay of the land," he said. "I'm Kevin, by the way. Or the Kevster, if you like. That's what the reverend calls me."

He dragged me around from office to office, collecting things and handing them to me as we went: a rough cut of a forthcoming DVD called *Faith at Home: Give God a Seat on Your Couch, Vol. 1.*, galleys to Holden's book *The Spiritual Road to Easy Street*, an Official Warren Holden bobblehead doll, and a stack of correspondences addressed to people in at least ten states.

"It's important to acquaint yourself with the product lines," the Kevster said, confident in a way that made him seem easily bored. "So, yeah, get to know this stuff. Oh, and also, you're going to want to put in some time watching game film." When it was clear that I didn't know what he was talking about, he said, "The podcasts. Watch the podcasts. Got it?"

"Got it."

He was now eager to be rid of me because, I sensed, he liked making the impression he was inordinately busy. He reached his arm through the doorway of a conference room and flipped on the lights without going inside. "Have fun," he said, urging me in.

Unfamiliar with the workings of the office, I did what I was told. I watched the DVD. I watched a little game film. The podcasts were heavily edited versions of Holden's services, sermons mostly, intercut with shots of him on "crusades," which looked a lot like regular services performed in different cities. There were also scenes of him with Isabella in the same third-world shithole from his commercial.

Next I read the letters. The one on top was addressed to a Calvin Rodgers, Dubuque, Iowa.

> *Brother Calvin,*
>
> *NOW IS THE TIME! It is no secret that we live in an uncertain world. Now more than ever we must forge a personal relationship with the Lord, JESUS. Amen. For if you do, miracles await. I want to tell you first, though, that what God asks you to do may seem unreasonable to a logical mind. The reason is that God's Word is not built on logic but faith and because you are devout, you will find yourself doing things which you'd never dream of doing.*
>
> *I've enclosed a gift for you, blessed shoe liners. What I want you to do is cut out the liners and place them in your bible at 2 CORINTHIANS 5:7. Fill out your prayer slip with your most pressing problem and put it next to the liners. Calvin, pray on it for 3 days. Focus on your desired result. Then take the prayer slip and place it in the enclosed envelope. Remember to include your SEED GIFT. You must plant a seed from which you will reap a harvest, Luke 6:38. The Lord has come to me and spoke about $2500.00. Pray on this. Finally, Brother Calvin I want you to put the shoe liners in the bottom of your everyday footwear. If you have followed these directions you will immediately feel the presence of GOD with you all of your days. His miracles will happen automatically. Your devotion is all that is required. When you mail the prayer slip do your best to include the amount God put on your heart for His Work. Once I receive your prayer slip it will be my honor to pray for you, to help bring about an end to your problems.*

The letter was a lot to digest. Holden's solicitation came nothing close in tone, appeal, and design to the letters my mother used at Franklin Avenue Community Outreach. The best she offered was a tote bag, budget willing (it almost never did). I marveled at the contradictory implication that without the seed gift the miracle wouldn't come, and yet all one needed was devotion. If the miracle never materialized, Holden had an out clause. How do you prove devotion? You'd think twenty-five hundred for paper shoe liners would do it. Dr. Scholl's was eleven bucks at CVS, with a money-back guarantee. I began wondering what kind of seed gift he would ask for the Chernobyl water. Holden said he couldn't charge for the miracle, but if this letter was any indication, it was a semantic argument he was making.

I was skimming *The Spiritual Road to Easy Street*, Chapter II: Avoiding Speed Bumps, when Kevin retrieved me. "Ready to see how the sausage is made?" he said.

He and I ducked into an elevator and, when the doors closed, he let out a deep breath and laughed, as though we had narrowly escaped a pursuing bully. The elevator descended into sub-lobby territory. The doors parted and we stepped into an undivided area the size of the entire level. To the left was a bank of computer workstations manned by operators in headsets; to the right a mailroom, with long metal sorting tables piled with overflowing plastic baskets and canvas bags. There were no windows.

"Cheese and rice got all muddy!" he said.

"Are we supposed to be down here?" I said.

"I'm the reverend's protégé, so it's okay. Now pay attention. The DVDs and books are fancy and buy us mainstream acceptance and, don't get me wrong, definitely generate revenue. But this is the bread and butter. Always has been."

Offerings were Holden's lifeblood, millions of dollars a month running through this room in credit card phone orders on the left and good old-fashioned checks, money orders, cash, and jewelry on the right. The letter I had seen was one of several weekly pleas the ministry sent out.

The Kevster said, "I heard that in the early '90s, Warren was sending out a hundred thousand mailing requests a month. Now he relies a lot on email, but he still works the mailing lists better than anyone I've ever seen. He refuses to go totally electronic. He's a genius. There are still parts of the country with spotty Internet connections. And old people can't work a computer. And they love getting mail. Everyone does. The reverend is all about the personal touch."

I asked him how many people the shoe liner letter was sent to.

"Just the Code 7 list."

"Are there codes one through six?"

We took a lap around the room as Kevin gave me the rundown. There were companies that compiled data on consumers and sold the information. "If you owned a landscaping business and wanted to do a direct mailer, a company would put together a list of people who were homeowners or who had hired a landscaper before or who bought grass seed. You might pay ten cents for a name and address. Code 7 is our most valuable list."

"Like a quarter a name?"

"Try five bucks."

"For a name and address?"

"Some cost more. These are big donors. Reverend Holden might drop fifty thou' for a list but the return is sometimes three or four hundred percent."

The Code 7 lists were so valuable that Holden put fake names on them with addresses that linked back to him. Only he knew which they were.

"If another ministry steals a list, he finds out," Kevin said.

We were back in front of the elevator. He pushed the button, the doors opened, we got inside.

"What's the deal with the shoe liners?" I said.

"I've seen miracles with my own eyes," he said.

I watched the digital arrow tick up. I didn't say anything.

"If you don't believe that, what are you doing here?" The doors opened on our floor. "Let's keep this between us," he said, and he took off down the hall.

Late in the day, Holden found me in the conference room. He looked crisp and spit-shined in a blue double-breasted suit with no tie. His cuff links were gold crosses the size of lug nuts.

"Hey, boss," I said.

"Where did the Kevster run off to? Never mind. So, this is where you're holed up? How is your first day going?"

"No complaints. But I'm glad you're here. I want to talk about a few things."

"What's on your mind?"

He caught sight of the letter to Calvin Rodgers, from Dubuque. He started to ask me something but then picked up the phone on the conference table and dialed an extension.

155

"Kevin, would you like to tell me why he has a Code 7 letter?" He listened. "Of course he shouldn't have them." Listened more. "You and I are going to have a long talk about this."

Holden gathered the letters. "I'll get these out of your way," he said, smiling. He pointed to the galleys of his book. "Tell me, what do you think? Of my five books, I'm most proud of this one. I really got to the kernel of my message this time."

Finally we got down to discussing what my job was to be. Holden explained that I was going through a probationary period in which I was to observe the day-to-day business, since it was easy to lose oneself in the grandness of his vision. Not to worry, though, he assured me. My matriculation to a full-time ministry member was but a formality, after which he and I would embark on a mutually-beneficial program of spreading God's word via my plant. First things first, I needed to attend a service.

March, 2005

This is a pre-paid call from an inmate at a federal correctional facility. This call is from: Alexander. *To accept, dial 5 now. To decline, dial 3 now, or just hang up.*

"Happy birthday, Alex, it seems odd that you should be calling me, when I should be calling you."

"It's just as well, Bubbe, my assistant is on vacation and I probably wouldn't have gotten the message."

"Haha, very clever. I'm so glad you're keeping your sense of humor. Such a shame you should be where you are. It makes no sense given your brains and your good family. So how did it happen? You can tell me, I won't judge."

"Guess I wasn't thinking straight."

"I was reading Money Magazine the other day. They rated the twelve best federal prisons. Otisville was number eight. I clipped the article. I've been meaning to mail it to you but my fingers hurt and I have such a difficult time addressing the envelope."

"Sounds like you need an assistant."

"Sure, to go along with my chauffeur and personal chef. The

article said Otisville has an active Jewish religious program. Do you know about that?"

"Religious program?"

"It might be a good time to give the man upstairs a shot."

"I don't know if it's for me."

"It was never my cup of tea, but what else are you going to do, take up water colors? I love you dearly, you have no idea, but I've seen you draw before. Arts and crafts are not your forte."

"Right, as usual, Bubbe."

"Sure, what do you have to lose? It won't kill you. Go see a rabbi. Go pray a little."

Sunday morning I was paired with Dolores in a backstage dressing room at the Church of the Abundant Valley, known by ministry staff, and most congregants, as "the Arena," on account of it being a stadium-like construction on ninety acres of farmland that had been bequeathed to Holden a dozen years earlier. Service was at noon, but the staff, me included, arrived by dawn. Dolores was a higher-up. She was sixty but looked shy of a hundred by about a week, a wax figurine left too close to a flame. She'd been on board with Holden for years, she said, since he ministered to her after her husband was killed one afternoon while officiating a varsity baseball game and took an errant line drive to the side of his neck, rupturing his carotid artery.

"How much time do I have before I start taking tickets?" I said.

"You, a ticket taker? Goodness," she said. She removed from a rack of clothes a blue blazer almost matching the color of the suit I wore at my Bar Mitzvah. "Blue blazers are for the ushers. Didn't anyone tell you this?" She held the jacket in front of me. "This looks like it will fit," and helped me into it. Like a tailor, she ran her hands over the sleeves, tugging the ends to see where on my wrist they terminated, and then buttoned the top gold button.

"I'm a high-powered usher, am I? Dreams really do come

true."

"Look at the mouth on you. I hope you're getting it out of your system. They're already lined up outside. You better be ready when we open the doors."

"Ready for what?"

"To do your job. And let security do their job. Don't get in the way."

"Are there a lot of unruly churchgoers?"

"Boy, you just can't stop. Our congregants are good people. They are hardworking and they love the Lord."

"Why the security?"

"Now you're asking the right questions. We have to be ultra-aware of so-called journalists weaseling their way in here. Those people are shameless. They want to mock the Reverend."

If what Dolores said made sense to me, it was because I'd had some experience with so-called journalists. "What do the ushers do?"

"It's an extremely important job. You're the first ones to welcome our guests. Find out where they're from, why they're here. If they're ill, you'll help them to their seats. Give them these prayer cards and make sure they fill them out." She passed me a stack of questionnaire-like cards, asking what needed praying over. "You're the first line in the Lord's army."

"God's cannon fodder."

"I sincerely hope there is a smart brain behind that smart mouth of yours."

Today's service was going to be recorded for a podcast on holdenministry.org and Vol. 2 of the DVD series. Maximum capacity at the Arena hovered around ten thousand. Holden could pack them in, a full house most Sundays, depending on the weather. If they came up short and it was a shooting day, the production crew simply blacked out the nose bleed sections. Editing tricks in post-production made the audience look twice as large anyway. The stage was carpeted in a luxurious red pile, threaded with gold so that it twinkled when the lights hit it just right. Thick blue curtains, a shade or two lighter than my blazer, hung around the stage and there were two gold-colored crosses, ten feet tall with sunbeams bursting behind them, located slightly downstage from Holden's lectern, or podium, or pulpit, whatever you wanted to call it.

"When you get out there," Dolores said, "remember to smile. It's a simple thing but you'd be surprised how easy it is to forget. So don't forget. It has to be sincere. They can spot a phony. That's why they're here. Because Reverend Holden is the real deal."

"Anything else?"

"That should do it. Watch the other ushers. Watch Kevin, he's such a sweetie, really impressing all of us with his devotion, unlike some people I know."

As I started to leave she said, "Where's your pin?"

"What pin?"

She rummaged through a drawer in the dressing room table. "This pin," she said, holding up a two inch version of the cross that adorned the stage. She hooked it onto my lapel as if she were my prom date pinning on a boutonnière. "This shows them you're not just another guy in a jacket. Stick it right up under their noses if you have to. It lets them know that you're part of the ministry and that they can trust you."

I took one last look in the mirror. My disbelief notwithstanding, I never felt more Jewish than when I wore that cross pin. I was as conscious of it as if it were stuck through my nipple. I left Dolores in the dressing room and walked the corridor to a side entrance of the auditorium. *Pray Like A Champion Today!* read the sign over the door frame. I continued through the theater out to the entrance gates where men and women in red blazers—ticket takers—waited for security to open the doors. The Arena was an apt name for this place. In the air was a luscious anxiety akin to competition and performance, as various employees and volunteers ran around making last minute adjustments.

Security popped open the entrances to admit an energetic crowd that paused impatiently while guards pawed at them with magnetic wands and inspected their bags, before moving on to the ticket takers. Once the folks in red blazers were satisfied, the crowd filed through the turnstiles and came straight at me. It was hours before the service, and these people had assigned seats, but they came in as if they were afraid of missing something unforgettable. Some advanced on crutches, some limped, exerting their life force to get inside, while others moved as if floating. To my right and left, I spotted other blue blazers. I couldn't say where they had come from, though I was thankful they were here. As I stood waiting for the crowd to envelop me, the other ushers rushed forward, eager and proactive. They introduced themselves, shook hands, smiled, hugged, took the weak and infirmed and elderly by the elbow.

It was time to get in the game. I smiled, as Dolores had instructed, and extended my hand to a beefy, pink-faced man, who simply barreled past me into a large crowd; and right then another usher intercepted the whole bunch, a feat made more amazing by how he did it. He just made himself available in a way that drew others to him, as if exuding Christian pheromones.

Damnit if it wasn't the Kevster. I hadn't seen him around the office the last couple of days but here he was, a blue-blazered brother. "I can see why you're a rising star," I said, "Man, you're good at this."

"Falling star is more like it. This is a demotion," he said, still smiling for all to see.

"I'm getting killed here. Any advice?"

"Off the top of my head, do a better job."

"I hear you."

"Good. Stick with me. Maybe I can score some points if I carry you."

Together we greeted the masses. I imitated everything he did, like a hero-worshipping younger brother.

"A great day," he said to a truly miserable looking woman.

"Really great," I flapped my lips, trying to approximate his natural pleasantness.

It worked. She failed to notice my poor mimicry. She grasped my hand and grabbed at my bicep, climbing my arm until she was clinging to my shoulder. "I try to tell myself that. But it's so hard sometimes."

Kevin peeled her off of me. "I'm glad you could make it ma'am.

I'm Kevin."

"Emily."

"Have you traveled far to be with us?"

"So far."

"Well, thank you for making the effort. I'm glad you could be here."

"I wanted to come for so long. Even today was almost too much. Sometimes it's just so . . ." he took her away.

That was how you did it. Like most everything else in life, it boiled down to confidence. I was an usher, a man with knowledge (of the seating chart if nothing else), and I needed to deliver that message. Next to cross my path was a family of four, a glowing Aryan couple flanked by two towheaded sons with the posture and gait of future all-American swimmers. Unlike poor Emily, they suffered no outward symptoms of sadness. A proprietary air radiated from them. They needed no usher. They needed assistance from no one save Jesus who, presumably, they were here to thank for their enviable attributes.

I slowed their advance by spreading my arms before them. "It's a great day," I said, reciting Kevin's opening.

"Good morning," the mother said.

"I'm Alex. It's a blessing to be here with you." I stuck my pin in her face and thrust out my hand to their older progeny, a boy of about thirteen. He said his name was Cody.

"Have you traveled far to be with us?" I continued from the script Kevin had left me.

"We're regulars," the father said. "Isn't that right?" he asked his brood.

"Have some prayer cards," I said, fanning out my stack.

He held up a few cards, already filled out. "We're way ahead of you. But please, take these."

"Great! Thank you so much. Please, right this way, I insist. Let's find your seats," I hissed through my clenched-jaw smile, forcing my will on them.

After dropping them off, I peeked at their prayer cards. The father implored the creator of all that is in heaven and earth for a bonus at work large enough to buy a new vacation home (*New* was underlined twice). His wife requested protection for her loved ones from "Islamo-enemies and all Chinamen." The younger son fretted about the soul of a Jewish boy at school, but mostly wished for a spot on the soccer travel league team. Outside the theater, I summarily tore up their cards.

Next, I assisted a man who relied on the Almighty's hand to pulverize his kidney stones, which he insisted were the size of blood diamonds, an elderly black man whose Border Collie's cataracts had reduced the dog to falling down stairs, a pre-teen boy who wanted a huge dong (his mother clipped him in the back of his head, and he complained, "What? It's true."), and a woman who never fully recovered from minor knee surgery three years ago ("Can you hear it clicking?" she asked, bending and straightening her leg. "It's clicking.")

For two hours this continued. They kept coming and I kept handing out prayer cards. There was cancer— boy, was there cancer! There were parents with disabled kids. There were others who weren't sick but faced endless money problems. I was more sensitive with them because I knew where they were coming from. For everything about this spectacle I disagreed with, I couldn't reject what these people felt. With so many impossible cases, there was something exceedingly American about their refusal to stand by and watch the foreclosure of their dreams. Then there were those who, like the vigorous Aryan family, had it all and very simply wanted more, more, more, and more.

At ten minutes after twelve, the theater lights dimmed and a series of multi-colored lasers and strobes burst from the ceiling, a futuristic assault from the heavens. The righteous glory of the Holden Ministry Orchestra (prerecorded) blared from the sound system a melody rousing, yet solemn, the sort of magnificent theme music that announced the arrival of a superhero.

And there was Holden.

He didn't step onto the glinting red carpet, peek around, surprised to find himself there. He *took* the stage. He leapt from the wings, a whirlwind of free-flowing energy propelling him from stage right to stage left, and then back again, and then back again. His arms were often out from his sides as he made his laps and, from the aisle where I watched, he reminded me of a small plane circling a corn field for a place to land. The audience was on its feet, stamping and clapping, savoring what was no doubt the highlight of their week. In time Holden found his way to the pulpit. Footlights were extinguished and one beam covered him from above. His forehead was damp and his black mane shone. He scanned the throbbing crowd before giving the command to sit.

"It's time," he said, "to forget everything hurtful, harmful, shameful, blameful, ignorant, intolerant, unfair, unjust. All the deceitfulness. All our *pain*. Because I know there is pain. It's time to let the unhappiness slip away. Go on, let it slip out! Tilt your head to the side if you must, if it makes it easier for the unhappiness to fall out, maybe through your ear. Did you ever get water in your ear at the beach and you had to jump up and down and hit yourself in the side of your head to get it out?" He came abreast of the pulpit and demonstrated. They laughed like they were supposed to. "That's what I want you to do if that's what it's going to take. Stand up and get it out of you."

More than a few people did. I saw them hopping on one foot, shaking their heads.

"That's not why Jesus died for us, so we could walk around feeling sorry for ourselves. That's not why we have the Spirit in us. *Oh, I can't pay my bills. Oh, I hate my job. Oh, when will someone love me for me?* Guess what? Someone already does. *He does.* He loves you for the person you are because he made you who you are. So go on, for the last time, let it all slip away this morning. It's a great morning. And it's time."

The orchestra came back, louder if possible, and Holden took a few more laps around the stage, revving himself up. He wound down and composed himself, feigned catching his breath, and said, "Earlier this morning, there was an accident on I-87, a very bad accident. I didn't know it at the time. When my car stopped in the road all I could think about was how the traffic was going to make me late. Me. I even turned to Isabella and said, 'Of all the times for this to happen to *me*.' The kids were in the backseat, growing impatient, God love them, and I wasn't your reverend just then. I was a frustrated man, sitting in traffic with his family, wanting to get somewhere he couldn't get to. Then I started getting angry, thinking about all of you, and how I needed to get to you, and how it was unfair that I couldn't get here, how *life* was unfair for making me late.

"When we rode beside the accident, I saw the twisted metal, broken glass and plastic, anti-freeze leaking a puddle, mangled bodies on stretchers. Praise God there were no fatalities. He saw to it they lived. Amen! I saw the police and the fire trucks and the ambulances and I thought to myself, 'What's the matter with me?' The accident had nothing to do with *me*, no one was out to make *me* late. There were people who were being tested, brothers and sisters just like yourselves, going through an ordeal, and all I could think about was my tiny little itty-bitty problem. It made me ashamed. I wanted Jesus to forgive me. I prayed right there on the side of the highway that He would let these people come through their ordeal and I prayed for His forgiveness. He forgave me. Do you want to know how I know?" He put his fingers to his temple the way he had when I met him. He closed his eyes, tilted his head to the ceiling. He said, "The book of Mark. Chapter 9, verse 6. 'But that ye may know that the Son of Man hath power on earth to forgive sins.'"

They erupted—*God bless!* and *Amen!* and *Praise Jesus!* Having them where he wanted them, Holden said nothing but smiled as if he was experiencing the same thing they were experiencing and not the architect of the whole thing, not the conductor bringing them to this emotional frenzy. He drifted down near the footlights which were on again, but muted, throwing off a shallow yellow light. So fired up was the crowd that he had to wait for their outburst to subside.

"I want to talk to you today. I have a few things I want to tell you, so please hear me out. Will you do that for me, please?" he said. "What I want to talk about is hope. This is an important subject for me. 'The Lord redeemeth the soul of His servants: and none of them that trust in Him shall be desolate.' Psalms 34:22. Now what does *desolate* mean? It can mean depressed, gloomy, wretched. It's how some of us go through life. It was how I felt in traffic: moody, unhappy. When you're desolate you're wanting. It can also mean barren, which we know is the opposite of fruitful. And herein lies the real meaning. The Lord redeemeth the soul of His servants. We stand here today as His servants. We live in His service. And none of us that trust in Him shall be desolate. Did you hear? None. Not one. The opposite of none is all. All of us. None of us shall be desolate. All of us shall be fruitful."

It was a nifty word game he played, even if the verse seemed to be about something else. I guessed it didn't matter because no one questioned his wisdom.

"So don't tell me that Jesus doesn't want to see us prosper, to see us live the abundant life. His Word is His proof. Is that not good enough? Is that what you're telling me?"

They emphatically denied it. His word was more than good enough for them. It was the only thing they needed.

"Oh, so you agree?" Holden said.

They did, obviously, they did, on their feet again.

"He wants you to have that loving relationship with your soul mate, the beautiful children, the dream job, the loving friends and family. He wants you to have that house, that second house, that third car, that vacation you've dreamed of for so long, the one with the palm trees and white sand and crystal blue water and the drink with the umbrella in it. None shall be desolate. That doesn't mean everybody *but* you. It doesn't mean your coworkers and your neighbors but not you. It means all shall be fruitful, as long as you're a servant of the Lord. Looking around this room today, that's all I see. Every single one of you.

"But here's the rub. Being a servant, even for someone as great as the Lord, is not a simple job. I have a musician friend who'd say, 'It ain't no easy gig.' It ain't. Being a servant of the Lord is demanding. It has to be. There is sin which we must contend with daily. And then we are tested in other ways, like our brothers and sisters in the car accident this morning. I know many of you here today are in pain, you suffer illness. Now what did I tell you? All of us shall be fruitful. The Lord means it. He's going to heal you. If you take Jesus Christ into your heart as your savior, He will heal you. None shall be desolate."

He paced around the stage, his head cocked to one side. He

stopped in one spot, shook his head, moved to another, resembling a man seeking better cell phone reception. He again showed that odd affectation of pressing his fingertips to his temple. He squeezed his eyes shut, sweat pushing through the pores on his forehead.

"Sitting amongst us today is a woman crippled by sadness, a woman who, on the sunniest of days, feels only storms in her heart, a woman whose entire life is gray." Holden dropped his fingers from his head and opened his eyes, gazing into the distance. "I want Emily to join me. Emily, I know you're here. Please join me." He stretched out his arms.

There was a stirring behind me as the woman Kevin and I met that morning stumbled into the aisle. She pushed herself to the stage where ushers near the first row helped her up the steps.

This hadn't been part of the podcasts I'd seen.

Holden placed his arm around her waist, propping her up.

"Sister Emily has been on a tough road since the end of her marriage."

Her head bobbed up and down, tears streaming, sobs coughing out of her.

"When Bruce left you and took Bruce Jr., you wanted to die. It hasn't gotten any easier, has it?"

She shook her head almost spastically. No, it had not gotten easier.

"Emily, have you accepted Jesus Christ into your heart?"

"Yes," she screamed, her voice unaided by a microphone.

"Are you a servant of the Lord?"

"Yes," came her plaintive wail. Behind her two ushers moved into position just as Holden reached out and palmed her head like a cantaloupe. She clung to his wrist.

"Heal!" He threw her backward. She fell with her arms flailing over her head. The ushers caught her and eased her onto the sparkling carpet where, laid out, she convulsed, babbling a monstrous gibberish. Holden stared at his healing hand, holding it up for the congregation to see, a dumbstruck look on his face. He staggered away from Emily, who the ushers were now dragging off stage. For a few moments, he rested his hands on his knees, as if exhausted by the stress of the Lord working through his frail earthly shell.

Holden recouped enough strength to call forward a man with sciatica so painful he seldom got out of bed in the morning. The new sufferer shuffled behind a walker and took forever reaching the stage. This guy is going to hit the floor and never get up, I thought. Only, when Holden grabbed him by his forehead and slammed him back into the ushers—"In the name of Jesus Christ, I say, Heal!"—the man jumped up and started boogying, lofting his walker over his head like a trophy. Was he a ringer? Were they all? They were actors, yes, they had to be, paid by Holden, each taking turns wearing disguises and inventing maladies. One day he might ask me to fabricate a slew of physical and emotional problems and then crawl down the aisle.

The healing session continued, his followers in the throes of fever, some collapsing in their seats, their eyes rolling up into their heads, speaking in tongues (I later learned this was called shouting—dancing in the Spirit.)

Once Holden could heal no more, when too much godly voltage had decimated his nerves, out came the offering pots. Large goldplated buckets, lined with crushed red velvet. Kevin handed me one and nudged me to the back rows where already wallets were in hands, purses opened, fists clutched cash. Growing up, the temple my family seldom frequented charged its members dues and didn't indulge in this sort of cash letting; however, I sometimes accompanied a Catholic friend to mass on Sunday, usually after sleeping over his house the night before. When the plates were passed around, his mother would press a warm five dollar bill to my palm so I could participate in the charity. This wasn't what was happening at the Arena. Here they fell over themselves to part with their money.

Holden said, "I need you to dig deep, to prove God. I need you to prove God by giving what you *can't* afford. That's faith. And he'll repay you for it."

The money tumbled in a flurry of green into my bucket. Andrew Jackson overwhelmed the blizzard of currency, along with Civil War legend U.S. Grant. I turned around and into the bucket fluttered Benjamin Franklin triplets.

If there were eight thousand in attendance that day . . . well, you do the math. Security rounded up the ushers and brought us upstairs to an office where Isabella sat before a counting machine. We handed over our buckets and before I was escorted out the door I saw her dumping the money onto a table.

I was downstairs in time for benediction. Holden looked depleted to the point of serenity. Gripping both sides of his pulpit, he said, "God be with you till we meet again; with the oil of joy anoint you; Sacred ministries appoint you; God be with you till we meet again. When life's perils thick confound you; put His arms unfailing round you; God be with you till we meet again."

The music returned, quieter than before, and the theater lights came on. The congregants, fortified for another week, shook hands, hugged. Smiles galore, radiant, sublime. My mysterious boss—black haired, black eyed, glowing-toothed Reverend Warren Holden—lingered a moment before disappearing behind the blue curtains.

Laura didn't make it all up. Don't misunderstand me, plenty of it was straight up bullshit. Some she just got wrong, though. And other parts of the story she exaggerated or tried to fill in blanks with speculations that weren't impossible to have happened, but just didn't go down that way. There was one episode in the book, however, that was factual and, more astonishing than that, emotionally correct, if rendered in her wretched prose. Here it is without comment or interpretation:

From *White Boy Bandito: How a Clever Suburbanite Became Death's Middleman for South American Revolutionaries*, by Dr. Laura Sullivan, PhD. (Verdict Press: 2006, 183-184)

Since the day Alexander was arrested, his family hoped against hope that it was all one crazy mix up. They wished it was just a bureaucratic mistake that could be sorted out in the blink of an eye. It was too inconceivable to be true. It was utterly unthinkable that he might actually be guilty.

Their son wasn't a criminal. Or was he?

On the flight out west, Robert and Judy had to come to terms with the hard truth that they hardly knew their son anymore. When was the last time they had seen him or spoken to him for more than a few brief minutes? The notion that Alexander, the boy they loved, had grown up to live a life so alien to their core values was about as big a jolt to their system as they could endure.

Their reunion was at the Ci Cibola County Correctional Institution, in Milan, New Mexico. As stressful as the meeting was for Robert and Judy, it was no picnic for Alexander either. He confided to me that having to explain why on earth he had been arrested was the hardest thing he ever did.

"Going in my plan was to sugarcoat it, to be as vague as possible," he said. "I'd been doing that my whole life. But when they brought us face-to-face, I lost it. I mean, I was fucking bawling. Everything just hit me at once.

"So finally I pulled myself together and spilled the beans. And my dad was asking me, 'What do you mean Ron's missing? Who the hell is Ernesto? Why did you give him a gun? Why did you have a gun to give him in the first place?' and I tried to say that I didn't give Ernesto a gun, but I couldn't really tell them what I was doing either because we were in the visitation room with guards around.

"And my mom, it was so sad, all she said over and over was, 'I don't understand.' It wasn't like she couldn't follow the conversation, she understood what I told her just fine. She was saying it like she didn't understand *how* this moment was even taking place, like it didn't compute. And I tried. I really tried telling her that, you know, it wasn't anything she did. The truth was I wasn't too sure right then how it happened myself, but she kept saying 'I don't understand.' The worst part was that she looked so ashamed that she'd let herself be blindsided by this whole thing, just totally embarrassed to be caught so off-guard like that. Like she should've known better if she was only honest with herself. Like if she'd really thought about it, it wouldn't have come as a surprise. That's when I lost it again."

SEVENTEEN

Rachel and Jelly were in the dining room. On the table were pieces of a Crown of Thorns plant that they had cut up into strips. The girls shared the ear buds to an iPod, dancing at the shoulders in their chairs, their hair whipping their faces as they grooved to the beat. They looked like a commercial for a fashionable lifestyle on the cusp of irrelevance.

"It's the Siamese Twins," I said.

Rachel pulled the tiny speaker from her ear. "What did you say?"

"I called you Siamese Twins."

"Conjoined twins is the un-racist vocabulary. Try it some time."

I was still clad in a tie (coolly loosened at the collar, I might add) and dress pants. Jelly said, "Hey, you're looking dapper."

I pretended not to notice Rachel's war face oscillating between her friend and me. "How was *church*?" she said, pronouncing the word as though she were saying hemorrhoid.

I watched them twist the plant pieces together. "What are you doing?"

"Oh, my God," Jelly said, "Rach had the best idea. We're making a Crown of Thorns into corsages. For prom. We told some of our friends that we were wearing them and they freaked out. Now our whole party bus is going to wear them. This is the prototype."

"I hope you're charging," I said. We couldn't spare any. With me working the service, my parents were running a stripped down booth at the flea market, with fewer than ten plants. Our second batch was going quicker than expected and Handley choked on his lunch when, in trying to pin him down on an exact number of plants available, I ordered a thousand. It was a bluff.

"Don't worry, this one has some brown leaves," Rachel said.

"Word up," agreed Jelly and they both giggled at the antiquated slang.

"Missed you at service," I said to her.

"Can I just say my parents are being freakin' weird lately? I think they're having a midlife crisis. They said they're having second thoughts about Reverend Holden. It sucks ass. They of all people should know that doubt is just the work of you-know-who," and she pointed down, indicating the depths of hell lay somewhere beneath my home, not an outlandish suggestion. "I feel rudderless without the reverend's guidance."

I left them to their crafts. So intertwined were my job and personal life that I wished to put everything on hold for just one afternoon and not feel guilty for wanting something as simple as free time. Of course, not an hour later, during a fantastic Yankees' five run, seventh inning lead over the Red Sox, Holden called. He needed to see me. "Can we hash it out over the phone, boss?" I said, at which point he shouted that I get my hell-bound ass to his house straightaway. So much for free time.

Isabella answered the door. "Warren's in the media room," she said, and led me to a closed door across the hall from his office.

She knocked softly. "Warren, baby."

"Is he here?"

She nodded that I should go in, then scurried away.

He was in a theater chair, fingering a laptop computer with one hand and the ice in a rocks glass with the other. Projected onto the screen at the front of the room was what looked like black-and-white surveillance footage. Just hours ago he was magnificent; now he looked like he'd been up for a week, his black hair matted against his head, his thin slits for eyes red and swollen.

"What's up, coach? Reviewing a little game film?"

"Get the fuck in and close the door behind you."

Before I could begin figuring out what I'd done to upset him, he started yelling.

"What is this?" He aimed his drink hand at the screen, ice clinking against the crystal. "What on God's earth were you doing?"

I followed his hand with my eyes and identified the grainy figure as yours truly. In my blue blazer I was standing in front of the strapping Aryan family.

"What am I paying you for? Even the brain-dead volunteers

know more than you."

"I thought you said you only work with the best," I said.

"Now you're pissing me off. Don't say another word. So help me, I'll rip your arms off. Just tell me, are you deliberately acting like a mongoloid to destroy everything I've worked for?"

"I was doing what Dolores told me to do, what the Kevster was doing."

"I have enough to worry about without listening to your bullshit. Am I totally out of my mind or did you and I have a conversation in my office right across the goddamn hall when I hired you?"

"Yes, but—"

"So, again—and I'm trying to stay calm—what did you think you were doing? Don't answer. *I'll* tell *you* what you were doing. Nothing! Except sit on your ass all week and then you go to the Arena this morning and act like you're new to this planet. Now you come in here pretending you're some kind of innocent? You don't think I already know?"

"Know what?"

"When did you plan on telling me you're selling a fake plant?"

"It's not fake."

"But did that stop you from cashing a paycheck, you shiftless cocksucker? The real plant is as big as a house. You couldn't use that one so you picked another. You know, Alex, you can't sell daisies and call them roses because you feel like it."

The situation here, as I saw it, was his problem. If I didn't live up to whatever misdiagnosed judgment he'd made about me then that was his fault. If I was a bad investment well . . . that was business. Ask my dad about bad investments. "Who do you think you're talking to? I've lived with killers."

That stopped him in his tracks. "Ha!" he said. "Let me apologize for the outburst. I get carried away. It's a failing of mine. Sit down, please."

I remained just inside the closed door. He had calmed down with an ease that suggested his anger was yet another showpiece.

"Come on, sit with me. Have a drink. I've got that superb

Russian vodka on the table back there." He pointed over his shoulder.

"No," I said.

"Suit yourself." He rubbed his eyes with his thumb and forefinger. "Well, where do we go from here? It's a decent idea but it's the wrong plant." This from a man selling paper shoe liners for over two grand.

"No one knows what plant was used to make Jesus' thorny crown. No one can prove there was a Jesus."

"What are you saying?"

"You trade in faith, not authenticity. This plant is a reminder of that faith." I was getting pretty good talking about my product. "The *Euphorbia milli* will be fine for us."

He seemed to be thinking it over. "You might have a point."

"What do you think?" I said.

"I think if we're going to do this, then we do this. All the way. Get the plants. Not now, but right now. Understand? I don't want to have this conversation again."

"I understand."

He pointed his drink at the screen. "You should know this wasn't all your fault. The game plan was poorly executed by everyone. Top to bottom. And it starts with me, straight down the line. Poor execution—that's what it boils down to." Now he indeed sounded like a coach explaining his team's loss to the media. "I can't live with these pathetic Sundays," he complained.

He coughed and for a second I thought he was choked up. From his laptop he made my image disappear, replacing it with his screen background, a photo of his five kids in white robes beside a lake.

"It will wreck my week until I get a chance to fix it. My congregation is forgiving. I only pray I didn't let them down too badly."

He had me coming and going. I just couldn't read him. Either he was wracked with regret or the greatest actor of his generation. What person's character became blurrier the more time you spent with him? Especially since there was little about Holden that was ambiguous. Vagueness wasn't his racket. He laid out his displeasure in specific terms and yet to grasp it at its source was like trying to hug a cloud.

"For what it's worth, I didn't think it was bad," I said.

"That's because you have no idea what a good service looks like. Alex, have a drink with me. Just like when I hired you."

He was looking at me in that wooing way. I wasn't touched exactly that he had stopped berating me, but I took it as a conciliatory gesture and I relented, poured myself a vodka, and sat down in the chair next to his.

"I'm four years old in Gloversville, New York," he said, "walking into a local newsroom in a double-breasted suit, with a bowtie, demanding to see the Editor-in-Chief because I have an announcement. That's right, I'm in town that weekend to tie the devil's tail in a knot. I have a lisp and I'm marrying people, officiating weddings, talking about the *th*anctity of marriage. Always wearing a fucking bowtie." His narrow lips disappeared in a frown.

At least I learned one fact about him—he was the boy-reverend all grown up—even if it tied him closer to his myth.

"You're looking at the third generation of Holden preachers. My grandpa was first. Next was my daddy. He was the real deal, washed in the blood like you wouldn't believe. He knew Scripture. I don't mean he had it memorized. He *knew* it, knew what a person needed to hear and could quote the good book as if it was personalized to a man. That can't be taught. Even I can't do that."

In the early '60s, Holden said, you could make a name for yourself on the revival circuit, the Sawdust Trail, but you still had to rely on families taking you in for meals, giving you a bed because you couldn't afford a hotel. There were a few vanguards—men like Oral Roberts and A.A. Allen—using the mail and radio and television in innovative ways, but most everyone else, his father included, scraped by. It was his mother who decided eternal salvation is wonderful but why shouldn't they all have a nice, long, comfortable life right here on earth before they returned to the Father?

"Mom was the one who introduced Daddy to the more lucrative way of ministering. She was the one who brought me on board. Four years old."

"That's a long time to do anything."

"What do you know about it?" he said.

"Warren, you can't expect me to be the best usher on my first try. That's what this is about, right? I'll do better next time."

"There never should have been a first time. And don't blame this on Dolores. She doesn't know what you and I are working on, our plans. Either you're on the same page as me or you're not."

I wasn't even sure what our plans were anymore. Again, I was backpedaling. "Mind reading's *your* power. If we're not on the same page, it's because you never gave me the book."

"If I haven't made myself clear before, I'll do it now." He began speaking slowly. "I'm busy. Very busy. I have to deal with a lot of things. It leads me, unfortunately, to get tunnel vision sometimes. That's where you come in. I need an idea man who doesn't look at me the same way my other employees do. I'm trying to reach the most people I can. Now, can you help me or do we part ways today?"

Parting ways was probably best. Even if we made a fortune together, it might not be worth it. But this decision affected more than just me. The Hudson Valley Flea Market wasn't enough for us. Also, let's face it, who was I kidding? I had no other opportunities. I didn't want to go back to Franklin Avenue Community Outreach. Yes, I was on the same page as him.

He smiled his benevolent closed mouth smile, his trademark Sunday service smile. "Good, I'm glad. Let's talk tomorrow."

As I was leaving, he said, "Oh, one more thing."

Though he broached it as an afterthought, he had carefully deliberated over what he said next. The ministry couldn't employ me. This didn't mean he was abandoning our partnership—he hoped our conversation today proved as much—but, in protecting his interests, while looking out for my interests as well, my relationship with the church should be unsullied by money. If, hypothetically speaking, his teachings inspired me to incorporate a business, and that business turned out to be a vendor of a product he endorsed, allowing for the fact that he, Warren Holden, personally, outside of his leadership of the Holden

Ministry, was an early investor in said product, again for appearances mind you, given his stature in certain communities, you understand, I should consider myself a wholly sovereign enterprise, free from his auspices.

"That's a hell of a way to say you want to distance yourself," I said.

"Absolutely not. When you think about it, it's the opposite really. I want people to know that ours is a genuine mentor-protégé relationship. I intend to give your business my blessing."

"Why do I get the feeling that if this goes bad, you walk away clean and I take it up the tail pipe?"

"How should I know? Maybe you're insecure. All I know is that everything I do has to promote my philosophy. Yours is not a philosophy. It's a reminder, I believe is how you put it. I hope you don't feel I'm using your words against you."

I had no room to bargain and he knew it. I had to go along with whatever he decided so his insistence on convincing me pointed toward something else. As a personality showcase, it didn't suit him as well as the irate coach or the tortured prophet or even the cold huckster. He cajoled me into one more shot of vodka and pushed me across the hall to his office, where he produced a checkbook from a locked desk drawer and wrote out a personal check from an account of Rev. Warren and Isabella Holden, payable to my mother ("Because of who you are, let's eliminate the chance for chicanery . . ."), and wrote in the memo, "Jeremiah 17:11."

Seeing his profane outburst through the prism of the check, I considered the meeting a test of my dedication. Had he doubted the plant, I couldn't have changed his mind. He planned on giving me the money before I got there.

"Use this for startup expenses and a little for your family," he said. "Don't forget to buy the plants. My accountant will call you in a day or two. He'll tell you how to draw up a promissory note and set up a payables account. Internal bookkeeping. Your father probably knows how to do this, so maybe just ask him."

And it was my father who was on my mind as I drove away from Holden's, the mansion cresting behind me.

"How's that for gate money, old man?"

November, 2006

Alex,

Mom got me a book for my birthday. Your mom, not mine. Harold Pinter plays. Fell in love with that stuff in college. Then forgot all about it. Never had time to read. Busy with work, you guys, etc. But . . . great stuff in there. So great. Takes me back. When you're young you have a funny idea when you reach a certain age, 30 or so, you turn into a different person. You won't care what you look like, you will stop wanting the things you've always wanted, no point in wanting because you are old. Even that is funny—thinking 30 is old. Anyway, not true, any of it. You care. You like. You want. These plays remind me of the young, strong Robert. I still feel like that person. Young, strong. Then I look in the mirror and the joke's on me. See if they have a copy in the library. If not, I'll send.

Wasn't going to mention this but, speaking of books, the exposé is finally out. Scandals, tragedies, family secrets—makes me feel like a Kennedy. A Jewish Kennedy. Imagine that! Trying to keep it sunny. Not always easy. I can take just about anything, never worried about my reputation, but your mom, Rachel. Everyone knows you didn't have anything to do with the book but that's us she's talking about. We are Wolfs too, don't forget. Our name is in there. My name before it was yours. My father's name before mine. On and on. We share in the pride and the shit. Welcome to the shit, sonny boy. This is not a judgment. A definition of family? Sure why not? Sharing the pride and the shit.

Don't get down on yourself. Nothing you can do about it now and it doesn't really matter in the long run. Wolfs have been in tighter jams than this. Just remember, like Pinter would say: "I'm chuffed to my bollocks" that you're my son.

Love,

Dad

EIGHTEEN

No longer a member of Holden's staff, I returned to my father's office. There was much to do to establish our business, and with the help of my family we pulled it off. Let me repeat: with the help of my family. It gives me feeble hope to report that, when I needed them, my people were there. Without thinking about it we shelved our gripes and for once stopped tracking who did what to whom and who was owed what, all that useless scorekeeping. An incomplete list of our tasks during this time included incorporating a company (Wolf Enterprises, Inc. d/b/a Crown of Thorns Offers, not the most original or inspiring name but it was short notice), obtaining a Federal Employer Identification Number (and unlike the ministry we were not tax exempt), opening a business checking account, registering a website domain (www.crownofthorns.com) and building a website, coordinating the website with our "Total Internet Store" (an account with an e-commerce company that provided us the software needed to take and track customer orders), leasing a credit card machine to process payments (First Data Global Virtual Terminal), establishing accounts with Fed Ex and UPS, arranging for Jerry Handley to ship orders from Cragg's Hill Nursery directly to customers, hiring a graphic designer to create a product logo, ordering stationary and letterhead . . .

The phone rang, someone looking for a copier. I wanted to shield my father from these kinds of calls, as if hearing his old business mentioned would trigger a nostalgic episode from which he wouldn't recover.

"Sorry," I told the caller.

"I don't get it. I drove by yesterday and the sign on the building says—"

"I know what the sign says, but I can't get you a Xerox. I'm sorry."

My father overheard. "We need to change that sign. From now on, we're Dynamic Seafood."

His remark assuaged my concern and also pointed to a larger

truth. If he were once a great salesman it wasn't due to any passion for the product. The fact was we could have become fishmongers and he wouldn't have cared. Selling a plant was no different to him than selling office equipment. Reclaiming his office, however, gave him buoyancy, and he seemed tickled that his dead business provided the facility for a new one. Gone was his attitude of resigned catastrophe, which by masking had only made it more noticeable.

My mother joined us a moment later, carrying in her arms a brown paper bag.

"I got sandwiches." She unpacked the bag onto my desk.

We dug into lunch, fine sandwiches that I might have enjoyed, if not for my anxiety. This association with the Holden Ministry was exhausting me. Look at what was riding on it, these unbearably high stakes. A temporary break, lunch with my parents, was what I needed. I looked forward to a time in the hopefully near future when we could meet for sandwiches under a sunnier pretext. But then I felt a pang that the satisfaction of our eating together was a product of its infrequency. I wondered if I'd come home to find the Wolfs otherwise thriving, would we have made room for each other in this way, or was joint desperation alone responsible for our united front.

"How's it coming at the house?" my father asked my mother.

I'd measured the progress at home by the growth of debris in the dumpster on the curb. After a bit of coaxing I convinced them to use part of Holden's money to begin renovating the basement. I doubt my words won them over. Our home was collapsing. What choice did they have?

She wiped crumbs from her mouth. "I'll say this, I don't miss seeing that stuff go. I thought I would, but it's not what I expected. We've lived there what, twenty-five years? I thought I'd be attached to everything but I'm not. Good riddance."

"A new start," my father said.

She took another bite of her sandwich, "I love when the tomato is really ripe. You don't usually get that until the middle of the summer."

April, 2005

She wasn't Dr. Sullivan yet. On her way. Close. ABD. And that was where we came in. The eight of us, her research group. Our job was to help her earn those three letters after her name: Papa, Hotel, Delta. In return we got something to do for a few hours a week and, according to the Chief Psychologist overseeing her study, much needed perspective about ourselves.

She was just *Laura*—that was what we called her—tall and healthy, prettyish, soccer player legs, impressive straight teeth, thick straight hair. No vitamin deficiencies, no congenital issues, you could tell. Robust was the word. I was anything but robust when I met her. I was adjusting poorly to my new home. I was constipated. I didn't sleep. I had rashes. My eyes itched. My lips were chapped. I sweated a lot. I joined the study because, like I said, it gave me something to do but more than that, Laura was researching first-time offenders so I figured I wouldn't be surrounded by career criminals. I let myself think I was in less danger around the other participants than around the rest of the population. It wasn't necessarily true, but it was something to believe in.

Laura was as assiduous as a fascist, but didn't give the impression of knowing which direction her research was supposed to be going in. She'd ask open-ended questions or give us prompts and then sit there listening, typing notes into her laptop. She recorded our sessions, everything we said. But I couldn't figure out what she expected us to say. If I described how all I'd pooped in the last three days was something resembling a petrified tater tot, I might get a good laugh from the group, but how was she to synthesize that factoid into a larger statement about the criminal justice system? She kept files on all of us in a cardboard box that she lugged around on a folding luggage cart. She stressed that, within the confines of the group, our sessions were a designated safe space. Since she didn't work for the prison, we didn't have to worry about her reporting us for rules infractions. It was confidential. She was obviously smart, but gullible too. She didn't seem to realize that without consulting each other, we instinctively lied to her. And once we realized that we were all lying to some extent, we started meeting at chow to come up with stories to tell her. No one was trying to sabotage her work or get in the way of her degree. We just needed something to do. Idle hands, right?

Maxwell Lukic, son of Serbian immigrants and a crooked day trader convicted of wire fraud, thought it would be hilarious if I told Laura that I was joining the Aryan Brotherhood for protection. I said there was no way she would believe it. Max was convinced she would. We wagered five dollars' worth of stamps over it.

Laura had barely sat down and turned on her recorder when he brought it up in session.

"I don't know if I should even be saying this, but someone I know, a friend, is about to make a terrible decision. I want to help him but I just don't know what to do. I don't know what's right in this hell hole anymore." Max was a smooth motherfucker. It was obvious why those investors gave him their money.

"You know you can say anything here. Please continue," Laura said.

He sighed, looked to the ceiling, stared at his hands. The burden was killing him.

"Have you ever heard of the Aryan Brotherhood? My friend has been approaching certain inmates. Gang members. He says it's for protection. He's trying to get in with them. I would love to tell you who it is, Ms. Laura, but my friend, oh Jesus, he's in this room. He's with us."

"Who?" she wanted to know.

"That's enough, Max," I said. "You've already said too much."

"You, Alex?" asked Laura. She flipped through her file on me. "Is this a mistake in here, or aren't you Jewish?"

"I am."

"And you want to join the Aryan Brotherhood?"

"I'd rather be a bad Jew than a dead Jew."

That sent her typing frantic notes, cross-referencing some page in my file, making sure her recorder was on. The delight in Max's cunning eyes, as the whole absurd scene unfolded, was worth the lost bet. How did we keep straight faces? Still, I almost felt bad for Laura, who took for granted that our voluntary participation in her study meant we cared about the outcome as much as she did.

Until:

"Fascinating. So good. Very strong data," she murmured to herself, typing, typing.

Never mind that I was full of shit or that the Brotherhood didn't even have active members in Otisville. For all Laura knew I really was contemplating betraying my faith and risking my life for a tenuous sense of safety. My confession elicited what in her, though? Empathy? Compassion? No, I was fascinating data to her. Nothing more, nothing else. I should have known right then who I was dealing with.

NINETEEN

I was running late to meet Holden, so of course Jelly was there to slow me further. She was leaning against the doorframe to Rachel's room. I was carrying one of the Crown of Thorns.

"Slow down there, guy. No need to speed through life."

"Taking it easy, as usual, I see."

"You know me. Slow and steady and winning the race."

"Where's my sister . . . or have you broken in?"

"Slutty Slutstein is in the shower. But you've got to admit, I'd make the most amazing cat burglar. I look hot in black and I'm ninja sneaky."

"You guys got hot dates tonight?"

"Wouldn't you like to know? Where are you running off to? Don't tell me you have a date." She reached out and cautiously touched one of the thorny branches on the plant. "The ladies like flowers, by the way."

"I have a date with a representative of the Lord. This is for him."

"You're seeing Reverend Holden? That's worse than you having a date. I'm seriously jealous now."

"Your parents are still out of the mix?"

"They think he isn't the man he says he is. They started calling him Reverend Who-lden, like they don't trust who he is."

"That's clever."

"I'm glad you think so because it's ripping my life apart."

"All right, I'm sorry. What happened?"

"Nothing happened. They're just so annoying. All I said was I wanted to apply to the college he went to."

"Why would you want to go to a bible college?" I said.

"You're just like them. I said it's *one* of the schools I'm looking at."

I told her I couldn't see why it caused a falling out.

"You don't get it," she said.

"Apparently, I don't."

"They said he didn't go there."

"Who said that?"

"Like an administrator. My mom spoke to the school. "

"And?"

"And there's no record of him?"

"Maybe he was enrolled under a different name," I said.

"That's what I said. But it's like he was never there. I tried telling them it's got to be a mistake, you know, but they don't want to hear it."

She looked as if she was about to cry. She placed herself in front of me, her eyes to the runner. I didn't want her to be sad. Fortunately, she puffed herself up and flipped her hair. Her blond highlights needed tending to. She was as buoyant as ever, slyly running her hand over the spikes on the plant. "Get your prick out of here."

Nice as it was bantering with her, she was right. I had to go. "Well, buddy, we'll talk soon."

Holden was working late at ministry headquarters. Since no other employees kept third-shift hours (except maybe those working in the basement call center) I roamed the labyrinthine corridors searching for him without success. When I texted him asking his whereabouts, he responded with *im here!!!* I was on the verge of leaving the plant on the receptionist's desk with a note for him when he popped up from behind the partitions of a cubicle in a state of vibration bordering on instability.

"Alex, me lad," he said. He came out to greet me, his arms outstretched, clutching me at my shoulders.

"Nice accent."

"'Tis the brogue of me family."

"I thought you were German."

"By way of Swansea, Wales."

Not that it was important one way or the other, just a different piece of the puzzle, I wondered if it was true. "Sounds Irish."

He dropped the voice, "Will you quit busting balls?"

"By the way, Jelly says hi."

"I'd rather not discuss that girl."

"I heard her parents quit the church."

"Her parents should be drawn and quartered."

"There are two of them. Drawn and eighthed?"

"This is a good night. Don't ruin it." He pawed at the plant. "Let's see it."

I handed it to him. He hefted its weight. He picked out a piece of dirt and rubbed it between his thumb and forefinger, then smelled it.

"Absolutely gorgeous. Come on, I want to show you something. Walk with me. Walk with me."

He took me to the editing suite of his production studio.

"Sit, sit, sit," he said, slapping his palm on the back of the chair. He put the plant on the desk and sat beside me. "I want to show you something, but don't judge it as finished. It's a rough cut. There's something a little off, something missing. I think I just figured it out. Let's see if you catch it. But it's good work. I'm proud of it."

He turned on the monitor. There was an HD digital image of a vast stretch of desert land, the word MOJAVE transposed over the dusty, cracked earth.

"What's this?" I said.

"Nothing you need to concern yourself with. Not yet, anyway." He closed the image and replaced it with one of him and Isabella, seated so close to each other she was nearly in his lap. He wore a preaching suit, a cross pin on his lapel, starched white shirt, multicolored silk tie—gold, red, purple. His hair shone like polished onyx. She wore an aqua blouse, embroidered with aquamarine and crimson beads, clownish eye makeup. They looked to be in a library, ornate bookcases behind them filled with wide, leather bound folios.

"Ready?" he said to me. He unfroze the image.

"Brothers and sisters, my dear wife, Isabella, and I want to welcome you to our home," said video Holden in his Sunday voice.

Isabella nodded.

Holden paused the recording. "That's not our home. We shot it right next door. Pretty cool, huh?"

I agreed it was. He resumed the video. His doppelganger said, "We're extremely excited to offer you today freedom from your bondage. It might be the bondage of debt, of loneliness, of sickness. That's right brothers and sisters, we have the keys to your shackles."

The video cut to a shot of a glass vial positioned on a maroon velvet pillow. The background showed a brook meandering through a stand of trees, not unlike one of the backgrounds at a JC Penny photography center, circa 1986. "Behold!" said Holden, in voiceover, "Miracle Spring Water, from a clandestine fount in Chernobyl, anointed by Jesus Christ of Nazareth."

The shot cut back to him in close up. "You see, I have love in my heart for those who rejoice in the Lord. It's all I can do to offer, free of charge, this blessing. Say Hallelujah. Just two drops of the spring water applied daily will guard you against illness and reveal the abundance of life. Won't you call today? Start moving your life in the direction you've always wished it to go!"

Holden could talk, that was nothing new, and the production value of his commercial was professional.

Isabella said, "This anointed miracle spring water has already brought joy to so many. Let me introduce you to a few of them."

The video cut to a man sitting on a park bench, two children flying a kite in the middle distance behind him. A caption identified him as Bradley Z., Vancouver, B.C. Bradley said, "God bless you, Reverend Holden, I ordered your miracle spring water and five days after it came in the mail, I got a new job that pays me $200 a week more than my last job. I'm going to buy a car thanks to you."

"It's no thanks to *me*," Holden said.

Isabella said, "Shall we meet some more?"

"The day I received your Miracle Spring Water, I said goodbye to arthritis forever," announced Annette D., from Princeton, NJ, wearing tennis whites and carrying a racquet.

There were a few more testimonials. In each, a grateful person praised the Chernobyl water as the source of staggering windfalls and a panacea for previously incurable illnesses.

Video Holden summed up, "What are you waiting for? Call now. Change your life. And remember, from the Holden family to yours, you are in our prayers."

Real Holden was standing now, rubbing his palms together. "It sings, doesn't it? Oh, Alex, this is going to be huge."

"Were the testimonials real?"

"Did you get that impression?"

"Just wondering."

"Those are actors. Dramatic reenactment, it's called. But the testimonials themselves are the result of two months' worth of independent market research."

"Why would you have to focus group a miracle?"

"Could you tell what was missing? You're new to this, so I won't fault you." He picked up the plant. "Product placement. This should be on the table next to me. I'll have to find a way to add it in post. CGI—Thank God for the digital age. How are you fixed for expenses? I hope you're getting receipts for everything."

I gave him a bank reconciliation, told him where we stood on funds. My report satisfied him.

"We need to discuss how we're going to introduce the plant," he said.

"I've already been selling it for weeks."

"And here's to you, king of the flea market. I'm talking about the real market. I don't want to rush it, but I don't want us to sit on our hands. Is two weeks too soon to unveil it?"

Because I didn't know what he meant by "unveil" I said, "No problem."

He sat with his eyes closed, mentally marking days on the calendar. Then, having come to an agreeable conclusion, he nodded. "Don't worry about what you're going to say. The script is being written as we speak."

"A script for what?"

"I'm going to bring you together with the congregation and you're going to sell it. I thought we were clear that I'm endorsing your product."

I must have flinched or flushed.

"Stage fright?" he said.

Stage fright, it wasn't. My longstanding vision of greatness often found me holding forth, my beliefs and anecdotes, my experiences and predictions, all of it the bedrock of my wisdom, which I felt obliged to share with others. No, what Holden spied in me was a fear of having to follow him and his relentless, captivating presence. I described the disaster as it would unfold. On the heels of his charismatic ministering, I'd come across as a bumbling profiteer, flop sweat stinging my eyes as ten thousand of his followers, so full of the Spirit it gave them holy indigestion, heckled me.

"I don't even own a suit," I said.

He leaned forward and grabbed my shirt. "You'll do fine because I believe in you. If I believe in you, they will believe in you. Tell me you understand."

"I understand." But I didn't.

"This Sunday you need to be with Isabella at the Arena. Since you haven't figured it out yet, that's where I want you. Then you'll know what I'm trying to do."

And it was from the Arena's production booth that I experienced a service far different from my first one. For starters, in one of the luxury boxes next door, Holden had a catered breakfast. Good stuff too: fresh fruits, juices, espresso, artisan pastries and jams, waffles, eggs, bacon. I couldn't have been happier. Nicer than the breakfast, however, was that there was no faking it on my end. I didn't have to declare the confident condition of my soul or pretend it was a glorious morning when the fact remained I was just me and it was just Sunday.

I ate to the point of sluggishness before joining Isabella in the command nook. It was from here that the production of the service took place. Monitors lined long tables, each corresponding with cameras on the floor that filmed the stage and audience. Each attendant in the room, including me, wore a credential on a lanyard around his neck, security clearance, and many wore a headset or held a two-way radio by which they communicated with a cameraman or a floor producer or a production assistant. Isabella was in charge. The staff called her Mrs. Holden. When there was a decision to be made, she made it.

As noon approached the atmosphere in the booth took on the heady and nauseating feeling leading up to a military operation. Or else it was heartburn. The structure behind the creation of the service contrasted the freewheeling revival on the floor. Down there, Holden was head barker, master of ceremonies. Up here, was strategic ground zero.

"Hank," said James, the assistant director, whose sandy

beard came up high on his cheeks, helping to disguise a permanently rosy complexion, "get that camera on baby legs right away. Mrs. H wants shots of the seated audience, in your section, Sport. Yeah, yeah, rows AA-EE."

Behind me, another man said on his headset, "I want you to change those gels quick. I'll tell you why if you just listen. We need accent light on the Rev when he comes out, that's why."

I wanted to make a pit stop at the men's room before the service got underway and ran into an extremely large, extremely pale man with a head of hair like Josef Stalin's. He was blocking the door to the suite and I didn't have to look hard to see that he shared the same latent malice as any number of COs at Otisville.

"I have to use the bathroom," I said.

"Mrs. Holden's rules, *sir*."

The condescension in that *sir* was too much. I immediately hated him.

"I'm grateful to your people for finding fire and inventing the wheel, but I'm her personal guest, not to mention Reverend Holden's, and neither of them, you fucking ape, want me to piss my pants."

Isabella put her hand on my elbow. "Alex," she said, her giant saucer eyes bobbing in her head, "Salvador isn't giving you a hard time because it's his pleasure. No one can leave right now. For security reasons." She leaned in my ear and said, "You're Warren's guest, not mine. Think twice before you insult a member of my staff again." Then reverting to her empty self, she continued, "Let's get you a seat. This is exciting."

Moments later, she told the room, "Everybody, I want silence." She pointed at a man operating a sound board. He worked a knob or two and the music of the Holden Ministry Orchestra filled the arena at ninety decibels. "Visuals," Isabella said and, from another control board, someone fired the psychedelic lights in the ceiling.

"Hello, Warren. Can you hear me? I love you," she sang into her headset.

The worshippers erupted when Holden came out and whirled

across his plush red racetrack. Even at a distance of several hundred feet, he looked no less in command than he had from floor level. His black hair, the luster of his suit and shoes, his iridescent smile—this was where the man belonged.

James operated a digital timer in the booth that counted backwards. His job was to ensure the timer and outline of the service remained simpatico. Holden spent seventy seconds peacocking across the stage. When the timer reached five, James informed Isabella. When it hit zero, the timer buzzed. Isabella said, "Pulpit," and Holden manned his pulpit. He spent the next ninety seconds welcoming the audience and describing the greatness of the day. Then the buzzer. Isabella said, "Book of John," and he recited scripture for one hundred seconds. And so on. Soon he reached his sermon —twelve and a half minutes— and, though his message was still God's-gonna-give-ya-whachu-want, this time his circuitous storytelling recalled an infertile couple who the Lord rewarded with a child.

Throughout the service, a woman sitting next to Isabella studied a fat stack of prayer cards, the kind I handed out and collected as an usher, and listened to headphones while taking notes on an unruled sheet of paper. By some rubric I couldn't decode, she thinned the stack and passed the harvested ones, along with her notes, to Isabella.

"Healing time, Warren. Need you to get pumped up. You're looking a little low. Step up your game, big guy. Fourth quarter. Pray like a champion," Isabella said. "Do you want a man or a woman? Amen for a man, hallelujah for a woman."

"Praise be to our Lord God and his only son, Jesus, Amen."

"A man it is," Isabella said. "I've got one for you. Alan Becker. Look to your left. Section 111. He's got Crohn's disease, whatever the hell that is."

Aside from the locked door, there was little about this that was surreptitious. If the audio guy knew what Holden really was, then it was common knowledge, right? Isabella recited names and illnesses; Holden transformed them into high art.

He stood on the edge of the stage, a hand to his forehead as if shielding his eyes from the sun, searching for Alan Becker, 43, estate planner from White Plains, husband and father,

Crohn's patient. "My brother, Alan, I know you're here with us today. Stand up, come to me. Let Jesus make you whole."

From the booth, Isabella said, "Plaid shirt, knit tie. Do you see him yet, War? Oh, look at him. He looks fine. What the hell? I've seen Heisman winners sicker than him." She glowered at the woman who gave her the card with Alan's information. "Who vetted him? I want to know who physically saw this guy."

"There you go, Brother Alan, get on up here with me," said Holden, beckoning Becker to him. The man came out of the shadows of the audience in a near sprint, so keyed up he hurtled the short staircase to the stage.

Isabella spoke into the headset, "Warren, baby, sorry about this one. He was diagnosed three years ago. His doctor's name is Bernstein."

"Alan, tell me, if it's not too hard, what was it like for you three years ago, when Dr. Bernstein sat you down and told you that you were afflicted with Crohn's disease?" Holden had the man by the shoulder and looked him in the eyes.

"It was one of the worst moments of my life."

It wasn't long before Holden, a true pro, broke him down. By making Becker relive his diagnosis and the details of his disease, Holden aged him ten years only to heal him, a palm over his head—"The power of the Lord commands you!"—shoving him into the arms of ushers who dragged him offstage.

Meanwhile, in the booth, the woman next to Isabella leaped out of her chair. "This should make up for the last one," she said.

Isabella listened to the other woman's headset. She was smiling when she took them off. "You ready, Warren? Put on your oven mitts because I got a sizzler. A scorcher. Francine Harrison. She's standing in the far back, past the last row. She's been talking to Kevin." Isabella began tittering. "Ovarian cancer. Great work, Kevster."

Francine was another sprinter, flying down the aisle as if chased. Coming up the steps, she tripped and sprawled face first onto the carpet. She lunged for Holden's shoes. He went to one knee and helped her up; not only a healer, he was chivalrous. He kept his routine brief because she was a fighter. She looked ready to cure her cancer by grappling with him, a no-holds-barred bout in which she would pin him down and count one, two, three. She tugged at him, yanking his lapels, wailing to Jesus. Then she turned on herself, falling to her knees, and rending her clothes. Holden stepped up and dropped her on her back with one violent shove of his palm on her forehead and a shout of "Heal. Praise Jesus." The ushers dragged her from view.

The parade of the ailing continued. Holden cured a third, a fourth, a fifth. Soon he had cured more than ten.

Isabella said, "Let's wrap it up. We're running out of time. Pull yourself together and let's get out of here."

On cue, the reverend recouped his strength in a matter of seconds. He located his pulpit and stood behind it. Out came the offering buckets and this was when Isabella left the booth with her missing link security guard. The tension in the room deflated in her absence. Nearing the end of the service, the techs smiled and joked. James apologized to me for not being friendlier. Next came Holden's benediction and it was over.

My opinion of faith healers, formed years before that day, was that like other flummery it was manipulative and unfair; but, unlike other flummery, the motives were less clear. The Nigerian prince so eager to share his vast inheritance with you via the World Wide Web knows that his royal genes and eye-popping fortune (which is presently tied up in litigation and that's where you come in!) are his own invention. The preachers on the other hand, even the most famous and mainstream, I could never tell how much they acknowledged as fake and how much was self-delusion. I mean, given enough hubris, wasn't it credible that a man might think God handpicked him and sanctioned superhuman abilities? And it begged the question of whether being a preacher duped by his own personality mitigated the sleaziness of his dealings. Was Holden a victim too, or if not a victim a product then, a good manufactured in the manner of our old time cars and transistor radios, the result of American ingenuity and determination, the consequence of Christianity shaping our country, the end effect of our society's interchangeable need for winners and leaders, the nutty convergence of a culture that acclaimed hard work and humble living while demanding every earthly luxury as a birthright, in spite of talent and intelligence and luck?

Regardless, to see the mechanism of Holden's flimflam, the coolness with which they pulled it off, floored me. The way they operated, the way Isabella in particular mocked the people who provided her with her wealth, the way they harbored no shame, almost made it okay. There was something about Holden that appealed to the same part of me that brought .50 caliber rifles to South America and figured it was a good idea to have sex with my prison psychologist. Since giving into this instinct rarely served me well, I had to decide if I really wanted to head down that road again. Opting for personal growth was the mature decision, but I saw no way to get there without costing my family our one chance to reverse course. Personal growth would have to wait.

May, 2005

"Lack of eye contact is one of the symptoms of autism," Laura said.

"It's also a symptom of liars and cowards."

"Is that how you see yourself?"

"No, doctor," I said.

"I'm not a doctor yet. I'm just Laura."

"If you insist."

"Why won't you look at me when we talk?"

The one-on-one interviews were conducted in a counselor's office at Psych Services. They were more personal in nature than our group sessions, thus the privacy. Since arriving at Otisville, as a survival method I'd stopped looking at people's faces. It was evasive behavior to be sure, and that was the goal: to evade interactions that could lead to trouble. But also looking at Laura made me uncomfortable for reasons I couldn't figure out.

"Your inner radiance is blinding. It's like looking at the sun, doctor," I said.

"Do you know what sarcasm is a symptom of?"

"A towering intellect? A girthy lover?"

"I haven't come across that in my studies."

"Maybe you need to brush up on your DSM-IV."

She turned off her recorder and looked to the door. I expected her to end the session, or to lecture me about the selfishness of wasting her time and undermining her work, an after school reprimand kind of thing.

"A woman went to her doctor and told him that she was in pain from being hit by a golf ball. The doctor asked where the ball hit her. She said between the first and second hole. Her doctor said, 'Well, that doesn't give me much room to work.'"

It caught me off guard. "You're resorting to dirty jokes? Didn't think you had it in you."

"That's my dad's favorite," she said. "What's even funnier is that he doesn't golf."

"Want to hear my grandmother's favorite joke? A wife wants to surprise her husband on their fiftieth wedding anniversary, so when he comes home she jumps out of the bedroom completely naked and says, 'Who's ready for super sex?' The old guy says, 'I'll have the soup.'"

"Your grandma sounds fun."

"She's a first class lady all the way."

From then on, our one-on-ones reminded me of the conversations two people have on their first few dates, getting to know each other and deciding if the other person is worth the effort. Laura revealed more to me than I did to her and at first I thought she was modeling the sort of openness she was after. Eventually I thought maybe she just liked talking to me, and enjoyed my company. How else did I learn that her parents divorced when she was fourteen, right after her younger brother's, Steven's, leukemia went into remission? And that it was the therapist she saw during this time who inspired her passion for psychology?

How could I, in good conscience, not reciprocate such honesty? After all, why would she have shared if she didn't really like me?

"I'm not joining the Aryan Brotherhood," I said.

"No duh, Alexander."

"You knew?"

"Obviously."

"Why didn't you call bullshit?"

"All your answers are valuable. The lies more than the truth sometimes."

Now, on top of starting to like Laura, I also began respecting her, so much so that I decided it wasn't a big deal that she'd called me "very strong data." I didn't even have the heart to tell Maxwell that I actually won the bet because my loyalties were shifting away from my fellow inmates to my new friend. At what point did she manipulate our camaraderie for her professional benefit? I never knew. I still can't believe she alone came up with the idea of embellishing (read: creating fiction) my life and then swearing to its veracity on every media outlet at her disposal upon publication. Whether she dreamed it up herself or was advised by someone else, it didn't matter. The conclusion was the same. One of us got to earn a comfortable living from that story and the other ended up sleeping on a convertible couch in his parents' house.

TWENTY

Turning up at the Arena that morning, I was guided by Dolores to a private dressing room. Her attitude toward me had warmed.

"I had you pegged all wrong. It's a blessing what you're doing."

"Do all blessings make me feel like I'm going to throw up?"

More than performance jitters, I was unmanned by the thought of simply being me in front of the ministry members. Present text notwithstanding, I hated opening up. Yet here I was, and to honor my promise to my family I was being asked to speak about myself in a basically sincere way to thousands of strangers in the hopes they took enough of a shine to me to buy my plant. I wasn't in a good mood.

She hugged me. Her old body felt made of bird bones. "You're doing a great thing today."

"You're sure?"

"I'm sure."

I dressed alone. My suit was different from the big-shouldered, double-breasted affairs worn by the reverend. Mine was black, sober. I could have buried my father in that suit. There was a copy of my script on the dressing room table. I took it with me to makeup. I'd memorized it a day after Holden approved the final draft but I wanted to keep my mind busy and I ran through it now so many times the words no longer made sense.

Holden met me backstage before the orchestra music started the service, both of our faces spackled bronze like warrior gods. "How are you doing?" he said.

"I don't know."

"That's not exactly what I was hoping to hear, but it's a little late in the day to help it."

"I have my concerns too," I said.

"The thing you have to remember, Alex, is that I'm going to be out there with you. I'll literally be by your side the whole time. You have to believe in me."

I gave in because he hadn't asked me to believe him, only to believe *in* him, a distinction that made all the difference in the world.

The music started, its reverberations rattling my chest. Holden was on stage, firing up the crowd. With so much confidence wafting off of him, how could I not believe in him? The sensation of never doubting your instincts, of trusting yourself beyond reason, drifted to me on the back of a deafening melody. I tried soaking it up, but it made me jumpy.

The service unfolded as it did every Sunday. During rehearsals, a point of debate arose over when to introduce me. I thought it was best to do it after the healings. I'd seen how the congregation grew impatient waiting for that moment. Let Holden give them what they came for before bringing me out. They would be grateful and amenable to my message. Holden refused. After the healing, everyone was spent, he said. They no longer had the capacity for new ideas. So I would come on after his sermon and a brief message about the Miracle Spring Water from Chernobyl. Now, by the time I realized Holden was talking about the water, the blood pounded so hard and constant in my ears that I could hear him only in the interval between heartbeats.

I don't recall my introduction, nor the sedated applause I received as I graced the stage (I've watched the podcast and it brings to mind no memory). I was in the midst of a realization, an honest-to-God epiphany really, that calmed me. I had to treat my speech as an actor's monologue, a soliloquy. Since these weren't things I would ever say, they must have been words belonging to someone else, a character I was to bring to life. He was an alternate me, the me of a parallel universe, the confessional me who lived without facade. At the pulpit, I shook hands with Holden, grateful I couldn't see the congregation for the stage lights. Just knowing they were out there was bad enough.

I took a deep breath and a sip of water. "Good morning. I'd like to thank you for sharing your morning with me. I don't take it lightly. I'd also like to thank Reverend Holden and his family for their generosity." I didn't describe the ways in which they were generous. The applause sounded anyway. The Holdens' bigheartedness was renowned.

"My name is Alexander Wolf. Some of you might have heard of me before. For those who haven't, I'd like to introduce myself. Until recently, I lived a life of confinement. I was told what time to wake up and what time to go to sleep. My every move was watched, my whereabouts always known. No, I wasn't married." I played this for a laugh and got one, much bigger than I expected. "I was an inmate in a federal prison. This is a fact. I cannot change it no matter how hard I try. I have no one to blame but myself. I understand now that my actions were the result of trying to fill a void in my life. In the place where Jesus should have lived, there was nothing." This was the first sentence I said with real conviction because it was bullshit. I killed with that line because it was false. It had a wonderful effect on the congregation. They knew the dangers of being empty in the Jesus parts.

"When I was released from prison, I found that my family had fallen on tough times. My father had lost his business. We couldn't pay our bills. Our house was sinking into the dirt. There was fighting. There was crying. We were tearing ourselves apart. And do you want to know what the funny part was?" You bet your ass they wanted to know. "The funny part was that I thought I didn't need the Lord's help. I thought I had it under control. Guess the joke was on me."

Next was the meat of my testimony and also my favorite part because it was plain stupid. "One day I was home alone, eating lunch. I didn't know it but the pilot light on the stove had gone out. The house had been filling with gas all day. I don't remember passing out but I remember waking on the kitchen floor to the sound of a voice. At first it was unintelligible to me. It sounded like noise. But I was able to stand up and the voice became clear. I looked around. I didn't see anyone. It was coming from the answering machine. It was a friend of my sister's, a remarkable young woman who is a member of the Holden Ministry." And where was Miss Jelly this morning? Was she even a member anymore? "She said, 'Is everything okay? I just had a feeling something was wrong.' This simple and caring message saved my life. I was able to get outside into the fresh air. I know it wasn't a fluke that she called when she did. There was something at work larger than me, a power that decided it wasn't my time. Jesus Christ was responsible. That was when I gave my life to him."

The party line says that testifying is about extolling what the Lord has done in your life. But as I gave my testimony, what I was really doing was consenting. *I'm just like you*, was my message, *I'm not a holdout. How bad a guy am I if we have this one great thing in common?* Once I proved my sameness to them, they would accept me. And having given them every reason to agree, "He's my kind of guy!" I brought out the plant. It was on a shelf behind the pulpit.

"The *Euphorbia milli* is the plant the Roman's used to make our Savior's thorny crown, when they proclaimed him the King of the Jews. And you can have your own, as a reminder of the sacrifice our Lord made for our sins."

When I introduced the website I made no mention of price or the "Total Internet Store" because it was inglorious to the moment. From the darkness, I felt them giving themselves to me. I became aware of—infinitesimal compared to what Holden must have felt—a sense of power. I was backstage before I knew it, the crowd again under their leader's guidance. He brought their grace to another level by healing them and taking their money. I saw none of it. I was distracted by the relief of finishing the speech and the happy exhaustion of surviving the last few intense weeks. For that matter, the fatigue of several years settled over me, as I could stop struggling against it and consent to it, just as I had consented to the rules and rites of the ministry. Before long the Arena was empty. I drove home to await the results of this experiment.

November, 2006

Alexander—

Here it is! Signed first edition. Courtesy of me, naturally. I hope you enjoy reading it as much as I did researching and writing it. Please do tell me what you think. As you know, I'm my own harshest critic, but you might be a close second. The initial reviews have been outstanding and my publicist says the rumor mill is in overdrive about me getting nominated for an Edgar Award (Best Fact Crime category). Could you imagine? Fingers and toes crossed.

You know I've always thought of you as "my inmate," but now your story belongs to the world. Don't fight it. We all know how you get sometimes. You should be happy. You deserve it. Congratulations! I'm so proud of us.

Love always,

Laura

TWENTY-ONE

These were our salad days or, befitting an obese nation (to honor my father's first post-Dynamic business idea), our festive-American-grill-franchise days, our waffle-fries-with-garlic-pesto-dressing days. We sold 99 plants in 12 hours following my speech. The posting of the podcast on holdenministry.org resulted, a week later, in cracking 700 plants sold. By the second week, in coordination with a direct mailer sent to a target market of 5,000 homes (locales in upstate New York, Virginia, and Florida, none coming from the Code 7 list), 1,600 plants. As our first month of business drew to a close (2,404 plants sold in 30 days), bills were once again paid in my house, credit card balances reduced. For all the optimism surrounding the good turn of events, it was reasonable to assume that this might be a flash in the pan and month two would yield fewer sales, with an even steeper decline the month after that. Unlike a job in, say, government, where the pay is steady and results almost never count, sales are a perpetual battle. Past successes hold no bearing on the future. Who knew this better than my father? To minimize any possible fallout, we embarked on an austerity policy, as we cleared financial headspace. This stung Rachel's muscular sense of entitlement, since precious little of our windfall was earmarked for, what my mother deemed, "extravagances."

"I'm not saying spend all of it. Why can't we have some fun is all? That's all I'm saying," Rachel said, her repetitious use of the word "all" signaling the thinness of her argument.

"We didn't get into this mess overnight and we're not going to get out of it by celebrating like it's party time," my mother answered.

"Now, Rachel, she's right. A buzz kill, but right," I commented over the top of a newspaper, lazing in my role of family savior. While they hadn't thanked me so much in words, we each felt a marked reduction in stress, and who do you think was responsible for that? Though I've always been suspicious of people who say things like "A weight has been lifted," or "I can breathe easier," to describe a lessening of personal burdens, in light of our improved situation, I was inclined to dabble in cliché.

"Ugh," groaned Rachel, "You're absolutely *no* help. And another thing, no one reads newspapers anymore. It's like keeping carrier pigeons."

I lifted the paper higher over my face, shook it disdainfully for effect.

"Some things never change. You're still a jerk," she said.

After browsing the paper a little longer, I said, "Well, I'm off to work. Another day in the salt mines."

In a lot of ways this was the perfect job for me. For one thing, there wasn't too much to do. Our "Total Internet Store" processed orders electronically and Handley shipped the plants. Another direct mailer was planned for western Pennsylvania and West Virginia that required no assistance from me. Holden plugged us into his mailing lists, though as I mentioned the coveted Code 7 addresses were off limits. I might have been the official face of the Crown of Thorns, but Holden gave us legitimacy. A large segment of his followers just assumed he was the man in charge. The link to our website on holdenministry.org helped drive sales in a way no amount of hustling on my end could have.

Most days at the office it was me and my father. The slowness of the daily routine left us with long stretches of downtime. It gave us an opportunity to continue the communication that started in prison letters, and to now reconnect in person, so that looking beyond a perfunctory obligation to a nine-to-five schedule, we could get to know each other as men. Only it turned out neither my father nor I was as good speaking what we felt as we were writing it. I, in particular, struggled to say things like: "I'm glad you're here to help me," or "I couldn't do this alone." Whenever I tried, I immediately began self-editing to mitigate the awkwardness of confessing my appreciation, when I knew there was really nothing dangerous or shameful about it. Also, I'd been so glib my whole life that I worried my father would look at my sincerity as the set-up to a joke.

So rather than force interactions I wasn't equipped to handle, or sit in bored silence, we retreated into a lingua franca of common interests that served to illustrate our sameness. We passed the time dissecting the overriding themes and finer plot points of our favorite Kung Fu movies, attempting to master our signatures with the opposite hand, studying take-out menus as if our lunch choices were tied to national security issues, and we read aloud to each other from that (according to Rachel) obsolete information delivery system, the newspaper.

We delighted in stories about bureaucratic efforts to solve community problems through well-meaning but asinine and/or cynical legislation, or bizarre crime stories featuring inept outlaws and vengeful, but preternaturally stupid, citizens—stories that reinforced the idea that we lived in a cracked world, inhabited by people whose ungainly maneuverings through it contributed to what journalists acidly called "human drama."

"Here we go," he said. "Council to Homeless: 'Stay Out of Our Park!' There's a town council in San Diego County that just voted to leave the sprinklers in their park running from eleven at night to eight in the morning to discourage homeless people from sleeping there. Keep in mind, Southern California is in the middle of a drought. The article says that between the price of utilities and the overtime paid to the public works department it costs taxpayers more than it would to extend services to these people. Still, and I quote, 'the council voted unanimously in favor of the measure.' Your mother would have a heart attack if she read this."

"That's a good one but, as usual, I can top it," I said.

My father reclined in his seat, threw a leg up on his desk. "Lay it on me."

"Dateline: Oklahoma. Two inmates were caught trying to break *in* to prison."

"I like where this is going."

"These guys had escaped, met up with friends at a bar and had themselves a little party. Around last call, it started raining. Their friends wouldn't give them a place to stay, harboring fugitives and all, so when they realized they had nowhere to go they decided their warm and dry cells didn't look so bad."

My father sat upright. "You ever think about escaping?"

"It's a nice way to kill an afternoon, that daydream."

Our first ballot Hall of Fame story involved the Lemon Juice Bank Robber, a man who, under the tutelage of a criminal luminary, became convinced that the application of lemon juice to his face would render him invisible to security cameras. Thus disguised, he broke into a bank one night after closing and was subsequently apprehended the next day when security footage ran on the evening news.

When police arrived at his home, the man confessed and said, "How did you find me? I was wearing the juice."

Which isn't to say there was no work to do. Customer relations were paramount. The website's *contact us* section required daily maintenance. I couldn't let dissatisfied customers feel as though their cries into the ether went unheard. Most mornings I tackled the inbox with a large cup of coffee, steeling myself against the problems therein:

> *Dear Sirs (or madams, or robots, or whoever is running this place),*
> *I purchased one of your Crown of Thorns for my mother's eighty-second birthday which is annually on July 9th and do you think it arrived on time? I'll save you the suspense, it did not. It came on July 12th, three days later. I want to say that yes it is beautiful and Mom loves it so I can't get too mad but promises are promises and I was promised the plant on the 9th. I don't think it's too much to ask that things show up on time. The worst is when I tried to call I found out there is no number, just this website. I doubt I'll ever hear from a real live person but maybe, just maybe, the automatons in charge of this website will 'fess up to the snafu and give me an apology.*
> *Warm regards,*
> *Susan (last name redacted)*

> Dear Susan,
> Our sincerest apologies. The United States Postal Service is a fickle, and sadly, untenable beast. An unbreakable wild horse perhaps? Though it may be called Priority Mail, it has recently come to this office's attention that they treat the parcels of everyone willing to pay a premium with equal urgency. It seems unfair that you should find your mother's birthday gift consigned to the same treatment as sundry unholy flotsam. As a token of our deepest regret, please accept a five dollar gift card redeemable at holdenministry.org.
> Yours in Christ,
> crownofthorns.com

Okay so I'm trying to buy a plant and it says my credit card "cannot be processed at this time." What do you want me to do now?

Dear loyal customer,
The crownofthorns.com Total Internet Store is open for your convenience 24/7/365. Please be sure that you have entered all sixteen digits on the front of your card and a valid expiration date. If that fails, please refer to the "Terms of Agreement" in the Check-out section. Your time is valuable to us so if you have further questions or concerns please feel free to contact us again.
Yours in Christ,
Crownofthorns.com

Dear Reverend Holden,
I wanted to thank you for this plant but there's no one to call. How odd! I guess that's my complaint. I want to thank someone over the phone but I can't. Talk about irony. Anyway, I hope this message finds you well. God Bless You and keep up the good work.

Dear Whoever You Are,
Reverend Holden is many things to many people, but you've got to be shitting me if you think he had anything to do with the development of this brilliant product. The Crown of Thorns is the brainchild of an exceedingly handsome firebrand who understands dopes like you can't help but throw their money away on any useless piece of junk placed within a mouse-click of them. That said, you bet your sweet ass I'll keep up the good work!

(However tempting, I didn't send this last reply.)

Our satisfied/dissatisfied customer ratio skewed to the former so most times I got away with referring them to another part of the website, hoping they would get lost and confused and give up. For those with web savvy, or who were just plain vigilant, those who chose to "contact us" again, I gave them a gift card. So far, no one had fought the system and demanded a refund. I suppose I would have given one. It might have been part of the "Terms of Agreement."

Mondays were busiest, a weekend's worth of questions, complaints, comments, and praises awaiting me. Sometimes I grumbled about it, but my father had no sympathy.

"Try selling fax machines in 1981 with a kid in nursery school and a wife volunteering at an animal shelter. Most people didn't know what the word facsimile meant. It was called telecopying. Faxes? No way. No small business had them back then. I went two or three months before I made a sale. I drove around all day, going into office buildings with a demo model. People thought it was a bomb."

He told me how the fax machine was a box with a rotating drum where you fed the paper, the message you wanted to send. A photo sensor moved down the page as it rotated. There was a line of little lights on the machine that lit up red to show its progress. Each page took a few minutes to scan.

"Then you dialed the number of where you wanted the message sent. You did this on your regular phone. When it started ringing, you placed the receiver in a cradle that was on the side of the fax machine. Then it transmitted."

"And it came on that glossy paper."

"That's called thermal paper. Chemicals on it turn black when heated." He looked proud to know this fact and to have played a part in the modernization of office communication. Then he took on a different look, one that showed he was nostalgic for the days of chemically treated fax paper and perhaps wary of where those days had led him.

"I was about your age. I would walk into an office lugging this machine, set it up and have someone at Dynamic send a fax over. I had my Bob Wolf shtick down, my gimmicks. I would find out the name of one of the managers or a cute woman in the office that everyone liked, and have a message about them come over. Employee of The Decade! Another thing I did on Mondays during football season was I'd get the Jets or Giants score faxed over. People liked that. Then I'd say I could predict the future and I'd have them fax me a score that I made up. I'd tell the customer that it was the score of the Monday night game, before it was even played."

"Clever," I said.

"I had to be back then. I had to do whatever I could. I had you to worry about and your mother."

He didn't sound resentful of his *had-to's*, but I could tell they were an enduring feature of the narrative he had constructed of his life. I enjoyed hearing his stories because they were entertaining and he was good at telling them, but also because they gave me a better, if still incomplete, view of my family's starting line. It was only by knowing the beginning that I could figure out if there was a definite moment when we veered off course, or if we had been using a faulty compass from day one.

"It wasn't for another few years before the fax really took off," he said. "And leasing office equipment? That's another story. People had never *heard* of leasing."

So that was the job. I did my best to relax and listen to my father's tales, just take things as they came. But you can't forget that this is a story about my family, meaning *him* also, this man who—especially when recalling his younger days—was so normal and not at all damaged. You see, it was his normal-sounding routine that put me on edge. It was when things were going well enough for them to unravel that I was forced to keep an eye out for signs of gambling and watched as he reverted into the damaged guy, even though *revert* didn't capture what would happen. He wouldn't change back and forth. He was always both those guys, the way I was both the jailbird and the son making amends by hawking shitty religious plants; and we were succeeding just enough that it was tempting to forget what was coming or imagine we had by some unproven method progressed beyond past failures. I was on edge because we were, both of us, comprised of more than one definite identity and these different identities couldn't quite jibe, were in conflict, and it was why I worried about the company because sometimes conflict is good in business but it's never good when taking place inside us, the inner turmoil dragging on us, slowing us like brakes from going as far as we needed in the right direction, continually pulling us up short. This was why I was smug to people who said things like "A weight has been lifted." It only wanted you to think it was lifted. It wanted you to breathe easier so that when it reapplied the weight, you really felt it. If my father showed up ten minutes late or had to leave the office for a previously unmentioned errand, I made a quick evaluation of his moods, searching in him for clues of that other guy clawing his way to the surface. Of course, this line of thinking assumed that the damaged guys in us weren't the dominant traits; for if they were, that would mean whatever good, normal instincts we had were recessive and predetermined to lose.

from: sparkmanasa99@yahoo.com
to: admin@crownofthornsoffers.com
date: Sun, July 6, 2008 at 10:47 PM
subject: Be Careful!!!!!

 I am trying to reach Alexander Wolf. If you are not him or cannot forward this to him please ignore the email. I'm an old friend of Warren Holden, old as in when we were friends it was almost thirty years ago. He lived with me for a time when he was a teenager, after he had moved away from his parents when he found out they stole from him. He didn't practice a religion. I was an older woman and I hate to say it but something of a surrogate mother for him in those days.

 I am writing to you because I have kept up with Warren's life from a distance, we do not speak anymore, and I have become aware of you from your testimony on his website. If I know him at all I would guess that you aren't what you say you are. That's fine with me, it's none of my business, but you should know that he isn't what he says he is either, and I don't mean that how you think. He has motives that are really "out there," dangerous if followed through on. I really don't want to involve myself in his life and I consider myself lucky to have gotten out long ago. On the slim chance you are sincere, I wanted to warn you that you are working with an unstable man.

"What do you make of it, Old Man?"

"Could be anything. Holden's a celebrity. Celebrities have obsessed fans, stalkers. This woman might be 'out there' herself, in love with him, delusional. Maybe they never even met. It could be a practical joke."

"Or maybe it's true," I said.

"Maybe."

"What then?"

"I don't know." He thought about it. "Whatever it means, this is a weird fucking guy we're dealing with, don't you think?"

I went back to my desk, agreeing that Holden was a weird fucking guy and that the email was consistent with everything thing else about my relationship with him: there wasn't much I could do but ride it out. Still the email had me feeling mixed up. It was so personal. Most emails were about the plant and I was the nameless entity replying to them. A direct warning was different.

After lunch a phone call came in from a man who identified himself as an editor at the county's leading (read: only) newspaper, Walter Janneck. He was hoping to run a few paragraphs about my transformation from ex-convict to spiritual entrepreneur.

"You've got some heat on you," he said.

There wasn't anything pushy about Walter, but I suppose coming on the heels of the email that morning, his call caused me low-grade paranoia. I mean how did he even find the office phone number? What if customers found it too? Then I'd spend my days listening to their voices. At least their emails were silent.

I just wanted to get off the phone. I cited my busy schedule as one of the many reasons I wouldn't be able to answer a handful of his questions.

"Maybe when I have less on my plate. Feel free to try me again in a few weeks," I said, hoping that by then a better story would have come across Walter's desk.

It was only later, when I kept thinking about his offer, that I realized I probably botched a chance to promote the plant and myself. Holden confirmed my suspicion. I didn't know how he heard about the interview, but his reaction was what I expected.

"He must think you're a real sucker to take free publicity," he said when he called

I pictured him at his desk, massaging his eyeballs with his thumb and forefinger.

"I get what you're saying, but you never had a book written about you. You have a very different relationship with the media from the one I've had."

"Do you ever bother listening to yourself? This is a newspaper that covers school board elections. If you're so worried, just ask for the questions in advance."

"Isn't that like cheating on a test?"

"Call him back, tell him you have an opening in your schedule and that you'd *love* to give an interview, you just need the questions beforehand."

So I did. Walter emailed the questions. They were boring and repetitive. The next day we talked on the phone. I got the impression he wasn't much interested in who I was, or what I was selling, and it made me think that the article would be contextually wrong. But it ran a week later almost verbatim to our conversation.

Holden said, "Congratulations! You have the media savvy of a JV basketball star!"

We saw a bump in sales after the piece ran and, in a surprising turn of events, the Associated Press picked up the article and reprinted it in newspapers across the country. This time the uptick in business was even bigger. I forgot all about the email warning me away from Holden. The story had legs, as they say, and I was invited to appear on several cable infotainment programs. I made one appearance: *Grady's World*.

Hal Grady had once conformed to that classic American archetype, the angry young man. At sixty, he'd long ago shed that righteous skin and got himself on the right side of the cash flow as a professional screamer. On his radio and television shows, he yelled down not only dissenting opinions but anyone he perceived to shift the focus, however minutely, from the self-assessed brilliance of his red-faced, sweaty, rhetoric. He declaimed himself a populist from his home in East Hampton and, with a net worth of fifty million, bemoaned the plight of the workingman, among whose rank he insisted he belonged.

Most people jumped at the chance to appear, for the publicity justified the abuse. But for those whom the show viewed as a tough sell, Grady let loose a booking producer named Jessica, the gentlest sounding girl I've ever spoken to, which I found out was as calculating a maneuver as Holden giving the Miracle Spring Water away for free. She sweet-talked me, begged me, broke down in tears saying she would be fired if I didn't come on the show. The act was unnecessary. I was high on the attention from the newspaper article and wanted more of it. I thought that reaching a nationwide audience, even one limited to cable television subscribers, would cause a spike in sales forever altering our business model.

Holden, of all people, cautioned against it. We were enjoying his backyard. The grass stretched the length of two football fields, ending at a sliver of lakefront beach. Behind us, closer to the house, his kids roughhoused in the pool.

"When were you planning on telling me that that black Irish piece of shit wants you on his show?" he said.

"How did you hear about that?"

"He wanted us both. I said no."

"I'm surprised. It's great exposure."

Holden stared at his lake and told me about his previous appearance on *Grady's World*, a notoriously brutal interview in which he and Grady played out their version of mutually assured destruction. This was why the show put Jessica on me. The producers were sure that as long as I was a satellite in Holden's constellation, odds were slim of getting me to show up.

"I was promoting my first book, *Got Wealth? God Wealth*, which had the distinction of knocking one of Grady's flag-waving tomes off the best seller's list. He was mad and wanted to take me down. I had no intention of being embarrassed. It got ugly. The thing that you need to remember is that Hal Grady is pro-Hal Grady. That's all he stands for. He's a piece of shit. You shouldn't go on."

"Why not?"

"He's going to eat your lunch."

"I can handle myself," I said.

"He doesn't talk. He *talks*. And not like you, with your cute little quips showing everyone how precocious you are. He lies, makes up statistics. He turns your own words against you. He will say one thing and, even though there will be recorded evidence, the next minute he will deny ever saying it. He will have no problem calling for a boycott of the plant. You're not established enough to weather it."

I was looking down at the water. For all his talk of my talents, Holden undervalued me. "I think you're giving him too much credit."

"What if I said I'd cut off support for the Crown of Thorns if you went on his show?"

"You'd do that?"

"No, but that's how big a mistake I think you're making."

White Boy Bandito: How a Clever Suburbanite Became Death's Middleman for South American Revolutionaries, by Dr. Laura Sullivan, PhD.

Review by Ellen X Marsh

Part rollicking true crime investigation, part rich psychological portrait, and part memoir, *White Boy Bandito* tells the story of Alexander Wolf, the eponymous gun-smuggling bandit, as seen through the eyes of his prison psychologist, Dr. Laura Sullivan.

By all outward appearances, Alexander Wolf was the last person in the world you would expect to end up supplying American guns to the People's Army. A perpetual wise guy and underachiever, Wolf finds himself several years out of college, shuffling paperwork at a suburban New York pool cleaning business owned by the family of his best friend, Ron Moreno. When the Morenos tell him of the terrible conflict engulfing their homeland, Wolf jumps at the chance to help in anyway he can.

First time author Sullivan delivers an irresistible page turner. Her depictions of tense showdowns at border crossings, of risky liaisons with violent militants, of the trial that tore Wolf's family apart, and of his search for redemption in federal prison, represent heart-pounding storytelling at its best. Sullivan bravely exposes herself as well, admitting that she crossed a professional line by having an affair with Wolf during prison therapy sessions.

Bottom line: *White Boy Bandito* will have fans of the genre delighting in this intriguing debut.

TWENTY-TWO

My mother stopped me in the hall. "I want to talk to you about maybe not going on that racist asshole's show."

"You too?"

"Who else?"

"Holden."

"Because Grady's a racist asshole?"

"Because he thinks I'm going to get my clock cleaned."

"Alex, hear me out. There isn't enough publicity in the world to justify helping that man promulgate his disgusting ideas."

"*Promulgate*. Good word. Can I go now?"

Dissenters aside, was there any doubt I would appear on *Grady's World*? Jessica was thrilled to hear from me (or pretended to be) and I was booked for Tuesday the next week.

The day before my appearance, Holden caved. "I can't have you getting humiliated in front of the whole country." He laid out a game plan. "When Grady introduces you, smile. I don't care how backhanded a compliment he gives you, or how inaccurate his description of you is, don't correct him. Just smile and thank him and act grateful because you only have about five seconds to get the audience on your side. Are you listening?"

"I should smile. Then what?"

"Keep talking. Even if you're not sure what you're saying. Just keep talking. If he yells, yell louder. It doesn't matter if you make sense. If he cuts off your microphone, start pounding the table. Your one chance is to look as passionate as he does."

"Any possibility we have a cordial interview?"

"Don't ask stupid questions."

Grady's World aired in prime time, but taped in the afternoon. I spent the early part of the program in the green room, clutching a Crown of Thorns to my chest and watching Grady on the monitors suggest we guard the Mexican border with Cold War-era nukes ("I believe our southern friends would think twice about crossing over if they had a few cobalt bombs staring them in the face. Now I don't promote unilateral hostility toward Mexico. Everyone knows that Mexico has no greater friend in the world than Hal Grady, but the drug violence on our borders..."). The only other guy in the room was some journalist who was sitting on the couch and so absorbed in his Blackberry that he didn't notice me. A production assistant came in and advised I take advantage of the gratis food and cocktails. A few drinks would have been perfect but I saw the hospitality as a trap.

My phone rang. I fumbled to get it out of my jacket pocket without dropping the plant.

"I forgot to ask. What are you wearing?" Holden said.

I said he sounded like an obscene caller. "I hope you have pants on."

"Not now. We don't have time."

It was the suit I wore when I addressed his congregation.

"On TV, you're going to look like Euro trash in that thing. Take off the jacket, lose the tie, undo the top button, maybe roll your sleeves a little."

I did as I was told. The production assistant came back and motioned for me to follow him. "You're up next. We have to get you mic-ed."

"Hey, Warren, they're calling me," I said.

"Did you bring a plant?"

"I'm holding it." The PA was in my face, tapping his finger against an imaginary watch on his wrist. "Seriously, I've to go," I said.

"Last thing, I know we haven't discussed it but at some point during the interview, I want you to mention that the ministry is making a pilgrimage next month."

"What?" I was following the PA down a corridor. He kept motioning for me to end my call.

"We're going to the Mojave."

I didn't connect what Holden was saying to the video image I'd seen in the editing suite.

"Desert?"

"No, the new fusion restaurant in midtown. Yes, desert."

"Why?"

"To see the face of Mary in the sky."

"What the hell does that mean?" I said as the PA grabbed

the phone out of my hand and ended my call.

"I'll give it back to you after," he said.

He clipped a lavalier microphone to my shirt, stuck a battery pack down the back of my pants. Grady was on the monitor over the door.

"Next on *Grady's World*, I'll interview a man who's gone from prison to the pulpit in a few short months. Amazing journey or the calculated move of a professional scammer? You be the judge."

A red light turned off over the studio door and the PA showed me inside to my seat at a round table across from Grady. He was big in person, two hundred pounds plus, a hot air balloon face, neck skin overhanging the pinched collar of his white shirt. At no point, not even when I said hello and extended my hand for him to shake, did he acknowledge me. Before leaving, the PA took the plant and placed it on the table. A young woman touched up Grady's makeup. He swatted her away and asked no one in particular if they had seen the president's speech that afternoon.

We began shooting and Hal Grady announced, "Welcome back to *Grady's World* and we thank you for joining us. Our next guest is a former gunrunner for a far left political fringe group. His incredible story was made into a movie. Let's watch a clip."

From the screenplay to *The Wrong Way Son* (H.E.L.R. Prod., 2007)

```
INT. SPECIAL HOUSING UNIT - FCI OTISVILLE - AFTERNOON

Two CORRECTIONAL OFFICERS lead a shackled Alex
down a dim white hallway. Alex carries a bedroll
and pillow, a small box of personal effects.

They stop in front of a GREEN metal door with a
slim window and closed slot.

One guard unlocks the door and the other shoves
Alex in.

The cell is tiny--6'x9'. A bed, a toilet, a small
water basin, and a shelf are the only furnishings.
```

> GUARD #1
>
> Welcome to The Hole.
>
> GUARD #2
>
> Ready for the grand tour?
>
> ALEX
>
> I think I can figure it out.
>
> GUARD #2
>
> Bet you can, bright boy.

The guards close and lock the door, and then slide open the slot. Alex pushes his wrists through and they unlock his handcuffs.

Guard #1 bangs on the door.

> GUARD #1
>
> Sweet dreams, Princess.

Alone, Alex surveys his new digs.

> ALEX (V.O.)
>
> My life is not my own. I'm told what time to wake up and what time to go to sleep. My every move is watched, my whereabouts always known. My name is Alexander Wolf, inmate #24799-051.

As the narration continues, he lays out his bed roll, his pillow.

> ALEX (V.O.) (CONT'D)
>
> This is a fact and I can't change it no matter how hard I try. I have no one to blame but myself. I realize now that my whole life I've been trying to fill a hole inside me. In the place where love should have lived, there was nothing.

He places his toiletries on the sink and sits on his bed.

> ALEX (V.O.) (CONT'D)
> Want to know the funny part? I
> thought I didn't need anyone's
> help. I thought I had it under
> control. Guess the joke was on me.
> You know, someone once told me
> 'You can't change the past, but you
> can change the future.'

Why did this cheesy monologue sound so familiar? Maybe because of its startling similarity to the speech I gave at the Arena. I couldn't believe it. Fucking Holden. Was he trying to activate subconscious associations the general public might have had about me, or was he just too lazy to come up with more original content?

The clip ended and Grady said, "Our guest recently found Jesus and has become an acolyte of the infamous Reverend Warren Holden. Alexander Wolf," and now he turned to me, "thank you for coming on the program and I give you credit right off the bat for having the *cajones* to take me on."

Here I was, smiling like a goddamn mental patient, per Holden, until my cheeks cramped, not even responding to Grady's inaccurate introduction other than to say, "Thank you, Hal. It's great to be here," when all I was thinking was that my genius boss had played me once again, and once again, I was the last one to find out. I couldn't even stew and rage over it now, because Grady leaned back in his seat and said, "Okay, let's get into it."

"My pleasure," I said, as if I knew what he meant.

"You sold guns to some very bad people. I don't know why, maybe you were a misguided youth, maybe you were a wacko lefty. But you did your time, you paid your debt to society, and now you're part of Holden's gang. Is that about it?"

"Well, that's *one* version of it," I said.

"You were convicted in federal court, there's no denying that's a fact. Now you consort with Warren Holden and others of his ilk. Tell me where I'm wrong."

I wanted to avoid looking him in the face but the studio lights bounced off the table so I couldn't look down. Surrounding me was the apparatus of the program: cameras and lights and cables and monitors and microphones and crew. I was hot and claustrophobic. Grady shifted forward. He had a receding hairline and limpid blue eyes. Burst capillaries showed through the makeup on his sun and booze damaged nose.

"Hal, I want to thank you one more time for giving me the opportunity to tell my side of things, but I would say you're a bit confused."

He licked his lips. "We don't like double-talk on *Grady's World*. If you think I'm wrong come out and say it. I know your record. I'm a student of the law and of your case in particular. I stand by my claim."

His certainty was astounding. There wasn't a speck of doubt on him. He scared me a little, okay. He was big and held an enormous home-field advantage. But how could he possibly know more about me than me? How could he be a student of my case doing three hours a day on the radio, and then another hour on TV? When he wasn't on air, he was busy with his speaking engagements, book tours, charity golf tournaments, and trumped-up political rallies with exaggerated attendance reports. How could he be an expert on all subjects, all the time?

"Just to clarify, then," I said, "what crime was I convicted of?"

"This is my show. You don't get to interview me. But I'm a sport, fine, I'll play along. You were convicted for your role in selling guns to General Aviles. And that's why you did thirty-nine months in Andersonville."

He was so wrong it was laughable. It almost seemed like a trap. I looked at the crew for clues that he was setting me up. Unable to get a read on them, I took a chance.

"First of all, no one ever accused me of selling guns. Second of all, I'm pretty sure Andersonville was a Civil War prison."

For an instant, Grady looked like he was coming over the table at me. "*Andersonville?* Don't put words in my mouth. You did time in Otisville. And let the audience be aware that you're being very cute right now saying you never sold guns. Your role with

Aviles' militia is well-documented. I encourage all citizens of *Grady's World* to investigate it on their own. Let's move on."

Under the circumstances, I should have been happy. He wanted to change topics. It meant we'd tied. Except he didn't know we tied. His arrogance wouldn't let him understand it.

"Seeing as how my role with Aviles is well-documented, could you tell me what it was?"

"I said let's move on!" It was the first time he raised his voice. He looked at me as though our families had blood feuded for generations. It forced me silent. I caught my image in the monitor, saw myself swallowing too hard, saw the creases on my forehead, which suddenly looked two inches higher than it normally did so that, on top of everything else, I began worrying I might be losing my hair.

"Why don't you tell me about this plant you brought with you?"

I found myself obeying him. "I'd be happy to. It is called the Crown of Thorns and it's available at www.crownofthor—"

Grady cut me off again so fast it felt like he severed my vocal chords. "I'll give you a chance to plug at the end. Why don't you start out telling the good citizens of *Grady's World* what it's all about?"

"As I was saying, this is the Crown of Thorns." In the monitor I saw the camera was on the plant and off of me and I relaxed. "It's the plant that was used at the Crucifixion and it serves as a reminder of our shared faith. A portion of the proceeds are donated to charity."

"Are you talking about the Holden Ministry?"

"Yes, I am."

"Your buddy Holden's been on the show before. I make no bones about not liking him. I've done extensive research into his ministry and found startling inconsistencies."

Now I understood that Grady had pivoted from my criminal record to the plant in order to get to Holden, to reposition himself on firmer ground. He got us there so fast, with such agility. I was impressed.

"All I can say is that Reverend Holden is a great man and his ministry serves people all over the world. Next month, in fact, we will be taking a pilgrimage to the Mojave Desert, bringing the message of the abundant life to the other side of the country."

The studio lights shifted a little, a directorial decision perhaps that brightened him and put me in shadows, made dark bags come out under my eyes.

Regally lit, Grady said, "Perhaps you'd like to comment on the misappropriation of ministry funds."

"I don't know what you're referring to." I really didn't.

"I'm talking about former members of his church, if you can even call it that, who lost their life savings."

"I'm not here to defend Reverend Holden. He's capable of—"

Grady slapped the table with his palm. "Because you can't defend him! I'll tell you something else, I've contacted the State Attorney's office about him. I'm not alone . . ."

It was exactly what Holden said he would do. So I started talking along with Grady, calmly at first. "I'm not here to defend him because he can defend himself without help from me . . ."

While Grady continued, ". . . as my investigation will no doubt be used as material evidence against your mentor . . ."

Then I got a bit louder, ". . . and I don't see how arguing with me proves anything one way or the other . . ."

". . . and best friend! Okay, you know what, I've heard just about enough from you. It's time for you to shut up. Shut up!"

Finally screaming in unison with him, my face as red as his, which I knew from the heat of my ears ". . . I mean, everyone's entitled to follow the spiritual calling in their hearts. It's only guaranteed in the Bill of Rights."

We were both quiet for a moment. Grady started laughing. "That's what I love about you left-wing nutjobs. Anytime you're about to lose an argument because your position stinks, you run and hide behind the First Amendment."

"You can't hide behind an amendment."

"Pardon me?"

"You can't hide behind an amendment because it is a right."

One of the ways I avoided trouble at Otisville was by assisting inmates with their appeals in the law library. The white collar convicts like my pal Maxwell never needed my help but many drug-related felons promised not to shake me down in return for my amateur legal services. For some reason they favored constitutionally based appeals and I learned the amendments this way. Grady, a student of the law, seemed confused.

I said, "It would be like saying a woman on Election Day is hiding behind the nineteenth amendment, or accusing a freedom loving African American of hiding behind the thirteenth amendment. Is that what you're saying?"

I didn't know exactly when the sound tech cut off my microphone but it stayed off until the end of the segment. Grady hectored me, reiterating his omnipotence on the topic of Alex Wolf, this time as it related to the Founding Father's true intentions. I challenged him mutely, wishing the interview, if that was what you wanted to call this bludgeoning, to end. At last, he said, as though the previous few minutes had been a lighthearted discussion about whether Red Delicious apples were tastier than Granny Smiths, "I guess we'll have to agree to disagree. Ladies and gentlemen, Alexander Wolf. His website is on the bottom of your screen and you can link to it from gradysworld.com as well. Alex, thanks for stopping by. You're welcome back anytime. Good luck with the plant."

"Thanks for having me?"

Staring at the camera, Grady said, "Coming up after the break, I'll be talking to investigative reporter Frank Valenti about his recent expose on the liberal progressive agenda to outlaw Christmas. It's a chilling report you won't want to miss."

The director called "Cut," my microphone was removed, and while I was being lifted out of my chair I heard a voice say, "Hey, is my nose bleeding?" It was Grady, talking to me. "You landed a hell of a jab with that 'you can't hide behind a right' thing. I didn't see it coming. Nice job."

I thanked him, hesitantly.

"Mind if I keep the plant? I told my wife I'd get her one. You can spare it?"

He thanked me for coming on, hoped that I got what I wanted out of the appearance. "Give Warren my best. Tell him to stop being a baby already. The segment he was on was one of the highest rated ever."

Accepting the car service Grady's World offered, I rode

glumly in the leather-upholstered, freshly-vacuumed back seat, watching a heavy, late afternoon sun impress its image upon the Hudson River. I was sure my interview would prove Holden right and show Grady handing me my ass to the delight of his millions of viewers. I had the driver stop at a liquor store in the Bronx and I bought a bottle of wine. With no way of opening it, I held the black plastic bag between my knees. Home, I skipped dinner and spent the hour before the show aired drinking the California red in my room, waiting for the inevitable end of my new career. I checked my closet for clothes to wear the next day when I went back to work at Franklin Avenue Community Outreach.

I couldn't make it through the interview. When I appeared on TV, I snorted at myself and said, "You're going down, sucker!" and then right as Grady finished his introduction of me and I heard my voice —a nasally, weaker version than the one I hear in my head—I lost my courage, wine or not, and turned it off. Five minutes later my phone was ringing. I didn't have to look to know who it was. I let it go to voicemail. Holden was persistent. I picked up on his fourth or fifth call.

"You did it, my boy!" he said.

"I was there, remember, I already know I got outtalked."

"Outtalked? Outtalked? For once you lived up to your potential."

What was he saying?

"You kept talking and that made it impossible for them to edit the show and pull everything out of context. You got your point across. That's as close to a win as you're going to get."

I was a winner. I won by not losing. This was a feature of success that had until then eluded me. Winning was about finding ways not to lose, which was different from finding ways to best your opponent. The phone calls continued, other ministry members, Dolores and the Kevster, even Salvador the Neanderthal, Isabella's director of security. I'd done the Lord's work today, they told me. At the mention of God, I thought for the first time about the religious aspect of the interview. Of the issues Grady pressed me on, he didn't accuse me of being a fake Christian. He barely touched on my conversion. I suppose it made sense to leave it alone because so much of being a Christian, as I'd seen, was a matter of proclaiming it. If I said I was saved, I was. The irony was that the most damaging thing Grady could have said to me—incidentally, the one that might have turned off his viewers, which is probably why he didn't say it—was the one that was true. It was easier for him to dispute the facts of my criminal record. I thanked each of my callers, saying, "I was just getting his message out," not knowing if *his message* was God's, Holden's, or even my own. Not like it mattered, they understood.

Now the wine was having its intended effect, buffing out the negative thoughts, polishing the positive ones, until my mental makeup was a high gloss. I went to spread the good news. My mother and Rachel were enduring each other in the kitchen. They looked as if they had argued earlier and though they resolved nothing, they no longer saw the value in confrontation.

"Ladies, it's a good night."

"What are you so happy about?" Rachel said.

"I take it you don't keep up on current events. I'm a TV star."

"I forgot," my mother said. "I've been so busy with the contractor. How did it go?"

"I won."

"Don't you find it depressing, Mom, that an ex-con is the breadwinner of the family? And he's like grabbed the brass ring by selling our religion down the river?" Rachel, a pithy wordsmith, could have had a cable talk show like Grady.

"What are you sticking it to me for?" I said.

"Guess where Dad is. Go ahead, guess," Rachel said.

"I don't know."

"That makes three of us."

"Your father doesn't have a curfew," my mother said.

"He should. I do. Big Al does, imposed by probation, I might add."

"You have a curfew because you're a minor. Alex has . . . you know what? I don't have to answer to you. You're an *adolescent*."

My mother was no lightweight either. She called Rachel an adolescent in the most disparaging sense of the word. It sent my sister from the room without a parting barb. The whereabouts of a psychologically competent man in his late-fifties, at 9:30, on a weeknight, shouldn't have been the basis for contention, not once you realized that even the west coast racetracks were closed, but I understood where Rachel was coming from. She wasn't adjusted to any other kind of life. Since she couldn't whine about impending bankruptcy anymore she loosed her irrational concerns in other areas because to do away with concern wholesale was to let go of a durable aspect of her existence.

"She's a delight," I said.

My mother began emptying the dishwasher. "I don't remember you being so acid at her age."

"That's because I was, and still am, wonderful."

"You were an obnoxious child."

"Me? Obnoxious? That's unimaginable." I put the utensils in the drawer, while she moved dishes back into the cabinet.

"I'm sorry about missing the interview," she said.

"It's on again at eleven."

"Let's see if I can stay awake that late. That contractor. He does fine work but if I don't stay on him constantly, he cuts corners. He thinks I don't notice."

"You're a regular hawk."

"Don't you start on me, too. Your sister exceeded my daily quota. So the interview went well?"

"I've been getting good feedback. I guess we won't really know until we track sales over the next week."

"It's a positively cockamamie idea you've come up with, but what do I know? I see how hard you've been working."

"Thanks. Well, I'm tired too. I get the feeling tomorrow will be busy."

My phone rang and it was Jelly screaming, "If you don't take me to the Emmys, I'm going to kill you."

"Emmys?"

"You're blowing up on the ministry message boards. Everyone says you killed it on that show."

"You didn't watch?"

"The news is so boring."

I gestured to my mom that my caller was an irritation I would rather ignore but that nevertheless needed my attention. I slid out of the kitchen, not in a huff like my sister, but on the light steps of a winner. Jelly was an unstoppable talker. After telling her that I wouldn't be nominated for an Emmy, she talked until I passed out, saying, "Then they're going to have to invent a category, like Most Kick Ass Guest on a Gross Old Guy's Show. Who do you want to present? You know, present the award? I mean, if you could choose anyone? I know I would love to see . . ." Of all my well-wishers that evening, she was the one I believed was sincere.

May, 2007

When Trotter wheeled the blue plastic cart onto the wing, it was one of the few times the mood in the place shifted toward the optimistic. Mail call. I know I'm not breaking new philosophical ground by saying hope is a large component to making it through any day, but I can't overstate that in prison it is elemental to survival. Not metaphorically, or spiritually, either. Hope is pretty much the only thing stopping you from tying a garbage bag over your head. That was why getting a letter or a card or a hometown newspaper really meant the world to inmates. It said, "You aren't forgotten. Even if you're never getting out, you aren't completely cut off." It meant somebody "out there" was thinking of you and made the effort to say so. I wasn't an exception. Mail call was the highlight of my day. If that sounds mawkish coming from me, suck my hairy beanbag. You want me to be glib about the look on an inmate's face when he hears his name called over the intercom to pick up "legal mail," when he's been waiting months for a sentence reduction letter to come through from the court? Sorry, I might be an asshole, but I can't help you there.

Officer Trotter, on the other hand, performed high-wire assholery without a net. He delivered the mail like he was not only doing you a favor, a huge one, but one he'd never let you forget. For over two years, the only people who wrote to me were my family and that was good enough. Then *White Boy Bandito* hit the bookshelves. I started getting fan mail like I was in a boy band. Trotter singled me out among the other inmates and started shit by telling them they couldn't get their letters because the whole staff was overloaded processing my mail, a total fabrication that put me in a very awkward position. It was easier to blame me when you didn't get a birthday card from your daughter than come to terms with your baby girl calling some other dude Dad.

(Semitic good looks aside) my notoriety made me quite the caged catch to a subculture of individuals attracted to criminals. They sought after me with discomfiting earnestness. Barring one or two missives from lonely men, women authored the bulk of the letters. They expressed the ways they wanted to get to know me, form a connection with me, understand me, become emotionally vulnerable to me, share intimacies with me, save me, save me, save me. As good faith offerings, they included photos of themselves in various states of nudity, in various poses of simulated fucking using sex toys that I could delicately describe as mining instruments. Of course I found the attention flattering, but I stopped enjoying the photos once I observed a direct correlation between the volume of mail I received and the number of copies of *White Boy Bandito* sold. It was enough to make me go twitchy with rage. Plus inmates' mail was pre-screened, meaning this kind of contraband was procedurally confiscated. I never could have gotten my hands on the photos in the first place without buying them, black-market-style, a tremendous risk on my part. Why did I even bother?

Because it wasn't my idea. Putting me in harm's way with the inmates didn't benefit Trotter beyond giving him a sadistic kick, so he got his hands on the nudie pics and threatened to "find" them under my bed roll during a random sweep if I didn't pay him. I had no money. The arrangement was my father wired this janky chiseler $35/week.

He held onto my letters until the end of mail call and then handed them off with such deliberate sneakiness, a mediocre actor in a TV version of a drug deal, painful to watch and worse to participate in. Everyone knew what was going on.

"This batch is extra filthy," he hissed, pimp that he was.

I grabbed my mail and started flipping through the envelopes, looking for letters I actually wanted.

Then he tossed off, "Shit, how'd I almost forget? Tell your pops, delivery price just went up. Fifty a week. Same Western Union account."

I worked my jaw, slow grinding my molars, staring at his mouth when he spoke. His underbite made him look like he was almost smiling, but he wasn't. "For a government contractor, you've really embraced the ethos of the free market," I said.

"Supply and demand's a bitch, am I right?"

"There's no demand, so you can stop delivering them. Market price goes to zero."

"Nah, we're not going to do that. Call it inflation, then."

"Fifty is too much. I can't afford it."

"Bullshit, inmate. Heard they're making a movie out of that book. I know you're getting that loot, you lucky bitch." He pulled back his lips on the underbite, a real smile now, flecks of Copenhagen dip stuck in his gums. I wished mouth cancer on him.

"You want that movie money, you call up Laura Sullivan. She's the lucky bitch."

"Damn! If you two kids couldn't make it . . . right?" He started laughing.

"I'm not trying to negotiate. I can't get that much for you."

"If I raise it to a hundred, it'll be a hundred. A thousand, a thousand. It's whatever I say it is. Right now, it's fifty. Do you understand me?"

"Yes," I said.

What was once my day's highlight had become a crude shake-down. Imagine what that did to my hope.

TWENTY-THREE

The next time I saw my father was about two hours after I got to the office.

"Morning," he said, on his way in.

"Just barely." I had worked myself into a bad mood, despite hearing from Jerry Handley that he was deluged with orders and expected a tremendous day.

"What's that?" my father said.

"Surprised you made it."

"So am I."

I followed him into his office. He opened two windows and sat at his desk.

"The AC is on," I said.

"Give me about five minutes and I'll be ready for you. You can tell me all about Hal Grady."

"Where were you?" I was going to get him to say it this time.

"Hospital."

"You don't look sick."

"Give me a couple of minutes and I'll be ready for you, okay?"

"Everything all right?"

"I'm just tired. I was in the emergency room all night."

"What was the emergency?" I was going to get him to admit there wasn't an emergency because there was never an emergency, never a flat tire, carjacking, amnesia, alien abduction. There was only ever one reason he disappeared, and I was going to get him to say it this time.

"Lenny," he said.

"What about Lenny?"

"Had a heart attack."

It seemed too sleazy an excuse to trot out if it weren't true. Based on Lenny's age and my lunch with him he seemed a candidate for heart disease. I doubted many cardiologists recommended a diet of burritos and tequila. "How's the mad dog?"

"Dead dog is more like it."

"Lenny died?"

"The man is dead." He said it as if he was talking about an ex-president who'd been pitching headlong into dementia for a decade, not one of his only friends.

I knew it was the truth. I was sorry to hear it. I liked Lenny. "Is there a funeral?"

"Tell me about the interview."

"It was fine."

"Fine?"

"Everyone said it was fine. Should we help with the arrangements?"

"His wife will do something. You sure it was fine? I know Holden was worried."

"It was fine. His wife will take care of arrangements?"

"I saw her last night."

"Was Lenny Catholic?"

"It doesn't matter, it's too late to help him now. Tell me about the interview. Grady was civil? Any news about sales? Is it too early to get a number on that?"

He wasn't being callous, just seeking a distraction. We might as well have talked business. I was about to tell him about Handley's call, but I noticed he was crying. It took me a moment to realize what I was seeing. It was obvious he lacked practice. The tears sort of leaked out of his eyes onto his startled face, like it was the result of an outside agent acting upon him, a snakebite, and he was afraid to move without exacerbating it. He sat at his desk, crying without acknowledging he was crying, and I was embarrassed for both of us, more for me having to see him this way. Don't get me wrong, I wanted to console him, the way he had soothed me, with varying degrees of success, the hundreds, thousands of times I cried, every day for the first few years of my life, but I didn't know what to say. I suggested he take the day off.

"Why would I take the day off?" he said, and stayed at his desk.

Handley called later with an update, said he was getting buried with orders.

"I'm in the weeds here. Literally and figuratively. I've never seen anything like it."

Thinking Jerry's news would cheer my father up, I went to his office. "Old Man, you've got to hear this."

He was sitting with his arms folded over this chest, staring at the wall in front of him.

"Yes?" he said. He didn't look at me.

"Nothing," I said.

We stayed at the office until he was ready to leave. It was after dark. If I had no words to comfort him with, I hoped my solidarity was in some way helpful. Rachel, of all people, was able to show him the affection I couldn't. The same girl who, one night earlier, blasted him in absentia now commiserated his loss over a man she never met and didn't know held a marker on his debt. As she hugged him I thought that her contradictions were at times so reasonable.

From the screenplay to *The Wrong Way Son* (H.E.L.R. Prod., 2007)

```
INT. CRYSTAL CLEAR POOLS - EARLY MORNING

Alex bursts into the office and barges in on Ron
Moreno Sr. and Luz Moreno. He is drained. Pallid.
Red eyes. Dry lips.

Luz tries hugging him. He squirms away.

          ALEX
     I don't even know where to begin.

          RON SR.
     No war is without casualties.

          ALEX
     Are you crazy?

          RON SR.
     He knew what he was getting himself
     into. He had no illusions.

          ALEX
     He's your son! Was your son. Is
     your son. Oh, God, I don't even
     know.
```

He starts sobbing. Luz brings him a cup of coffee.

>   LUZ
>   We are grieving too.
>   ALEX
>   No. No.
>   LUZ
>   But he died a hero.
>   RON SR.
>   If you want to honor your
>   friend, you know what you must do.

Alex takes the coffee. Composes himself.

>   ALEX
>   I'm only going to say this once.
>   This is it for me. The last buy.
>   Then I'm out. Do you understand?
>   I'm never leaving America again.
>   I'll spend the rest of my life
>   trying to remove my every memory
>   of your goddamn country, and if
>   that means I need a lobotomy,
>   so be it.

His eyes land on a framed photo on a filing cabinet. He runs his thumb through the dust on the glass. 2ND GRADE CLASS PICTURE. Young Alex and Ron stand side by side, arms around each other's shoulders, smiling gap-toothed smiles.

>   ALEX (CONT'D)
>   You're all crazy, do you know that?
>   Why do you even care who those
>   people want to be their leader? You
>   live in America. Ron is an American.
>   Was an American. Is a... He wasn't a
>   hero. He was a little boy. We both
>   Were.

He breaks down again.

Lenny Marino was waked on Sunday. My father went alone. He didn't want company. I was back at the Arena, watching from the control booth with Isabella and her crew. Below us, Holden performed the razzle-dazzle of his grotesque vaudeville. During his sermon he formally introduced the Mojave trip.

"Brothers and Sisters, I am delighted to announce the First Annual Holden Ministry Pilgrimage. Say Amen! We're heading west, to the desert, to a sacred spot where Mary, mother of God, reveals herself. Ah, yes, the dessert. Like Moses with the Israelites. Like our Lord, Jesus, in the wilderness. The *desert*. We wish you could all join us. But those of you who cannot make the trip, you too can share in this momentous occasion with your very own, one-hundred-percent authentic, photograph of the Virgin Mary, as she appears in the desert sky, by making a simple seed gift. Bring the marvels of the spiritual world—the miracle spring water, the Crown of Thorns plant, the photograph of Mary—bring these into your home."

After service, I got the details. Holden was taking us to the desert, as he said, in August no less, leading us on a pilgrimage. The trip hinged on seeing something in the Mojave sky. He wasn't pulling it out of blue sky either. It was documented, sort of, by a dubiously sourced online encyclopedia.

Our Lady of The Barrens

Our Lady of The Barrens is an unofficial title of the Blessed Virgin Mary based on apparitions witnessed by "Sister" Maria Damaris De La Cruz. In 1991, "Sister" Maria claims the Virgin Mary appeared to her standing atop a cloud, in the Mojave Desert. She returns to the desert on the same day every month, where she has encountered Mary countless times. In subsequent years, word of her visions has spread and attracted a growing set of followers. The site has since become the location of a minor Roman Catholic pilgrimage, visited each year by thousands seeking miraculous healings.

Initial apparition

On the morning of February 13, 1991, Maria Damaris De La Cruz was walking her dog in a desert region ten miles north of California City, CA., when she looked up at the sky and saw "a woman of indescribable beauty" standing on a cloud and watching her. The woman instructed "Sister" Maria to turn her life over to the Holy Trinity. At the time of the vision, De La Cruz had recently abandoned chemotherapy treatment of metastatic squamous neck cancer. Without treatment, doctors gave her less than a five percent chance of recovery. The remission of her cancer soon thereafter was regarded by her physicians as scientifically improbable. De La Cruz hailed her recovery a miracle, and credited it to her vision.

Historical precedent

The day of the 13th is historically significant. On May 13, 1917, three shepherd children in Fatima, Portugal purportedly saw a lady "brighter than the sun, shedding rays of light clearer and stronger than a crystal goblet filled with the most sparkling water and pierced by the burning rays of the sun." She asked the children to pray for an end to war. Reports of the story quickly became well known throughout the village and over the next few months thousands of people flocked to Fatima. Between May 13 and October 13, 1917, witnesses are said to have seen six visions of the Virgin Mary.

Pilgrimage

Monthly pilgrimages to the site in the Mojave Desert take place on the 13th. Up to several hundred people arrive early in the morning, bringing beach chairs and picnic lunches. Most are Southern Californians, Catholics, and Latinos. "Sister" Maria is the unofficial spokesperson of the gatherings. Today it is accepted by pilgrims that apparitions are seen by photographing the sun with a Polaroid camera. The Virgin Mary's image appears on the developed Instamatic film.

Controversy

Although she wears a full length white habit and is referred to by followers as "Sister" Maria, De La Cruz is not a Catholic nun. The Roman Catholic Diocese of Fresno disavowed reports of the apparition, stating that pilgrims were "in danger of being misled." Such warnings, however, have done little to diminish the popularity of the pilgrimages.

Looking to increase his market share, Holden was targeting the West Coast. He reasoned that if you were willing to travel to Lourdes, you would probably come to the Arena. Or at least offer a seed gift. He said my family and I would join him on his private jet; as compensation for a job well done, I wouldn't have to travel with the rest of the staff and select members from the Code 7 list who would be on a chartered 757.

"It's been in the works for a while," he said. "You might think it's counterintuitive, what with them being Catholic. But my research shows that Catholics are leaving the fold like never before. I hope you understand how big this trip is going to be. A pilgrimage," he shouted. "We're going west! It's one of our most romantic myths."

"Christian myths?"

"American."

"Why do you want my family to come?"

"Don't you think it's time we met?"

"I don't know," I said. I didn't think I needed to protect my family from him. I just wasn't sure I could do my job with them around. What if Holden asked me to testify again? It had been hard enough getting through that unsavory part of my job without my parents watching. I started making excuses for why they might not be able to make the trip, but Holden had made up his mind. The issue was settled.

When I got home from the Arena, Glen Holtzclaw, my probation officer, was waiting for me in the living room with my mother. He sat on the couch, rolling a bottle of water between his hands. It took me a moment to contextualize this sack of bureaucratic potatoes moldering in my house, and even after I did, I was taken so completely off guard by the situation I'd walked into that all I could do was stare at his water bottle. Glen's pink hands, chewed fingernails and cuticles, moved the bottle back and forth, back and forth, the crunching plastic the only sound I heard.

My mother, who should be credited for trying to keep him company, interrupted my daze. "He's talking to you, sweetie," she said.

"I'm sorry, what?"

"I asked if you know why I'm here," he said.

In both the spirit and letter of the law, I'd violated my probation. I hadn't reported to Glen in the last month (or was it two?), during which time I'd changed places of employment without notification.

"A few things come to mind," I said and pulled off my tie.

"It's rare for someone in my caseload to fall through the cracks."

"And yet here we are."

"Yes, here we are." He opened a file folder that sat on the cushion beside him. "I'm quick to rectify the situation, even if it means making a house call. On Sunday. Let me get to the point. I was watching TV the other night. Care to guess who I saw?"

"You're a citizen of Grady's World?" I asked.

"I am," said Glen.

"Mr. Holtzclaw, I want to apologize for any miscommunication between us. It's no doubt my fault."

I realized how smarmy I sounded, but for once I was sincere. This wasn't a case of my arrogance deciding that the mandates of federal probation were helpful suggestions that I could take or leave as I thought best. By throwing myself so totally into my work I'd forgotten my freedom was contingent upon appeasing this man's strict interpretation of the law.

"I would say so," Glen said.

Which sucked because, yes, ignoring him meant I broke the rules, but my intentions were good, my intentions . . . it didn't matter. Regardless of my reasons or excuses, I felt he was going to report me in violation of my probation and sort out my story later. The surest way to retrieve me from the cracks in his caseload would be to bring me before a judge.

"Where were you this morning?" Glen said.

"Church of the Abundant Valley. I work with the Holden Ministry." It sounded like an admission of guilt.

"I got into this line because I wanted to help. But it's really just a lot of paperwork and headaches. And sadness. One tragedy after another. I deal with the worst our society has to offer. Evil. I work with evil."

"You stop right there, Mr. Holtzclaw," my mother said. "You're in my house and you don't get to call my son evil. How dare you? I should throw you out right now."

"It's okay, mom," I said.

"It's not okay. You're a lot of things, but you're not evil. I do *not* have an evil son."

"What I'm getting at, Mrs. Wolf, is that Reverend Holden makes it manageable."

I wouldn't have pegged Glen as a believer.

"The reverend teaches us humility. I know it might sound silly, but I didn't report my new job to you because I didn't want you to think I was bragging. Also, I love what I do and I don't think of it as work," I said.

Now there was some pretty unsubtle bullshit I was serving up. Were it not for Holden I wouldn't have risked it. That was his grip on his followers. Even if I explained who he really was, laying bare the mechanism of his scam, the information would have bounced off Glen's intransient faith like a stone off a tank.

As if the tension in the room hadn't already reached its apex, it was at this moment, as my mother and I waited for Glen to decide my fate, that my father shouted from upstairs, "Is that moron still here?"

I didn't miss a beat. "He's talking about me. It's kind of my nickname. That and King Dipshit."

My probation officer shook his large, balding head. I'm sure he'd been called worse. "I'm going to need to verify your employment and a few other things," he said. He wanted to talk to Holden.

"Of course. No problem."

Then he left. That was it. To quote Holden: I was "free to pray another day."

"Thank you for defending me," I said to my mother.

"That's my job," she said.

My father soon joined us.

"What the hell, Old Man?" I said.

"How was I supposed to know he hadn't left?"

"How was the wake?"

"I'll see you later."

"Where are you going, Bob?" my mother said.

"Nyack," he said, shorthand for the Off Track Betting in Nyack, a rare concession in that he didn't insult us with a lie. Like Glen before him, he went out the front door.

"What the fuck was that about?" I said.

"Language, Alex. He's very upset about Lenny."

"He better snap out of it."

"He's grieving. It isn't something you snap out of."

"We're going to the desert and he needs to hold it together."

"Who's going to the desert?"

I told her about the pilgrimage without using trigger words like "pilgrimage," or expressions like "visions in the sky," doing my best to make it sound more like a secular vacation than what it really was.

It was her turn to serve up some bullshit. "I'm not sure I can take time off from work," she said.

"If Dad goes, I need you to go too."

"Perhaps he's not going."

"We're all going."

August, 2007

Hola Alejandro (I'm trying nicknames for you until one sticks),

Oh man, you really did it this time! Dad saw a commercial for that movie we're all supposed to pretend isn't happening. This actor Jim Belushi, who I never heard of until I googled him, is playing Dad. Yikes! The commercial even said it. Starring Jim Belushi as Robert Wolf. He changed the channel so fast, Mr. Chill, moving right along, nothing to see here, but you could tell he definitely wanted to kill someone. Maybe you! Consider yourself lucky there are guards all around protecting you. Later I heard him say to Mom "Why couldn't it be Mandy Patinkin?" He was serious! It's so freakin' weird. It's like that game where you say "Who would you want to be you in the movie version of your life?" The girl who plays me is cute but she's a nobody. Even in a movie I can't be famous. Oh, well. I'll just go on a crime spree. Then I'll get some attention. It worked for you, right? I'm supposed to look up to my big brother, right? You're a real role model, right? I made honor roll again this quarter but you're all Mom and Dad have talked about in forever. Poor me! Anyway, I was kidding about Dad wanting to kill you. I just thought you might want to know. The whole thing was pretty funny.

Peace!

Rach

TWENTY-FOUR

I was glad to be leaving town. Which isn't to say I had no reservations. After all, my family was coming. On top of that, Rachel was bringing Jelly. I didn't even want to know what they said to Jelly's parents to get permission. Whatever story the girls cooked up was between them, I certainly wasn't *in loco parentis*.

Of course my family would go on to chafe me as well as they could, but at least on the morning of the flight, the Wolfs showed themselves in finer form than the Holdens. Isabella met us on the tarmac, in the shadow of a Gulfstream G-IV, Warren nowhere in sight. She stood rigidly at the jet's stairs, a carry-on briefcase of grained leather clutched in her hand. Her kids, ignoring persistent warnings from the ground crew, ran all over the place. The sight of the jet produced in Rachel and Jelly a tender and worshipful whimper.

Isabella looked once at Jelly. "You and I are going to have a little chat about this," she said to me.

I should have sized up the state of affairs. It wasn't vacation jitters. Here was a frosty woman on a brutally hot August morning, whose sense of reason and humor appeared to have been confiscated as if in violation of TSA regulation. She stared down her thin, Gallic nose at me, surgically reconstructed nostrils flaring, pupils contracted against the sun. I knew better than to argue. Heat waves bent the 757 at the next gate, where over two hundred of the ministry's richest faithful boarded, stowing their luggage in overhead compartments, I imagined, and then holding hands for a short but inspirational prayer before ascending thirty thousand feet closer to God.

Holden now materialized at the door of the jet, puffy and red, a white shirt rumpled and untucked but buttoned to the collar, shuffling his sockless feet back and forth. Disheveled as he was, I still expected him to say something important. He swayed in the open door like he might fall out. Isabella rushed up the stairs, pushing him from sight.

This was the start of the First Annual Holden Ministry

Pilgrimage. On board, I admired the teak decorative sidewall panels, the dual zone, temperature controlled, fresh-air system, and the softest leather seat my ass has ever had the privilege to rest upon; while Isabella, adroit as an Australian shepherd, corralled her family to the front section of the cabin. Holden fell straight asleep in a seat with a telescoping footrest, and her five kids huddled together on the three seat divan with portable DVD players. Thus free of them, she took me aside and we had the little chat.

Jelly was my problem for the trip. "Which might just be the way you like it," she said, before warning (echoing my own concern) that God help me should Jelly be here without her parents' say-so.

Throughout her tirade, I continually cleared my throat as if on the verge of making a strident point of my own. Provided I knew more about the pilgrimage than the very little I did, I wanted to say, I could have taken the necessary steps to protect our agenda, but I suspected that Isabella preferred to keep me in the dark, and I didn't want to give her the chance to rub it in.

I looked past the top of her head to her snoring husband and said, as nonchalant as I could, "Russian flu?"

She was ready to cut my throat. Her nostrils flared again. "He isn't drunk. He hasn't slept in three days. He works very hard for his family. Unlike someone else's father," and it was her turn to glance past me to where my Old Man was examining one of the gorgeous bone leather seats.

Before we further slandered each other's loved ones, we were interrupted by a tall, athletic blonde with impeccable teeth, a throwback to the kind of woman who used to pursue a career in commercial flight, back when flight attendants were also registered nurses and air travel was a celebration of conquering gravity. Blondy said we were preparing for takeoff, and I was able to retreat to the part of the cabin claimed by the Wolf clan.

"Jelly," I said.

"'Sup?"

"Just so I know, am I harboring a runaway teen?"

"Oh. My. God. Is that why she was giving you the business? Everyone can just chill, okay? My parents know I'm here."

"Really?"

"It's not like I have a permission slip on me, but yeah, they know. Trust."

Trust. As if I had a choice.

Aloft, we were free to enjoy the luxurious appointments. Chrome serving dishes containing a buffet spread were laid out in the galley. Rachel and Jelly eased into the new standard of living with confidence: drinking pomegranate juice in champagne flutes while scarfing jumbo shrimp, and bacon-wrapped scallops, then later partaking in massage therapy, reclining in their seats, flipping the glossy pages of tabloid magazines while an Asian woman in a smock pedicured their piggies. My parents, on the other hand, scrutinized the amenities as if expecting a trap.

My father said, "We used to have a jet, but it was a G-V. A plane like this," and he gave a dismissive wave to his surroundings, "I guess this is good enough for *some* people."

"That was the one we kept at our chalet in the south of France, dear?" asked my mother.

"No, at our villa on the Italian Riviera."

I laughed along with them at this wealth we would never know. We went back for seconds, my father even made a small third trip. Soon after that Isabella and Warren emerged from the lavatory and walked over to us. Holden was almost entirely revived. His face was again sharp and his black eyes were clear of red swelling. He had changed shirts, donned socks and shoes, and with Isabella beside him (her face an invitation to admire her husband) he introduced himself to my parents.

"I'm glad to see you're having a good time," he said, his teeth reflecting sunlight through the cabin window.

"The food was very good," my mother said.

"You're very welcome," Isabella answered. Everyone was the heart of politeness.

Our blonde attendant sidled up to clear our table. My mother waved her off. She grabbed our plates and began moving them back to the galley.

The attendant, furrowing her sun-kissed forehead, said, "It's my job, please."

My mother wouldn't hear of it. They had done so much

already, she said. As deferential as she was acting, I knew otherwise. What the Holdens couldn't understand was that, by refusing to let anyone clear our plates for us, my mother was saying in her own prideful way that, though her life would never be as easy as theirs, she was better than them. And, as if guessing that this small gesture was too subtle for their broad sensibilities, she then decided to use this meet-and-greet to show them that her soul was as fundamentally clean as our table.

"Reverend, I'm glad we have this chance to talk. I don't know if Alex ever told you but I'm the director of an outreach program."

"He has, and God bless you for it," he said.

"I was just wondering then if you realized that families make up almost eighty percent of the homeless shelter population in this country and that one in four children under the age of five lives in poverty."

Isabella's multi-ringed hand fluttered to her mouth. "Could that be true? That's so sad."

"I'm afraid so," Holden said, rocking back and forth on his heels. "This is why Mrs. Wolf's work is so important."

"Judy," my mother insisted, and then made her pitch. "I have years of experience working with religious organizations of every stripe."

The reverend winked at me as if to say, "How much is this little shakedown going to cost?" He told my mother that as soon as we returned from California, he would have his vice president of philanthropy (a position I'd never heard of) contact her. He thanked my parents again for coming and said that he and I had business to discuss. We sat facing each other at the front of the jet. Our attendant delivered two rocks glasses and a bottle of vodka—from the tiny distillery in the woods. We drank for a while with Holden outpacing me at least two-to-one, possibly more. If Isabella was right and he wasn't drunk when he got on the jet, he had to be drunk now.

"Now I see where you get your hustle. It was the same way in my family. My mom pushed me on the world. That was her ambition," he said.

"I wouldn't worry about it. She's been drumming up donations for so long she just doesn't know how to turn it off."

Holden fixed a terrible look on me. He was frightened. "You're right. It's impossible to turn it off." Then he refilled our glasses and led me spiritedly into his madness. "Are you aware that they passed a law in California because of me? Because of me, you have to be at least sixteen to be ordained. When they write legislation around you, that's bigger than fame. Mom taught me to read just so I could memorize the Bible, so I could learn sermons. She choreographed the whole thing. We had codes. She sat right up front. If she said, 'Amen,' it meant I needed to get more energetic. If she said, 'Praise Jesus,' it meant I had them where I wanted them, don't let up. If she said, 'Hallelujah,' that meant I should bring out the offering plates. We had plates back then, not buckets."

He trained his eyes on his children, who were rehearsing a song (*I don't know what the future holds/ but I know who holds the future* ...) "I'm not going to let them do this. I'm giving them the choice I never had. Of all the advantages I've given them, this will be the most important one."

My father wanted me to find a career more fulfilling than selling copy machines. I was thirty and look where my freewill had gotten me. The best Holden could hope for was that his children would make their own mistakes, not his. It wouldn't be his fault either way, of course, just as it wasn't my parents' fault.

"Making your kids preach is just about the worst thing you can do. It's worse than putting them in beauty pageants," he said.

For the first time I believed he was telling me the real truth, different from the legend of his self-invention. I was dizzy from alcohol and cabin pressure, which seemed to be squeezing my brain, not causing pain but adding gravity. Out the window, I searched for the charter flight of religious pilgrims, as if we were on a highway and they were in the next lane.

"Mom orchestrated the whole thing and then she and Daddy ripped me off. I was about fifteen when I learned the money wasn't building churches in Africa like they said. They ripped off my money and my childhood," Holden said.

The vodka was making me sweat. There was no nozzle of air overhead. Maybe you only got that flying coach. I wiped my face on a napkin.

Holden went to the bathroom, stopping on his way to steal a chicken finger from one of his sons. He came back wearing a different shirt and had our attendant bring us cans of Diet Coke. He looked soberer than he had minutes earlier, unless I was drunker and couldn't tell the difference.

"To answer your question," he said, apropos of no question I asked, "I lost my way and for a few years I didn't think about the Lord. I didn't think about anything. I was in the wilderness. It was a dark period in my life. Then I met Isabella and the two of us built everything you see."

He told me, in the beginning, their setup was less elaborate than it was today, but some things were the same. They used the same kind of prayer cards except now they were printed on a better stock of paper. Isabella, then and now, scouted the audience for "hot ones." He and Isabella used to record hours of conversations with sick and depressed and lonely people, to learn the way people spoke about themselves and their illnesses, so he would be fluent in the language of their suffering.

"She would ask them, 'Oh, what's your name? And where do you live? And is Jesus going to heal you? Well, how long have you been sick?' And she would record all that stuff and radio it to me during the service. She carried a battery pack in her purse and a transmitter under her shirt. It's funny, Alex, I tried to escape my calling and I couldn't. No one can. You can run for a while but, when the Lord taps you, sooner or later you fall in line."

He was too mixed up in the contradictions of his own story to know how absurd this sounded.

"I wonder whose divine plan says it's cool to rip off people," I said.

"Who do I rip off? I rip off nobody." He took a sickeningly large gulp of vodka. "This is the truth: healing is a very small part of what I do with my ministry. It's a holdover from my youth, a tribute to my parents who don't deserve one, but who taught me the business. It's a bridge to those who've been with me the longest, the ones who remember what it was like in the tents. Back then, my grandpa would heal a thousand a night, every night. Me? Ten? Twelve? A week?"

"I don't want to start a fight or anything but let me ask you one thing. You don't even have to answer. How many people would call you a great man if you didn't pull a rabbit out of your hat every Sunday?"

He laughed at me, not in derision, but in genuine shock of hearing something unexpected. "I'm starting to think less of you. Here's the test. Bring me an amputee. Ask me to have God regrow his leg. Get ten thousand people to pray on it all at once. Now tell me what happens."

"You would never let an ampu—"

"Now if, on the other hand, you bring me a guy with high blood pressure, maybe that's me easing the tension in his arteries or maybe he started taking aspirin every day. See my point?"

"Not really, no."

"The guy will believe it's me. They want to believe in God's grace as much as I believe in it."

"Warren, how can you say you believe any of it?"

"That's not fair," he said, his mouth a rictus of misunderstanding. "Why would you say that?" He repeated it several more times, to himself almost. "I mean what gives you that idea? I believe more than anyone I've ever known, including Daddy."

The caffeine kicked in and I started emerging from my vodka haze. "Forget I said anything. Too much potato juice."

He couldn't let it go. "No, you're wrong. Everything I do is *because* I believe."

After his falling out with his parents he didn't think about preaching anymore but when he got together with Isabella his faith came back.

"I was preaching my ass off." Holden wanted to get God's attention, and thank Him for giving him a second chance. The problem was that God snubbed him. "No matter what I did, no matter how many souls I saved, He ignored me. So I decided to get His attention any way I could. Surely, He couldn't ignore me if I started to heal again. He couldn't ignore me if I preached that He wants them to be stinking rich. That's literally the opposite of what Jesus taught. There was no way He could ignore me if I mocked him in an arena, with a laser light show and that *rah-rah* music and made myself into a god on earth in

His name. But He has. Every step of the way. Not a peep."

I began wilting under the friction of his restlessness. "Excuse me," I said, and locked myself in the lavatory. I remembered the anonymous email telling me Holden's motives were "out there." No kidding. I would have preferred him to be a straight up conman. That I understood. Trying to get God's attention? This was beyond me. On my return from the bathroom, I tried sneaking back to my family's side of the jet. He called me over and was no less intense.

"A few years ago, I was tinkering with the idea of taking an academic position. I wanted more respect. How could He pretend I didn't exist if the world looked at me the way they look at Billy Graham? But I never went to high school. I didn't have the right pedigree. You know what I did? I just gave myself a doctor of divinity degree and dared the university to call me on it. For a million dollars, I couldn't tell you what state that school is in. What balls! Still nothing. I mean, Miracle Water from Chernobyl, are you kidding me? Fucking *Chernobyl*? For all of it I haven't felt even a stirring of His presence."

"Hiring convicts?" I said.

"That's actually one of the more Christian things I've done. But don't worry. Don't you worry about me. I'm not worried. I'm going to get His attention this time. On this trip!" He eased back his seat, relaxing like a man who, having surveyed all possible outcomes of a situation, was at peace with his decision.

December, 2007

I hadn't seen them since the trial, nor had we written to each other during my bid. It was a surprise to see them sitting at a table when I walked in the visiting room. Felix was grayer in the temples but Ron Sr. and Luz looked the same as they always did. Not even their son's death shrunk them, physically.

"Fancy meeting you here," I said and nothing else. To say I once considered them family would be a stretch, but we'd bonded through mutual affection for Ron and the secrecy of our crimes. My reticence now had nothing to do with antipathy for them. I'd always gotten along with all the Morenos, even Felix. I didn't blame them for my arrest and if I ever judged them responsible for what happened to Ron—and I had—enough time had passed to understand that faulting them was just a way to reverse engineer some little logic onto an event too difficult to otherwise process. I sat across from them in the visiting room, not speaking, because their showing up here after three years of radio silence made me think they wanted something from me. I was right.

Felix, speaking on behalf of the family, said, "We saw that movie. Crazy shit. They should be sued for making us look like a bunch of dirty cowboys shooting up the rainforest."

"Artistic license," I said.

"Mentiras," said Luz, *lies*.

"What do you want me to do, bring a lawsuit? Is that really why you drove up here? How about maybe we don't keep beating it into the ground. Maybe we just let it go."

"Calm down, Alex, we don't want to sue anyone. We came here to tell you something."

Felix said the movie made them irate when they saw how Laura Sullivan and the production company that bought the film rights had taken advantage of me. It was unfair that so many other people were finding success with my story, but not me. "After we saw the way this doctor used you, we were so mad for you and your family. But it was Ron Sr. here who spoke the truth. We used you too and if we were mad about the movie then we had to be mad at ourselves."

Ron's father nodded in agreement.

"You didn't use me. What are you talking about?" I said.

Like many people, I dabbled in the hobby of viewing my life as a sitcom in which I was the star and everyone else served as supporting cast members—satellites orbiting throughout the Alex-centric universe—functioning as eccentrics and nuisances that I coped with in the B-story of each week's episode. What Felix said next, however, opened me up to another perspective, one in which I was the weird neighbor whose lack of self-awareness was an endless fount of studio audience guffaws.

"We didn't need you to buy the guns. We could have done

it ourselves, but we thought, hey, if he wants to do it for us, let him. He wants to act like our hero? Go for it. But you weren't our hero. *El chico de oro* was a joke, man. We just knew using a white guy at the airports was better for us, safer. And Ron loved you so much, loved having you around, you were his brother. That's also why we shouldn't have let you in. Because you weren't his brother and you didn't belong with us."

Felix's bluntness wasn't to hurt me, I didn't think. It was as though everything he said was common knowledge and therefore powerless to cause insult. Still he'd yet to come to his point.

What they wanted from me was forgiveness.

"You fucked up your whole life when we should have kept you in the office, billing our customers and making everyone laugh. My family is sorry."

Rarely had my self-perception been so thoroughly run aground in the shallow sea of reality.

"Don't worry about it," I said. "Apology accepted."

Later I took their names off my inmate's visiting list.

TWENTY-FIVE

We deplaned at Mojave Airport and shuffled to the baggage carousel to meet the charter flight, whose pilgrims let off a deafening cheer when they saw Holden. He wore none of the effects of flying cross-country and drinking most of a bottle of criminally potent vodka. He led them in prayer, thanking God—the same God who ignored him no matter what offenses he dreamed up—for our safe arrival, and asked Him to bless the pilgrimage. A fleet of rental cars and shuttle vans awaited us in the unthinkably hot desert and I climbed into one of the cars with my mother at the wheel. I was still groggy so that our convoy was already en route when I noticed our party was incomplete. "Where's the Old Man?"

"He got his own car. That way if one of us needs to go somewhere, the rest of us won't be stranded at the hotel."

I didn't think to ask where one of us would need to go. After hearing Holden confess his real motives, I'd readjusted my expectations. I only wanted to make it through the trip intact. I felt like the private whose commanding officer tells the platoon on the eve of battle, "Half of you ain't coming back."

We followed the long procession out of Mojave twenty miles to California City where we turned off the road at the Gold Spur Ranch and Spa. Given the dearth of anything resembling a real town (a complete list of area attractions is as follows: 1. Edwards Air Force Base. 2 . . . um, I'm thinking, give me a minute . . .) the ranch was an oasis. Just beyond its requisite post-and-rail fence—its name crudely rendered in forged steel on a wooden arch over the entrance—lay 350 acres in the foothills of the Sierra Madre Mountains. The word *ranch* is a folksy and misleading name for what was a resort with a golf course, tennis courts, full spa facilities, archery range, skeet shooting, equestrian center, and petting zoo. The First Annual Holden Ministry Pilgrimage had booked the whole place for a three night stay, sixty-two rooms and eight luxury bungalows, one of which was reserved for my faction.

Before I could appreciate the bungalow's wraparound patio,

or wonder aloud as to what was keeping my father, or tell Rachel and Jelly that, for the love of God, please stop talking so much, I saw my mother sneaking out. From the window I watched her get into the car. I flagged her down.

"Going somewhere?" I said, jogging down the patio steps.

"To the Tejon Indian Reservation. The Kawaiisu Tribe lives there," she said as if she'd already told me ten times.

"Of course they do."

"I spoke to their chair, Laughing Horse."

"Fuck," I whined.

"His Anglo name is Richard. I've volunteered at the reservation for two days."

"Of course you have." I stared at the sun hoping to blind myself and when I looked at my mother again, images of the sun floated in circles of color over her face.

She took her foot off the brake and rolled a few feet away.

"Bakersfield is about an hour from here. I'll be back with plenty of time before we leave. Can't see what the big deal is."

"That's why you're leaving without telling anyone?"

"You know my objections to this ministry business."

"It's a little late for that, Mom. It's thousands of dollars and a remodeled basement and a jet flight too late." The sun pounded the back of my neck.

She rolled farther away. "Are you at all interested to know that fifty percent of Native Americans live below the poverty line?"

"I am not."

"I didn't think so." As she drove off, she said, "I can't do any good here. Let me do some good."

"I'm telling Dad," I yelled after her.

Inside Rachel and Jelly had changed into bathing suits and were perusing a room service menu.

"We're getting lunch and then hitting the pool," Rachel said.

"Want to come with?" Jelly said. "And yeah, no Speedos allowed. I'm talking about banana hammocks, homie."

Their giggling tore through my head, pulling something loose in there. I dropped to the couch, rubbed my eyes with my palms.

"Big Al doesn't look so good," Rachel said.

"Do you know about Mom going to some Indian reservation?"

"Sure, she told us all about it. She's really jazzed up. I'm happy for her."

"Do you know where Dad is?"

"No idea," she said. "Chicken Caesar salad, *yes*. If I order beer will you sign for it?"

"We'll totally stay in the bedroom when the guy comes," said Jelly.

They were treating this like the vacation it was. "Get me some water," I said.

"What's the magic word?" Jelly said.

"This is what you get for slamming shots with the reverend," Rachel said, who found bottled water in the minibar and brought me one. "Forget about signing for the beer. There are some in this fridge."

I emptied the bottle in one sip and looked around the living room, the western furnishings. With the time change, it was early afternoon. Through the window sunlight washed out a swath of land made green by a landscape architect and preserved by an irrigation system hissing water in perpetuity. Rachel and Jelly had the right idea. This was a vacation. I should take advantage of it. I'd kept up my end of the bargain, operating to this point under the assumption that my family was basically good people. I judged our happiness as linked; I couldn't have any unless they had some. Watching my sister and her friend drinking and burping, knowing my mother couldn't be more content driving a rental car to help out a bunch of Indians, not knowing where my father was but having a pretty fair guess—I was starting to think my job was done. The Crown of Thorns did the trick. That was enough. Maybe I should hit the pool too, get a bite to eat, ride a horse, shoot a gun (probably not wise, that last one), Cowboy Alex on the frontier. Maybe I should invite Jelly to the resort's 3-star restaurant for dinner, the whole thing on Holden's tab.

"It says they'll deliver room service to the pool," Jelly said.

"Pool service. Ready, Miss Skanksalot?" Rachel said, and they grabbed towels, magazines, sunglasses, and hats.

"Coming?" Jelly said.

"I'll meet you there."

"I sincerely hope you brought sunblock," she said.

They closed the door behind them. I welcomed the silence. A couple of minutes to get my second wind, then slip into vacation mode. Holden could annoy God for the rest of his life, it was none of my business. He had been at it before me and would be at it after I retired from the plant game. My parents were set in their ways too.

There was a limit to what I could do for any of them. I wasn't an agent of change. Far from it, I was barely awake.

The room phone rang. Thinking it might be my father, I answered right away.

"Alexander?" a voice said.

There are only three people who ever called me Alexander: my grandfather who, when he was alive, often modified it with "The Great," my mother when she was angry with me, and Laura Sullivan.

"You've got to be kidding." I breathed loudly into the receiver.

"I recently read the most interesting thing about you. At least I think it was you. There could be more than one Alexander Wolf in this world and isn't that a scary thought?"

"How did you find me?"

"I did a little research when I saw you on Grady's World and I visited your website. . . . Is it true you're a Christian?"

"Since when does the truth matter to you?"

"You know who you're like? You're like a guy who plays the same lotto numbers every day for ten years and on the one day the deli closes early and he can't buy his ticket, his numbers win and he spends the rest of his life blaming the owner of the deli for everything that ever happens to him."

"Your narrative skills are as sharp as ever." I tried picturing her and kept seeing her at Otisville, where she didn't work anymore, elbows on a desk, fingers in her hair, slumped from a long day. I couldn't see her anywhere else. That she was able to find me in a bungalow at a resort in the Sierra Madre foothills seemed almost supernatural.

"Did you ever stop to think that my book helped you?"

"Board of Prisons was tickled pink about the chapter where

you claimed I seduced you."

"You have your version and I have mine. And mine is about to come out in paperback. It's why I'm calling."

She was in Los Angeles. She lived there now and was scheduled to appear at a few book signings and readings to promote the paperback edition of *White Boy Bandito*. Laura wanted to know—since I was out west anyway—if I would join her. "I've heard of this Warren Holden. He's certainly a big shot in the faith healing community."

"I've got to go."

"Alexander, hold on. You just *have* to come. People are going to go crazy when they find out you've been saved—not that I really believe it. It's the final piece to the story. You know, between you and me, the largest criticism of the book was your lack of redemption."

"I thought it was your lack of talent."

"The average male reaches full cognitive maturity around age nineteen, so this type of juvenile insult is to be expected. Anyway, as a writer, I always liked your stubbornness. It made for an interesting character study. But fans want a happy ending. We can give it to them. What do you say?"

I hung up. Vacations no longer interested me. I lay down in the bedroom and closed my eyes. In a minute I would unpack.

I woke up in time to catch the end of dinner. Holden waved me over to his table. Excusing myself through the dining room, I saw culinary wreckage on all sides. It was like touring Antietam and picturing the carnage. This was an all-inclusive package the pilgrims had paid for, and they had no trouble squaring spiritual superiority with sinful gluttony. After all, these two hundred pigs were only adhering to Holden's Gospel. Dinner was among their earthly rewards. I shouldn't have been surprised by the Herculean task left for the busboys, the courses running together so that dregs of New England clam chowder spilled over onto the dressing drenched remnants of a chef's salad, which itself covered greasy pork chop bones. Coffee and desert were being served with third helpings of shrimp cocktail.

"Alex, my lad, you made it," Holden said. He slapped me on the back. "Eat fast. You and I are going for a walk."

"Any chance you've seen my father?"

"I can't say I've been looking for him. Come on, eat. I want to see the sunset."

Outside, early evening, it was still triple digit heat, though a dry heat, as the saying goes.

"That was a good meal and now we're having a good walk. I want you to learn to savor these moments," he said. We were over by the golf course, taking the cart path from the clubhouse to the first tee, and Holden sauntered along, not as if he was conserving energy but as if, in his self-satisfaction, he expected the world to meet his pace.

His phone rang and he answered. "Listen, listen, I'll get on a plane right now, come over there with a hunting knife, and field dress you in my backyard. I'll dog paddle in your viscera." He hung up, shrugged at me, and said, "Pool guy. You used to work for a pool company. Were they any good? I really need to switch services."

"Laura Sullivan called. She wants me to go on some book tour with her."

"Isn't it funny the way things work out? I've been thinking about your Phase II. I wanted to know what opportunities you were pursuing. And then she calls. Coincidence, some might say. But I think we both know who's responsible. You should do it. I also think that at breakfast tomorrow you should work the room a little. Are you aware of how much money is sitting there, eating all that food? Your plant won't carry you forever."

"Right now I'm thinking I'm done with the business."

He bent and tied his shoe. On one knee, he looked out toward the mountains on the horizon. The sun was beginning to melt into them. "He created all of this."

"Are you listening?" We started walking again.

"These pilgrims want to get the biggest return on their investment, spiritually speaking. Just because they're loyal to me, doesn't mean they won't hedge their bets with you."

"Thanks for the tip."

"Good," he said as if we actually settled something.

At the first tee was a foursome looking to get in a few holes before the end of the day. One of the men came over and Holden blessed his driver.

"A woman goes to her doctor and says that she's in pain from being hit by a golf ball," I said. "The doctor asks where the ball hit her. She says between the first and second hole. Her doctor says, 'Well that doesn't give me much room to work.'"

Holden didn't laugh. We took the path back toward the clubhouse. The tops of his ears were almost purple. He was getting that deranged expression on his face. I got the feeling he might take a run into the mountains just to see if they were really as far away as they looked.

"You remember our conversation on the plane?" he said.

"Vaguely."

"Everything I told you was true. But, here's the thing. I'm not a stupid man. I've looked at it from every angle and the only reason that fully explains why I've failed to get His attention is, as unlikely as it seems, what if He doesn't exist? I don't think that's the reason, and I get uneasy just saying it, but I mean there is the chance, right?"

"Warren, I have no idea," I said. His crisis was so unimportant it bordered on the meaningless.

"You don't believe in anything. You could tell me your secret, but you won't. You like to play it close to the vest."

"I don't know what the future holds, but I know who holds the future," I said.

It wasn't what he wanted. It put him in a snit. "You should run along now. I'd like to enjoy the sunset alone."

So I ran along, or walked away with my pride intact, having escaped without giving him what he wanted. I walked around a while, thinking, trying to figure everything out. Did I really want to quit the plant business? I couldn't see the next step. Quit this and do what? *I don't know what the future holds* . . . I really didn't. I just knew I took no comfort in believing things happened for a reason. What I could have told Holden was that such an idea scared me. If true, it meant I was trapped. I'd have to cope with whatever was in store for me, to just take it, because at some point, struggling against it would be nothing more than trying to uphold an idea of myself that was irrelevant to whoever was calling the shots. A random existence was what heartened me.

In an anarchic universe, I could move freely, like I was doing now. I walked a while longer, trying to sort it out. Soon it was dark.

As I approached the bungalow I heard music and voices exploding into the night. There was Rachel and Jelly, with two boys wearing plaid shorts and pastel polo shirts. The boys straightened up when they saw me, but they were drunk and young and brazen enough not to hide the beer. Rachel and Jelly, in shorts and bikini tops, didn't see me. They were busy giving the boys a secular crash course. Out here, in the lawless west, Rachel had finally cut loose. She and Jelly were dancing, hopping from foot to foot as if standing on hot sand. The boys sipped beer, no longer interested in who I was.

"Party's over," I said.

Jelly spun around and ran the length of the porch and threw her arms around me. "Hey there, you. I'm kind of glad you're here, you know? You were with Reverend Holden, right? I can't believe it, he's here and you're here and I'm here."

She smelled like cigarettes. She tried pouring beer into my mouth. I pulled away and it spilled down the front of my shirt.

"Rachel, we need to talk."

"Don't be pissed," Jelly said. "These guys are seat-fillers. I mean, give me a little credit."

My sister took each boy by the hand and swayed with them, pretending she couldn't hear me over the music. I felt bad for her. "Rach," I said, louder. "Rachel!"

She dropped their hands and walked past me, into the bungalow through the open front door. Insects covered a lampshade on an end table, their shadows projected huge against the wall.

The real party was in the living room. Twenty or so teens and college-age kids, even the Kevster, draped themselves over the furniture, sun reddened and sweating, drinking and smoking, shouting their conversations over music and laughter. They had laid waste to the minibar.

"There he is," yelled Kevin, pointing a lit cigarette at me. "There's the man!" He gave me a solo ovation. "Someone get this man a drink!"

Rachel and I went to my bedroom and she started looking at herself in the mirror. "That boy, Derrick, his brother told him I'm prettier than Jelly."

I couldn't tell if this surprised her or affirmed what she already believed. She flopped down on the bed, her arms and legs positioned as if she were about to attempt a snow angel. "When I do this the room spins."

"Then don't do it." I sat down next to her.

She sat up. She smelled like beer. Her forehead, nose, and the tops of her shoulders were pink. "Knock knock."

"Who's there?"

"Dad."

"Dad who?"

"That's the joke."

"Not bad," I said.

"I found those tickets with the numbers on them. A few weeks ago, in the washing machine."

Now I laid back and stared at the ceiling. Hearing it from Rachel was tougher than hearing it from the late Lenny Marino.

"I wasn't joking this time, Alex."

"I never said you were."

"You're laughing."

I was laughing because I hadn't realized until then that, in Lenny's death, the old man skirted his debt. One less note to make good on. "I'm thinking of something else."

"What are we doing here?" she said.

"This is my job."

"What's the deal? You're kicking everyone out?"

"Laura Sullivan called. She wants me to go to L.A. with her."

It was the wrong thing to say. Rachel started crying. She moved up the bed and turned away from me. "What? What's the matter?" I said.

"Now you're leaving too!"

I said I wasn't going anywhere.

"Then why bring it up?"

"I was just thinking that this probably shouldn't be my job anymore."

What I really hoped for wasn't a new line of work, I realized, but relief—relief from having to worry about people who weren't even here right now. I just couldn't understand the degree to which our parents took for granted the tremendous work we had done to get to this point. How could they not appreciate how far we'd come? More than anything Holden ever said, this situation struck me as a persuasive argument in favor of a guiding hand—one that, in our case, had judged us primed for ruin. Though it contradicted my entire outlook, I wanted to believe it because the other option meant accepting that Bob and Judy Wolf might simply be shitty people. At that moment I preferred a disapproving God to asshole progenitors.

I repeated that I wasn't going anywhere, as much to convince myself as Rachel. She walked over to the mirror and wiped her face. She snorted a little laugh. "Maybe we should call it a night. I'm hideous." She ran her hand through her hair. "Thank you," she said.

"Sure. What for?"

"For sticking around." She dabbed at her bloodshot eyes with a tissue. "How did you manage to become the most reliable person in this place?"

"I hope that's not true."

"The bar wasn't that high to begin with."

September, 2007

This is a pre-paid call from an inmate at a federal correctional facility. This call is from: Alexander. *To accept, dial 5 now. To decline, dial 3 now, or just hang up.*

"Who is this?"

"You have more than one brother in a federal correctional facility?"

"Oh, hey Big Al, what's up?"

"Big Al?"

"I told you I'm trying out nicknames until one sticks."

"I guess it beats Alejandro."

"Okay then, Big Al it is."

"What's up with these questions you sent me?"

"What do you mean, what's up? I explained everything in the letter. It's a project for my communication arts class."

"Your teacher assigned you to interview an inmate?"

"I can interview anyone I like. I chose you. Consider yourself honored. I was going to interview the guy who pulls down his pants outside Franklin Ave. Community."

"Hilarious. You know I only get fifteen minutes a call, right?"

"Let's stop screwing around then. You have the questions in front of you?"

"I do, but Rachel, what the fuck is this? Some of these questions."

"What's the problem? They're regular questions: *Do you regret what you did? Have you made any friends in prison? What do you think it will be like when you re-enter society? What's your greatest weakness?* Fine, that one sucks."

"*Beyonce or Rihanna? Do you have a girlfriend?*"

"What? That's human interest."

"*Have you ever killed anyone? If so, how many people and how did you do it?*"

"That's legit journalism."

"*What's your drug of choice? How old were you when you lost your virginity?* What the hell kind of class is this?"

"Can I be honest with you? Some of the questions really are for my project. The other ones—oh, God, I don't want to talk about this—it's just that since that movie about us was on TV, things have sucked for me at school. I'm being harassed. I mean it, really. It's not cool."

"Goddamn it. I'm sorry. Fucking Laura Sullivan."

"It's not her! It's you! *You* did this. It's your fault. So here's the deal: I'm selling you out to the kids at school to save myself. I'm going to give them a bunch of gossip and then maybe they'll leave me alone. I don't want to, but that's the way it is. You can answer the questions or not, but you'll be screwing me over again if you don't. And I'll probably just make up answers anyway, okay?

"Okay, let's start at the beginning."

TWENTY-SIX

For all its first-class amenities, Gold Spur Ranch and Spa never caught on as a venue for the arts, not for the owners' lack of trying. At one point, they envisioned their hotel an entertainment destination, like Lake Tahoe. Through private investors, they raised funds and constructed an amphitheater, hoping to attract entertainers who couldn't book Vegas anymore but, on more nights than not, were still capable of flooring a packed house. California City, they should have known, was no has-been Vegas, or poor man's Tahoe. During the first performance, a strange but lively showcase of celebrity impersonators, scorpions scuttled in the aisles and, while no one was stung, two audience members suffered heatstroke, and a third became sick from the odor emanating from nearby horse stables. With investors already impatiently awaiting a return on their money, the owners couldn't walk away from their plan, and they borrowed against equity on the vast property and built a roof over the theater. Even that didn't change their fortune. Stuck with this theater in which all but the most desperate acts refused to play, and all but the least discerning vacationer refused to pay for a seat, they got as much mileage out of it as they could. Talks of teaming up with the Air Force and turning it into a planetarium fell through, and it functioned now as a meeting place for businesses on corporate retreats and a chapel for the occasional wedding. On Sunday, August 12, it was the location of Holden's service.

 The service was to be a stripped down affair. At a staff meeting after breakfast, Holden said that Monday in the Mojave, with Mary's grand entrance, was the main event. It wasn't his style to phone it in, he was a pro, but he wasn't going to waste A-material on a service that would never make it to podcast or DVD. He was content to let the music and lights do the heavy lifting, perform a few of his more histrionic prayers, and wrap it up, encouraging the pilgrims to partake in the resort's many wholesome diversions. Knowing them as well as he did, he figured correctly that they would bring to the service their goodwill and optimism and fill in any blanks. That meant no healing. Healing was tomorrow.

First, though, was breakfast, notable as it marked the reappearance of Robert Wolf. He was seated with the reverend, the reverend's family, Dolores and Salvador. I hated to admit it, but I was relieved to see him. It was one less thing to worry about.

They made room for me at the table. At another table, Rachel and Jelly broke bread with the adolescent pilgrims. The same junior degenerates who raided my minibar and burned cigarette holes in the furniture were now holding hands, saying grace.

"Sonny boy, I recommend you don't try keeping up with the youngsters."

"You heard?" I said.

"He couldn't keep up with me either. I mean, good God, Bob, he looks old enough to be *your* father," Holden said around a bite of toast.

"You see, Alex, the trick is clean living." My father downed half a glass of grapefruit juice.

"He's frowning," Holden said. "Come on, cheer up. Have an omelet. We're just having fun. There's no law against having fun on the Lord's Day."

"Where were you?" I said to my father.

"Here and there. You thought I was gone?"

"It fit the evidence."

"I told you when Dynamic closed I wasn't about to drive off into the American west."

"A man of your word, right?" I said.

"You bet your ass." He stood and kissed the top of my head. "After the service, you, me, and Rachel, let's ride horses."

"The Good, the Bad, and the Ugly."

"That's not a nice thing to say about your sister."

"She's the Good," I said.

"I know. I was kidding. Find me after the service."

Following the staff meeting, I made it over to the theater. Isabella was taking the day off and the production crew acted like a classroom of students with a substitute teacher. There was talk of jetlag and a general complacency in the booth, the rigid tension of a service at the Arena replaced by a lazy, jokey attitude.

James, today elevated from A.D. to director, said by way of a pep talk, "Let's power through it and get out of here. Easy peasy. Anyone who's interested, I'll be holding a service of my own at the rifle range. First round is on me. Get it, round?" He looked at me and said, "This guy knows what I'm talking about." Like a lot of folks in the ministry, James didn't drink, smoke, take drugs, or use profanity, and this is what passed for humor with him.

Holden hit the ground running, quoting from Acts. He said, "'Then Peter opened his mouth, and said, Of a truth I perceive that God is no respecter of persons.'"

"No shit," I muttered, and James told me to be quiet.

The reverend said the quote meant that God didn't play favorites. He said that if the pilgrims were blessed, it was because they had given their lives to God. It was an interesting message to deliver from a resort, an hour removed from a breakfast that looked a lot like a Viking feast.

I stopped paying attention and only caught snippets of what Holden said. "'So pray to the Lord of the harvest to force out and thrust laborers into His harvest.'"

He rambled on about what they could expect in the Mojave, really using the power of suggestion to get everyone primed to see what he wanted them to see, to preemptively quash skepticism and dissent. We had to be nearing the end of the service when James got all of a sudden very excited.

"Where's he going? Does anyone know what he's doing? Keep a light on him," he said.

I looked down at the stage. Holden wasn't there. He was standing in the aisle near the first few rows, greeting the people sitting there, his microphone at his side, making it difficult to hear what he was saying.

"What is he doing?" James flipped though some pages in front of him, an outline of prayers to be recited, Holden's blocking on stage, the pacing of the service. "He's riffing. He's not wearing an earpiece? Can we find a way to communicate with him?"

No one knew. Confusion ruled the booth. Holden was walking

up and down the aisles, the microphone at his side, who-knew-what he was saying. He kneeled in front of a girl about six or seven and refastened a buckle on her white patent leather shoe.

"We're flying without radar here. On your toes," James said.

Holden made it to the back of the theater, resembling a guy ambling through a park at dusk, when the crickets were waking up, with nowhere else in the world to be, expected by no one, without responsibilities or obligations. He wore a look of freedom I'd never seen on him. Even at his most focused and determined, he was always torn in some way, some chaos only he understood pulling and pushing him, his crazy schemes and incompatible beliefs making him pulse. Even when sipping vodka on his private lake, counting his money and appreciating his fame, he wasn't free from the thing that drove him, the thing he chased and that chased him, the thing he named "his calling." Well he looked free of it now, standing at the back of the theater. The pilgrims turned around in their seats, necks craning, trying to get a look at what he was up to. A thud came over the speakers when he dropped his microphone. We heard it rolling away from him. He wasn't wearing a tie and his shirt was open at the collar. He undid the next button and massaged his throat. Then, with the same sense of freedom, he jogged down the aisle. As he built up speed, the congregation began cheering, clapping. When he reached the stage, he turned around and ran back up the center aisle toward the doors, and this time I thought he was going to bust through them, take them right off the hinges or leave a Holden-shaped hole in them, like in a cartoon.

They were cheering, "Go! Go! Go! Go!" They didn't know it was improvised. They didn't feel the discomfort overtaking the production booth. Only those of us on the inside knew that these services, though they looked made up on the spot, were as regimented as a military funeral.

Holden hit the back of the theater and spun around, faster now, careening. On his return to the stage it looked as if he might outrun his feet, fall on his face, rip a nice rug burn on his forehead.

"Can someone get Isabella, please?" James asked. He turned to me. "You're his boy. Did he tell you about this?"

Beyond his immediate concern for his job, there was a fear, I sensed, that James was witnessing his own disillusion. The crew glanced at each other, worried too that they were seeing the unraveling of Holden. I wasn't sure Holden had a mind to lose, not after his talk on the jet of trying and failing to get God's attention. I remembered him saying that he was going to succeed on this trip. It struck me as ridiculous that a cardio workout was how he planned to go about it.

By his third or fourth lap, a sweat map in the shape of Brazil stained the back of his shirt. James directed a sound tech to follow Holden with a boom mic and the poor bastard trailed after him. We heard them both panting. This went on long enough that the clapping in the audience fell out of rhythm and the chant of "Go, go . . ." lost its insistence, as if some people were starting to wonder *where* they were encouraging him to go. About halfway up the aisle, Holden stopped, causing the boom operator to almost collide with his back. He caught his breath, his hands on his knees. He straightened up, walked to the stage, climbed the stairs, and took his place behind his pulpit. The sound guy followed him.

"That was fun," he said. He slapped his palm on the pulpit. "I've got to tell you, I'm feeling the Spirit like never before. I'm bursting with it and I'm going to pass it on to you. You know, in the Book of Matthew . . . oh, forget that. When you feel like I do, there is no scripture that can describe it. Just raise your hand if you know what I mean."

If he had lost control of himself, even for a moment, he never lost his followers. They felt it too, the Spirit, the natural high that was the reward of the faithful. Their hands shot into the air and James, beside me, sighed. "All right, we're back. Back on track."

Holden was glistening with sweat. "We got any sickies here today? Because I've got a surplus of Spirit in me and it's only right to share. It's only fair. Come on, tell me, where are you out there? Where are you? I've got your number today, Lord."

Maybe he hadn't planned it, just got struck by an impulse and gave in to it. James stated aloud what we already knew. "There are no healings today. What does he think he's doing?" And there was real heartbreak in his voice. Here was Evel

Knievel launching himself in a rocket over Snake River Canyon. You were positive he wasn't going to make it, but you wanted him to, you needed him to, because you found inspiration in his rejection of the laws of gravity. He was going to will himself over the gorge in his Red, White and Blue rocket. So why was there pain in your voice even before the rocket sputtered and belched a cloud of white smoke and dropped Evel in a parachute into the limbs of a tree? Why was James already brokenhearted before Holden called his infirmed onto the stage? It was because you lived vicariously through this man in the past, but things had gone too far, and now you had to impose your limits on him, you had to saddle him with your mortality. This made you sad for everyone because, just this one time, you were the clairvoyant and saw the end before he did, saw how it was going to play out, and you were frantically trying to rewrite the finale before it happened, trying to change the unavoidable.

"Yes, you, young lady," Holden said, pointing to someone in the middle of the theater. "Yes, I remember you. You come up here and tell me what Jesus can do for you. Tell me how Jesus is going to make you whole."

It was the little girl whose shoe he refastened. The girl, shy from the attention, tried to bury herself in her mother's lap, but the woman pushed her into the aisle, knowing that this was the kind of gift that changed the trajectory of a young life.

"Come on, honey. This is going to be fun," Holden said. He waved her up. In the aisle she stood shaking her head. The mother stepped out and led her, half dragging her up to the pulpit. Holden did his Q&A, bleeding the story out of them, extracting the drama. Only there wasn't much of a story. The little girl, named Grace ("Did you know that I named one of my daughters Grace, too?" Holden said, making those connections with people the way great politicians do), had picked up a head cold on the flight here, wreaking havoc on her sinuses. "What's the matter, my girl?"

"I'm *th*ick," she said, her congested speech getting a laugh. "My head hur*th*."

"Well, Grace, I've got good news. God is going to fix*th* you." Which got even more laughs.

"Do you think he'll really go through with it?" James said.

Two things made me confident to say, "He's going to do it." The first was that Holden didn't heal children. I liked to think it was too cold a trick to play on a family, even for Holden. But maybe there was a technical reason. Kids were unpredictable. An adult might fool himself into transitory good health because he needed it to be true. A child might shrug it off. The second thing I realized is that I had watched Holden cure cancer, diabetes, infertility, hepatitis, endocarditis, diverticulitis, prostatitis, meningoencephalitis—hell, all the "itises"—in addition to correct botched surgeries, mend broken hearts, and reverse crippling depression. If he was going to waste his incredible power on a stuffy nose, it was only because he was really trying to cure it.

He was praying, "God, give me the strength," over and over. He was begging God to acknowledge, for once, not that he was a great man, but that he simply existed. That was all he wanted, God to say, "Yes, Warren, I see you." He put his fingers to the girl's face and pushed on either side of her nose.

"Ouch," she said.

"Grace, I need you to pray with me. Mom, I need you to pray with Grace. The three of us have to pray like we're trying to move the world." They huddled together, and I watched Holden's sweat drenched back heaving up and down. "Please Lord, rid Grace of her burden." He was psyching himself up for it.

I was already embarrassed for him. Finally, he pulled the trigger, laid his palm over Grace's forehead and shouted "Heal," but it sounded like a question, not a command. The girl fell into her mother's arms. She and Holden helped Grace to her feet, and awaited the results.

"How do you feel? Did the Lord heal you?" the mom asked.

"*Th*ort of," said Grace.

It was agony in that instant. The production crew was silent. The worshippers were silent. The mother was silent. I was silent. Holden looked like he was facing a firing squad. Then, right as the entirety of his failure was sinking in, Grace sneezed. Without a hint of irony, someone called out, "God bless you."

She sneezed again. A snot bubble formed on her nostril, shone under the stage lights, and burst on her face. She sneezed again, this one turning her nose into a faucet. Greenish mucous overran her upper lip, into her mouth. After each sneeze, someone else called out "God bless you." Grace must have sneezed ten, twelve times, eruptions that shook her little body. Her mother and Holden backed away as if the girl might detonate. She was raised to be polite and she tried covering her face with her hands, but she was sneezing so frequently and violently her hands couldn't make it to her nose. In full view we watched as she drained more snot than seemed possible for one nose to contain.

James pounded me on the back saying, "He did it. Holy God, he did it. I can't believe we're not filming."

Grace's father jogged down the aisle and he scooped her up with one arm, reaching out to shake Holden's hand with the other. The mother closed in around her husband, their family united, their blessed snot-smeared child waving to the pilgrims who, though they had seen high-order healings before, found sublimity in a job well done. Miracles were miracles and who were they to rank them? Holden, however, was nonplussed. He went back to his pulpit and needed it to hold him up. His face blanched, still the sweat poured, his black eyes closed against the stage lights. He whispered a benediction and ended the service.

The crew scrambled to close the show. The Holden Ministry Orchestra played its theme music and the house lights came on. James kept saying, "He did it."

While the pilgrims greeted one another, Holden remained at the pulpit. People yelled up to him their messages of peace, but he was muttering something to himself. They filed out of the doors at the back of the theater. Holden stayed where he was, unready to cede the spot of his one true miracle.

From *White Boy Bandito: How a Clever Suburbanite Became Death's Middleman for South American Revolutionaries*, by Dr. Laura Sullivan, PhD. (Verdict Press: 2006, 278-279)

Like many women, I'm attracted to the Bad Boy, and Alexander was that in spades. I knew I was developing feelings for him. He could be quite playful when he wanted to be. It was never boring when I was with him. Even when he drove me crazy as my most rambunctious participant in the group, there was always something unpredictable about him that excited me. He kept me on my toes, walking on eggshells. A smile from him could melt my heart and a cutting glance could tear it to pieces. I knew it was wrong to get involved with an inmate, and yet it was as if I couldn't help myself. Alexander had a kind of power over me.

Finally I succumbed to my primal desire. It was toward the end of my research, after a group session. Alexander had a habit of tipping his chair back and balancing his weight on one foot. It forced his legs apart, thrusting his crotch out, and leaving little to the imagination. You can be sure my imagination was running wild. When he caught me staring, he gave me a look that said it could all be mine if I wanted it. I wondered if the other inmates noticed the crazy energy flying back and forth between us. How could they not?

The session ended and everyone left to go to the dining room, or "chow hall" as they called it, for dinner. Only Alexander lingered.

"Need any help carrying your files?" he said. He stared at my bosom with a shameless brazenness.

I began feeling feverish. The next thing I knew I was in his embrace. What did he say to me? What were the words he used that made me surrender to our passion? I can't remember his words. We didn't need words. We were beyond the language of words.

"We can't," I panted. "What if we get caught?"

He grunted like the wild beast he was and hiked up my skirt, tore my underwear, his fingers exploring my wetness. I tried speaking again, this time to tell him "Yes!" but his lips were on mine. I'd been dreaming of kissing those lips for fortnights and now I really and truly was. Our tongues danced a slippery tango. He unsheathed his turgid member. My entire body was on fire. He thrust his manhood into my sex. I was impaled on his skin sabre and I clung to him for dear life, like a bull rider hoping and praying not to get tossed off. It was ecstasy. It was madness. I came instantly.

TWENTY-SEVEN

Did I believe that God, via Holden (or Holden, via God), opened the spigot in Grace's nose, decanting her filthy snot? Was it most plausible that the omnipotent being, who to this point ignored each of Holden's ploys, finally decided to reward the maniac with the one thing he wanted, validating his atrocious behavior? I was thinking about it while heading back to the bungalow to meet up with my father and Rachel to ride horses, and the conclusion I kept drawing was that I didn't care. Holden would make this episode into what he needed it to be. That it contradicted my reality didn't matter, not from where I stood, because I was standing in the same spot from the day before (I was actually in a worse spot but I wouldn't find that out until later). Right then, I wanted what I'd wanted since we landed—to relax on vacation.

At the bungalow my father told me that Rachel was off with Jelly and a bunch of other kids. They were going to barbecue or do something else—I don't remember what he said. I only remember that it wasn't what she ended up doing. At the time I was glad. Finally, I thought, I could go to the pool, take a dip, eat a sandwich, and close my eyes while my body baked in the dry desert heat.

It was four years since I was last in a pool, and the Gold Spur Ranch and Spa had a very nice one, blue tiles and clear water, a diving board from where I hurled my body in a pantomime of Olympic glory. I stretched to my full length underwater, popping up in the shallow end and floating on my back, paying little attention to the other swimmers or to my father who had made his way down from the bungalow, wearing a hotel bathrobe, a newspaper tucked under his arm. When the glare off the water became more than I could take, I retreated to a chaise and the shade of an umbrella.

I was pondering lunch choices, when my phone rang. It was a call I'd been waiting for, even if I wasn't sure when it was coming or who it was going to be from. I'd waited for it since we sold our first plant. I'd waited for it in the office with my father, day after day, listening to his tales of sales history. It was a call I'd waited for my whole life. I always knew it was coming, maybe not the details, but the message. It was Visa, looking for the account holder of a Platinum Plus card, account number ending 9763, Wolf Enterprises Inc., d/b/a Crown of Thorns Offers. Trevor wanted to verify a series of transactions, cash advances, taken over the last three days, some in New York, some in California, totaling close to $10,000.

Does Visa always make calls on Sunday? *Visa was committed to fraud prevention 365 days a year. It was part of the total protection package that I received as a Platinum Plus member.* That's mighty white of you. *Had my card remained in my possession during this time?* It had (Hadn't it?). *Good. Had I authorized the charges?* There was the option of denying them, submitting a claim to the fraud department, but where would that get me? Yes, I made the charges, I told Trevor. *Was I aware that my balance was over its limit?* Now that you mention it . . . *Would I like to be transferred to the payment processing center so I could avoid further overdraft fees?* Nothing would make me happier.

I paid down the balance using funds from our operating account, which is another way of saying I took the money out of my own pocket.

Which left me staring as best I could through the brilliant play of light on the surface of the pool at my father, a man on the far side of middle age, with a physique to prove it. He was up to his tits in the water, a hairy egg bobbing obliviously in a pot. I met him by the ladder. Staring down at him I saw his wet hair was thinning a little on top but decent coverage for a man his age. I noticed it because he should have been bald from stress, or from pulling it out in self-flagellation.

"I wish I placed the bets myself," I told him.

"What bets?"

If only he'd just admit he fucked up. Admit it once and maybe that would have changed something.

"I would've had a chance to win, at least. I would've had fun or felt the excitement or whatever it is that made you steal from me." I was calm saying this, or I wasn't yelling.

Dripping wet and indignant, he heaved himself up the steps to the deck. "I'm your father. You don't . . . I'm your father, you remember that," he said.

He started leaving the pool area, forgetting his robe, sandals, newspaper. I matched him step for step toward the gate.

"You took my credit card. How is it that I have to explain why that's wrong?"

"The card's in the bungalow. I'll give it to you right now," he said as though the credit card was the problem, and I was complicating a simple matter.

"And the money?"

"There's money left. You can have it."

"Oh, may I?"

"You just remember, I'm your father."

"I can't help you anymore. Any of you." I kept going, out of the pool area. I looked back once and saw him with his arms resting on the fence. I went to the bungalow to retrieve my money and credit card.

Which was where he said it was—the card, not the money. The money I couldn't find after turning out his pockets and dumping the contents of his dresser drawers. The bungalow was still in post-party disarray, another reminder of how far off the rails this trip had gone. This was my fault, I thought, not just the trip, but all of it, one more example of wanting to be special, to be great, of believing I could help, when I should have known from the beginning who I was dealing with, should have seen my family for who they were, and seen who I was, and realized it was patent delusion to believe that I, Alexander Wolf, of all people, was the one to fix us, to believe that we were fixable, that I was fixable.

I went to the hotel to escape the wreck of the bungalow and eat lunch, avoiding the pilgrim vomitorium, better known as the dining room, opting for the restaurant. For close to an hour, I lingered like a grateful lover over an architecturally-sound turkey club and a basket of duck fat fries. *Duck fat*, the smell alone hit the snooze button on my most pressing problems and returned me to a state approaching normal. Their aroma heightened my sense of smell, opened up the whole world through my nose, so that I discerned the mountains and desert, the hardscrabble flora, the nocturnal reptiles sleeping under rocks and in cracks in the earth. I could even smell Laura Sullivan's perfume as though, traveling from upstate New York—a fragrance jailbreak—it eventually reached me years later. Faint at first, the way it lingered on my fingers and face whenever I left her, now it grew stronger, overtaking the smell of the fries and the crisp, yet meaty, applewood-smoked bacon in my sandwich, so that it was like a dining companion. And that was what it was, because when I looked up I saw her.

Laura had spent a lot of money on her appearance. Gone was the fresh-scrubbed, clean-faced girl with her hair pulled back so tight she looked perpetually surprised. Her new iteration was tan, though her freckles were well concealed with makeup, her hair highlighted and layered, falling down to her shoulders. Her purse looked Goodwill but probably cost thousands. I'm sure Rachel could have told me who designed it.

She was laughing at me. "I've been sitting here for two minutes. What if I was an assassin?"

"You'd be doing me a favor. Fries?"

"I'm on a raw food diet. I've never felt better. And I'm only saying this as a friend but, if you want to die, your lunch is helping big time." She waved the waiter over and ordered hot water with lemon. "I make a great number of speaking engagements and my voice is the worse for it," she told him.

"You think he gives a shit?"

"You're right, but being around you makes me feel like I must defend my every move. Would you look at this scene? The two of us together, like old times. It's as if I've seen the whole world, only to land in the same spot I started."

"'The universe is shaped exactly like the earth, if you go straight long enough you end up where you were.'"

"Is that Zen?"

"Isaac Brock."

"Who?"

"Why are you here?"

"Oh, Alexander, not this again."

It was impossible to argue with her because she disallowed my grievance. There was no basis for contention from her standpoint, so any bitterness I felt was misdirected self-loathing.

That was unfair to her—couldn't I see that?—when all she'd ever done was try to help me.

"I had to see this with my own eyes. You, a convert," she said.

"You really don't get it, do you?"

"You never give me credit. This place isn't right around the corner. I've been driving all morning. Just hear me out: tomorrow, I'll come to the desert with you. We'll see Mary. That should be weird. God, those fries do smell wonderful. Okay, I'll have just one," and she picked through my basket.

"Who's Mary?"

"The First Annual Holden Ministry Pilgrimage is hardly a secret. Reverend Holden has quite an Internet presence. A digital footprint like Sasquatch."

"Why are you talking about him like I don't know him?"

"Damn, these fries are good," she said, ignoring me.

I asked the waiter for my tab. "I've got to run, Laura. It was great catching up, but I do have work. God never sleeps."

"I don't think you're being sincere. Alexander, you didn't answer my question."

"You didn't ask me a question."

"Can I stay with you tonight? The hotel is booked and the motel in town looks like a crime scene waiting to happen. It has a very bad aura."

"Let's not wait a couple of years to do this again." I signed my bungalow number to the check. She followed me outside. I kept a few paces ahead of her to avoid talking.

"Fine by me," she said to my back. "I prefer meditative silences over bickering anyway."

August, 2005

Sex is like murder—it comes down to means, motive, and opportunity. That's pretty hard-boiled for this type of story, I know, but it's also a fitting description of how things went down between me and Laura. It's impossible to know whether I would have been attracted to her if we'd met on the outside. I met her in prison and can only speak to things as they happened. I liked the way she looked and I liked her, and I mistakenly considered her my friend despite the total imbalance of our positions. We could never be friends. Our situations were too different.

Still, friend or not, Laura was a female in a place where there were few females. And I was deprived of any physical contact and hunting for masturbatory inspiration wherever I could find it. Even if I had hated her and found her repellent, I nevertheless might have envisioned a scenario, born of my still-adolescent concept of hot sex, in which she took all five and seven-eighth inches of my dick into her mouth and, while simultaneously tonguing my scrotum, recited in perfect elocution a Brendan Behan witticism about British colonialism.

Not that I planned on pursuing her or noticed the vibe had changed between us, some heightened connection formed on this day. What I remembered was feeling grateful for the air conditioner in the office where we met for our one-on-ones. It was a big rattling window unit with a coffee mug on the floor under it to catch drops of condensation. It felt wonderful in the office.

I also remember Laura being upset. She was often stressed out, but her attitude seemed different from the usual high-achiever pressure she put on herself. It was as if she was distracted by a gnawing, but ultimately unimportant, matter, her mind elsewhere. Since I had gnawing matters of my own to deal with, I didn't ask her what was bothering her.

But she brought it up. Mike emailed. Out of the blue, she said.

"Mike's my ex-fiancé."

"Really? When were you engaged?" I didn't have a life outside the prison so it was easy to forget that other people did.

"For a few months, junior year in college, but I ended it after a semester abroad in Italy."

"What did he want?"

"To send me an invitation to his wedding. He doesn't have my address up here. I guess he finally found someone who will go through with it. I'm kidding, he's a really great guy. We were just too young."

"Are you going to go? Would that be weird?" I said.

"Want to see something funny?" she said. "It's so embarrassing. After Mike and I broke up, I got a tattoo. Want to see? Going once, going twice . . ."

"Sold," I said.

She came around the desk. I didn't expect her to unbutton her pants but that was what she did. At the crossroads of her hip and groin, poking out from her underwear, was the pointy-eared, pointy-chinned, horned emblem of arrogance and entitlement: Duke University's Blue Devil.

"I make it a habit to root against Duke in sports . . . and in life," I said, which was sadly my idea of flirting.

"Everybody hates us. It's because you're all jealous." She started brushing her fingers over the ink. "I've had it forever and it still feels like it's raised off my skin."

Then she took my hand and rubbed my fingertips over the tattoo. "See? It's not actually above the skin."

That we came very close to playing out my jerk-off fantasy, minus the scrotum tonguing and Behan, was a shock to me, even as it was happening. When I slid her underwear to the side, I found her pubic hair a tad untended to (though not unruly), letting me think that this encounter was as much of a surprise for her as it was for me.

"What do you want?" she said.

"Huh?"

"Tell me what you want."

"Um . . ."

"Do you want to fuck me?"

"Yeah, of course, totally."

"Say it to me."

"Oh, I get it. Dirty talk. Sure," I said. "I want to fuck you."

"We can't. What if someone catches us?" she said.

"Right. What was I thinking? Duh." I pulled my hand back.

"No, we can," she whispered in my ear. "We can." She grabbed my hand, putting it back in place. "You're not good at this, are you?"

When we got into it, it was slick with sweat, smelling faintly of brine and bleach and a chilled mildew odor blew on us from the air conditioner. I remember she palmed my butt with both hands, which I thought was funny. But we didn't finish. A clattering noise in the hall had us jumping away from each other like similarly charged magnets. I rearranged my boner to hide it as she tucked her shirt back in, buttoned her pants. Then I left the office without saying goodbye, assuming this was a one-time thing.

At the bungalow, more surprises. Head of security, Salvador, on the couch, and the mess from the previous night's party was gone. "Did you do this?"

He pointed into the bathroom to a stack of folded towels on the sink counter. "Maid."

The good ladies in housekeeping had mercifully restocked the minibar. I reduced its supply of tiny bourbon bottles by two. I knocked back one of them. "Anyone want a drink?" I said, ever the generous host.

"Mrs. Holden needs to see you. It's an emergency."

"Hear that, Sully? The man says it's an emergency. Got to go now."

I left with Salvador, sipping my other drink as I walked. Laura tagged after us, too determined to be dissuaded. We hurried to the large private house where the Holdens were staying.

At the front door Laura shot out her right hand for an introduction. "Mrs. Holden, I'm Dr. Laura Sullivan and—"

"Don't care," Isabella said, leaving Laura's hand floating between them.

The look on her face!

"I'll take a walk, Alexander, and we'll meet later," Laura said.

"At least this one is age appropriate," Isabella said.

She brought me to the dining room and sat opposite me at the table, flanked by Dolores and Salvador. They looked like national security advisors in possession of imminent danger intelligence. Dolores offered everyone water. Only I accepted. It was tap water and tasted like someone let a sulfuric fart in my mouth.

"Do you know what happened at the service this morning?" Isabella said.

"I was there."

"The thing that makes Warren great is that he knows his limitations. Maybe he doesn't know his limitations, per se, but he knows he has them. If he starts thinking he can really perform miracles, I don't know what he'll do next."

"What does he have to say about it?"

"Warren is missing," Mrs. Holden said.

I nodded.

"Are you nodding because you understand what I said or because you already know he's gone?"

"The first one."

"I don't need to tell you that tomorrow is a huge day for the ministry."

"Maybe he's just taking a breather. I'm sure he'll show up."

Her face lit up with what I assumed were images of my murder. My reassurances made her hate me. But she spoke with a firm, flat voice, the joy of picturing my death secondary to the matter at hand. "I hope you're right." Then she tossed this off. "Do you know he was seen driving away with your father?"

"They were awfully chummy at breakfast," Dolores said.

I choked down the farty water, buying time while I figured out what she meant. "I just saw my dad. Not too long ago."

"Take my word for it, they're gone," Isabella said.

"I don't know where they are."

"Normally, you're the last person I'd come to for help."

"Thanks a million."

"I find you extremely average."

"No one can be extremely average. That's what average means."

"You're an idiot," she said. "But Warren is a better judge of talent than I am. He likes you. If you can find him, maybe you can convince him to come back."

"I'm not a bounty hunter."

"I know very well what you are and are not. You can recognize an opportunity when you see one. I'm talking about money, of course. Find him and bring him back. If you do, I'm ready to pay you a percentage of the offerings collected tomorrow. There's your motivation."

I stared at my empty water glass. "Why me?"

"Didn't you hear what I said? Warren's with your father. I suppose you have a way of reaching him, a phone number." She stood up, signaling the end of the meeting. "This information cannot get out. No one outside of this room can know. Not even my children. Let's hope, no, let's pray, that you track them down."

They felt the weight of the predicament so I forced its heaviness upon me, my way of telling her that I was, as usual, part of the team. Isabella knew I was game, but if she saw dollar signs in my eyes, she was wrong. My eyes were seeking the horizon. I knew exactly what I was going to do. There was no chance I was looking for Holden. Here was my escape plan. If he pulled a no-show on the biggest day in the history of his ministry, it might signal the end of the ministry. Or, at least, the beginning of the end. With its downfall, I would have no way of helping my family, a commitment that—forgetting what I told my father—I would still consider mine. I just would. It wasn't sensible but neither were we. We were family.

Laura was sitting on the porch steps. She was up and on my heels, flitting ever nearer to me. "It's a hundred and ten degrees and that woman made me shiver. Not at all like the person you see on those commercials for the spring water. What was the problem?"

"Who said there was a problem?" We came up the stone path to the bungalow. "This reunion has been more magical than I ever dreamed possible but, like all good things, our time has come to an end."

"Where am I supposed to stay tonight?"

Inside, Jelly was on the couch, crying and more than a little drunk. One of the pastel twins was standing in the middle of the room. He couldn't even look at me. It was from him that I knew something was wrong by adult standards, not wrong in the way that a wasted seventeen-year-old girl can see the end of the world in a dirty look.

She crawled up from the couch and lunged at me. "I'm sorry.

So sorry." She was sweating vodka, and not the good stuff Holden drank.

For the first time Laura seemed to understand that coming here was a mistake. A sequel to our story must have looked sexier in L.A. I hoped she was beginning to realize that most sequels weren't as good as the original anyway. Sure there was material here, more than enough if she was willing to root around in it (and she didn't even know that Holden had deserted with my father), but she'd already done her slumming at Otisville. Now she wanted painless speaking engagements that lined her pockets, solidifying in the process her brand as an expert in a psychology-related field. Linking herself to a religious huckster working a three thousand mile con on the flock of his deceived could do what but tarnish her image?

Jelly had yet to come out with the bad news. "I'm so sorry," she continued to wail on my shoulder.

"She needs real help, Alex," Laura said.

Was it not clear that I was the closest thing resembling real help? I danced Jelly over to the couch where we sat, her body folded over on itself in my lap. There seemed to be a direct ratio between the horrendousness of the information and the length of time I was kept uninformed. The pastel kid was staring at the floor. "You. Who are you?" I demanded.

"Derrick, sir," he mumbled. The formality of *sir* skewed the ratio closer to catastrophe.

"What happened?" I said to him, but it was Jelly who burst out with an answer.

"We were riding these things, you know like motorcycles but like with four wheels, but fat wheels—"

"ATVs, sir," Derrick clarified.

"And Rach was driving it and there was a hill and it rolled over and . . ." Her sobs finished the story.

"Well, is she alright?" I said.

They couldn't confirm my sister's condition. She was on her way to the hospital. That was all anyone knew.

I tossed Jelly aside and stood up. Derrick backed away from me as if I had judged him responsible. "You're so fucking stupid," I said, directing my message at everyone in the room, myself included. I hauled Derrick outside by the collar of his polo shirt, not to thrash him, but because I wasn't going alone to the hospital. Laura and Jelly ran after us.

"Where's your car?" I said. Laura led us to a Mercedes, desert grime covering its Obsidian Black metallic paint. I made a note that the German coupe was likely paid for by my prison sentence, if indirectly, and was as fucking stupid as the rest of us: over-priced, overrated, overly coveted. When its V-8 blasted to life, I also decided that it was overly powerful in a world of peak oil. The mellifluous disembodied voice of the navigation system told Laura where to go. She tried putting on the radio, but I said, "No music. I need to think." But that wasn't why I wanted silence.

If Rachel was dead, or dying, or in a persistent vegetative state (a fate worse than death, all her youthful, pretty features melting into flabby pockets of unresponsive flesh, her long brown hair chopped to a butch cut that was easy for nurses to wipe food from, her orthodontically perfected teeth falling out of alignment in the permanent gape of her mouth), or in some other way maimed, I didn't need a soundtrack to go with it. I would not be ambushed by grief years down the line on an otherwise forgettable day because I heard a pop song and was immediately returned to Laura's car and our drive to the hospital. The kids in the backseat were warned not to make a sound. I didn't want to end up hating Jelly because I associated her voice with Rachel's death.

June, 2004

The last time I saw Ron Moreno, who was my best friend before some pop-psychologist called him that in a trash exposé of my life, he was eating a ham sandwich. He had a particularly unappealing way of making it, sifting onto the mayonnaise-smeared Kaiser roll a half-inch of table salt. He named his sandwich Salty-Ass Ham. It became a sort of running joke. Like whenever he got angry I called him Salty-Ass Ron. That kind of thing.

He was in his kitchen, building one of these monstrosities for lunch, on the day before he made the trip from which he would never return. I always said that if I had been with him, I would have disappeared too, and that was true in the sense that whoever killed him would have had no reason to spare me, but it wasn't as if I was supposed be on that trip in the first place and survived due to a stupid reason that I later ascribed to destiny or divine intervention, like some asshole who, because of his mind-bending hangover, overslept and missed his flight, which turned out to be American Airlines flight 11 that forty-seven minutes after takeoff crashed into the North Tower of the World Trade Center. Ron traveled alone because we weren't taking guns with us. I didn't know what his agenda was. I wasn't privy to many details outside of my limited purview as the gun guy. Beyond that, I didn't know and didn't want to know, purposive ignorance my modus operandi of choice at the time.

When someone close to you dies, what do you choose to remember? Or do you not have a choice? I ask because here was what I remembered being the last thing I ever said to Ron: "Those sandwiches are going to kill you."

Oh, the ever-loving fucking irony.

I told him that eating those sandwiches would kill him and he dug in, cramming it right in his mouth and moaning with pleasure. But was that the actual last thing I said to him? It couldn't have been. I must have said something else before leaving his place. "Later, Chump," or "See you when you get back," or "What are you doing this weekend?" Or, "Your breath smells like cured meat." Yet, my last fixed image was of him going to town on his disgusting lunch.

TWENTY-EIGHT

The nurse at Tehachapi Valley Hospital's emergency room desk was held by an unflagging devotion to protocol and failed to meet my panic. She consulted her computer at her own pace to see if Rachel had been admitted, while I was about ready to conduct my own floor-by-floor, room-by-room, search. Then I saw my mother emerge from the bank of elevators at the end of the hall. Somehow she got there ahead of us.

"Rachel's fine," she said. "Well not fine, she's banged up, but she's awake."

Jelly cried some more, her face swollen and raw from repeated swipes of tissue, relieved that her best friend was alive.

Dr. Sullivan introduced herself, my mother absently taking her hand.

"Don't ask," I said. Priorities being what they were, Laura was a secondary concern.

"Can we see her, Mrs. W?" asked Jelly.

"Not all at once, okay? Alex, come with me."

We waited for an elevator. "Why didn't your father ride over with you?" my mother said.

"That's kind of a long story."

The elevator doors opened and we got on.

"He said he was on his way," she said.

"You talked to him?"

"Of course."

"Where is he coming from?"

"I assume the ranch."

She said Rachel fractured her right clavicle and ulna on her right arm. She had a mild concussion. "Alex, where were you when this happened? Why was she left alone?"

"I don't know, maybe because her mother was busy saving Cherokees from small pox or whatever it was you were doing, and her father was, well, that one's a doozy," but I let it drop. There would be time later to assign blame.

We got off on the third floor, turned the corner to Rachel's room. "Have you slept? You look tired," she said.

"I need a vacation from this vacation."

I didn't know if the doctor gave Rachel something for the pain or if it was the booze. Either way, she was in high spirits.

"There's my Broski," she said, her wrist set in a fiberglass cast, pink (no surprise), in a sling to immobilize her collarbone. "How's it hanging, Big Al?"

"Don't be vulgar," my mother said.

"I'm getting by," I said.

"I got a busted wing."

"I heard."

"Other than that I'm looking good and feeling fine." She sipped from a can sitting on a food tray. "This is, like, without a doubt. Know what I mean?"

"She's a mess," my mother said.

"Oh, my God, you guys, without a doubt, the best juice ever. You've got to try." She nudged the can at me. "Delish, am I right? No need to thank me."

"Sure thing, sis."

So, tragedy averted. I was grateful. However, if days like this were supposed to realign your perspective so the truly important things stood out against so much triviality, I wasn't seeing it. The doctors and nurses knew the truth and that was what kept them slightly aloof and guarded: Your crises don't stop the rest of the world from happening. My father was on his way? With or without Holden?

When the Old Man did turn up, he was alone, striding into the room in that Robert Wolf way, smiles galore, arms bursting with hospital gift shop swag. Rachel had little use for a desert vista calendar but cuddled with a flight suit-wearing teddy bear as if it had been with her since infancy. He came around the bed and kissed the top of my head. No mention of misappropriating company money or the resultant poolside nastiness. No point to it. There we were, the family dynamic intact, however tenuously.

It was my mother who brought up the pilgrimage, asking what she believed was an innocuous question. "What did I miss?"

I didn't know where to begin. I told them, but my father mostly, that Isabella planned to pay me if I brought Holden back.

"That's quite an assignment," he said.

"Why do you say that?"

"He's not coming back."

"Back from where? Where did he go?" my mother said.

"Yeah, Daddy," Rachel said, "Where'd the Rev go? Did he rev up his engine and go home?" She thought this was the ultimate in hilarity.

"I left him at the craps table," he said, and my mother winced as if a gunshot victim, handcuffed to a bloody gurney, had been wheeled into Rachel's room.

It went down as I'd suspected. After healing the snotty little girl, Holden was convinced that God had heard him and, with his life now justified, lost his reason to continue mocking his creator. But now he experienced the first unintended consequence of his enlightenment: His life disproved the idea of luck. How could there be luck, knowing what he knew? That was just how ignoramuses made sense of a world they couldn't understand, what losers chased and romanced but never caught. There was only God, and Holden now knew that some people lived nestled in the hollow of His collarbone. The rest of us clung to whatever part we could, all of us the Lord's fleas. Right around the time I was taking the first bite of my turkey club, Holden ran into my father by our bungalow. He was eager to test his newfound certitude, and persuaded Bob (I can't image this was a tough sell) to take him to a casino in Rosamond, Jackpot Joe's, "no bigger than an IHOP," said my father, a slots haven with a smattering of table games. It must have been a riddle to Holden—What do you call a game of chance when you no longer accept its basic premise? House edge? The arrogance of the house to think they held the upper hand in anything. To demonstrate this, and with only a passing knowledge of the dice game, he went on an immediate and prolonged winning streak.

"Warren can roll the bones," my father said. "He was up a hundred grand in an hour."

The table cheered him and rode his streak. "I got on him early, bet for bet. Of course his handle was a shade bigger than mine."

Holden made every point and the table went crazy. If my

father was able to appreciate the gift Holden was giving them, he also saw the sadness in it. Those who ringed the table jumped up and down, high-fived, ordered more drinks, tipped the dealer and waitresses, while he stood by, mirroring silent Holden, who took no joy in his winning. Here was the second unintended consequence: Winning doesn't exist in a vacuum. Only the possibility of losing gives winning its flavor. This fact, so simple to my father, who in his way based his life on it, never occurred to Holden until then.

"I can't say it was exciting. It was supposed to be, but it just wasn't. It was like heads I win, tails you lose."

"Am I the only one who doesn't understand a word he's saying?" Rachel said.

"We're whole on the credit card and then some. You don't have to worry about it," my father said to me.

I still worried about it, it loomed too large not to, but I took comfort in remembering that he was redeemable. Because while it was true that the money fell in his lap, he'd first needed to see the windfall as a corrective. He could have given the winnings straight back to Jackpot Joe's. That was the easy thing to do, and what I expected of him.

"What credit card? And why were you gambling when you should have been supervising your daughter?" my mother said.

I waved a hand at her, as if saying you shouldn't ask questions when you already know the answers.

Rachel started waving like me, laughing. "It looks like I have a lot of fingers when I do this."

"Everyone in the place dropped what they were doing. The floor supervisor was watching, the pit manager came over, even the casino manager checked it out. Warren had the weirdest look on his face, like he was alone, staring in a bathroom mirror," my father said.

It wasn't the story itself that made me think Holden was gone for good, but that the details were wrong. My father didn't mention Holden's lunatic black eyes squinting down to nothing, or his guzzling vodka on the rocks. He didn't say, "Goddamn, that guy kept putting his fingers to his temples." Who knew what Holden was thinking in the shooter position at the craps table, but my father's description was unlike anything I ever observed in him. Given the likelihood that he wouldn't be with us when Mary took to the sky tomorrow, I started thinking about my goodbye to the ministry and the Crown of Thorns business. What sort of person was I to think that the only way out was through failure? There had to be a way to capitalize on the situation, a high-level escape plan that left me, us, in a better tomorrow. If I had imagination and courage . . .

"This thing's starting to itch," Rachel said, pawing at her wrist.

Just wait a few weeks, I thought. If it itched now it was going to be hell later. At least it was a short cast and she might be able to dig a finger or chopstick in there, scratch around. It wasn't the whole arm, or leg, one of those femur casts to the hip. Those always looked unbearable. I pictured my sister head to toe in pink fiberglass, a Pepto-Bismol-colored statue of the girl who rolled an ATV after swilling bargain liquor on the Lord's Day. That image, and the possibilities I saw in it, stirred me up. That image—there it was, the other option for us, the other *adios*.

My plan, if you could even call it a plan at this point, demanded of me at least one quality with which I first impressed Holden: an ability to ingratiate myself with difficult people. The person whose favor I needed to curry? The implacable Isabella Holden.

An orderly entered the room and said if the patient was feeling up to it she could see visitors.

"Yeah, *dónde están mis amigas*?" Rachel said.

"I'll bring them up," my mother said and headed to the door.

I stopped her. "Why not finish on a high note?"

"Finish what?" she said.

It took a lot of talking, mostly because I was plotting it out on the fly, amending and revising the specifics as I went. I made it clear that this was the last time I would impose on them, preemptively addressing their doubts and obligatory resistance. Not one of them pointed out I wasn't in a position to make such a promise.

"What do you need from us?" my mother said.

"Imagination and courage."

I also needed money. It took a decent amount of the gambling winnings to grease a nurse who was unhappy with desert life in general and her working conditions in particular. By the time we let other visitors into the room, my sister was in something close to a body cast, ankle to hip on both legs, matching the cast on her broken right arm and the decorative cast on her other arm that wrapped around her shoulder and upper torso. Jelly and Derrick and Dr. Sullivan and a few other kids who had since shown up, crowded the small room took turns graffiti-ing my sister with a Sharpie pen. My father and I moved into the hallway.

"I hope the nurse stays quiet," I said. "She could really screw this up for us."

"You paid her enough."

There was laughter from inside the room, echoing into the hall. The astringent smell of hospital disinfectant was strong in the air.

"Dad, you have to quit. This can't happen again."

"I was at a bar upstate once that had a slot machine in the corner, a mechanical model, a real One Armed Bandit—5 cent Money Honey. I doubted it worked, just something to give the place character, but when I asked the bartender, he said, 'Of course.' People were always fussing with it, jerking the arm and setting the reels spinning. I should have a go at it. For fun.

"At last call I was still dumping nickels into it. This, after the bartender twice told me to give it a rest, the bar wasn't licensed for it, it was a fucking novelty. As long as I was standing in front of the machine nothing could touch me. I was so plugged in and focused. I even got a little irritated whenever the cherries or pineapples lined up and I had to wait as the jackpot poured out because it broke up my rhythm, took me out of the zone."

"See? That's what I mean. You've got to stop."

"The reason I'm telling you this story is because if you understood how I felt, you would never ask me to stop."

From *White Boy Bandito: How a Clever Suburbanite Became Death's Middleman for South American Revolutionaries*, by Dr. Laura Sullivan, PhD. (Verdict Press: 2006, 326)

Four brilliant Liverpudlians once famously opined, "Life goes on." Alexander Wolf is scheduled to be released from prison in 2008 and his life is far from over. I do not know what he has in store for us next, but I would not bet against him. If I can end on a hopeful note, I would like to say that I've witnessed his potential firsthand. He is capable of succeeding at whatever he puts his mind to, provided he has learned what his mother knows is all so true: the world is a better place when we help more than ourselves.

In no time the pilgrims descended on the hospital as if it was one more activity to wedge between skeet shooting and a couple's massage. We let enough of them visit Rachel to spread our message, our message being that she was injured but brave, ready to tackle the long road of rehabilitation and praying for full recovery, God willing. We would be beside her until she was "out of the woods." Hospital staff succeeded in kicking out everyone who wasn't family. While my parents and I sat with Rachel a little while longer, we shared the excitement of our plan, and wondered if we could pull it off.

My sister was coming down off her buzz. In her haze she'd agreed to the superfluous casts without much resistance, but now that the pain was kicking in, she had one extremely pressing question regarding the irrespirable body armor she was wearing.

"What's my cut?" she demanded to know.

"*Our* cut, sweet sister. Our cut. And I don't have the details on that. I still have to talk Isabella into it."

"Wait, she hasn't said you could do it?"

"A mere technicality," I said, and got out of there before she could unload on me.

I set out for the ranch. It was now night. The Gold Spur came into view in the distance, blurry yellow illuminations in the foothills, like brush fires.

Isabella impatiently heard my report, a version of events that saw my father drop Holden at a motel about a half hour from the ranch and continue to Bakersfield to pick up my mother from the Indian reservation. I left out Jackpot Joe's in case Holden was still there.

"That's it? That's everything you know?"

"I was up to my ass in my own emergency."

"Yes, your sister. I heard. It's all anyone could talk about at dinner. How is she?"

"Not good."

"This day," Isabella sighed. "Have you ever seen anything like it?"

"Nope."

She asked again if I knew anything else. I heard her five children stamping around upstairs. Where, I wondered, did they suppose their father was?

I said I didn't think Holden was coming back.

"What are you basing that on?"

"Warren told my dad that he always expected the sky to look different on his first day of retirement, but it didn't. He said he probably needed a few days to adjust." All of it lies.

It was hard to tell where her concern lay: that he wasn't coming back to the ministry or that he wasn't coming back to her.

She sent Salvador to the motel. "Don't confront him. Just make sure he's there."

The security director did as he was instructed, and of course returned with nothing Isabella wanted to hear.

"He's wandering around this hick town in a three thousand dollar suit and no one's seen him?" she said.

Salvador tried answering, couldn't, and ended up shrugging.

Dolores spoke up. "I guess we'll have to cancel tomorrow."

"I don't remember asking for your opinion," said Isabella.

The old woman's face collapsed a little. Holden's desertion didn't mean a promotion for her.

"This is impossible. What the hell am I going to do?" Isabella said.

Dolores respected the question as rhetorical; I saw an

opening. "I have a contingency plan. It involves me."

"I wouldn't say we're off to a winning start," Isabella said.

I would fill in for Holden.

"What are you babbling about?"

I paced back and forth, hoping my side-to-side movement proved hypnotic. "I agree it's going to be a little confusing when I come out instead of Warren. Some people might even be outraged that he's not there. But they'll be outraged quietly. Who's bold enough to desecrate the day by heckling the understudy? Storm off and demand their money back? And go where? No, they'll stay because in their shirt pockets, close to their hearts, will be Mary's image on Instamatic film."

"You think you can do what my husband does? I can't even fathom your ego. Or is it idiocy? Are you just plain stupid?" Her dislike of me was so calcified as to be unbendable.

"I don't think I'll be good. I just think I can survive it."

"I don't feel well."

And then Salvador spoke up. "Forgive me, ma'am, but he has stage presence."

"*Excuse* me?"

"We've all seen the podcast. Onstage, he's less of a weasel than he is in person. Doesn't come across as full of shit."

"I didn't know I was surrounded by talent scouts."

As surprised as I was by Salvador's vote of confidence (Alex Wolf: less weaselly and almost poop-free!), I worried that Isabella might feel ganged up on, dig in her heels out of principle. I backed off a little. "Then you should go up there."

"I'm graced with enough self-awareness to know that's not an option."

"Let's think of some other options," I said. "We can go Dolores' route and cancel. Or we can tell everyone the truth. Or let's just light out like thieves in the night. We could be hundreds of miles away by dawn, sipping burnt diner coffee before the pilgrims realize we're gone."

The subtext here was as plain as my supposed stupidity. I was the miracle cure for the lost cause, as yet unproven in humans, performed only by a discredited former-Soviet doctor. Better than that, I was, to keep the metaphors religious, the Hail

Mary pass, fourth down, no time on the clock, the entire season on the line. "I'm the best worst alternative!"

"There's no way you're doing this in the spirit of charity," she said.

"Meaning?"

"What do you want in return?"

The balls on her to try to make me feel guilty. "The same deal as before. A percentage of tomorrow's take. Slightly higher percentage. Negligible, really."

"I need to be alone." She walked upstairs.

I took refuge in my cell phone. A text from my mother read that Rachel was finally asleep and my father and she were en route to the ranch.

Isabella trod softly on the carpeted stairs back into the living room. She produced an envelope, inside of which, she said, was the service outline and a sermon. She refused to hand it over before talking me through the production.

"There are details in the sermon specific to Warren that won't make sense if you say them. I'll tweak it and get you a finalized copy by morning. But familiarize yourself with this one."

It doesn't cheapen the significance of the sermons to point out that they followed a rigid template and by picking a topic and flipping through the Good Book at random, shoehorning the wisdom therein to fit whatever message I needed to impart, I probably could have cobbled together my own without assistance. But I heard her out the same way I'd listened to my father at length the first time he handed over the car keys when I was sixteen, knowing now as then that the lecture was mostly about their anxiety. Little of what they said would make a difference when the moment came. I didn't know what the tipping point had been for Isabella when she went upstairs, or if she'd already resolved by then to let me get on stage. What was clear was that she would attempt to salvage the pilgrimage and save the ministry. If she hated me, I can't imagine what she was feeling for Holden by forcing her into this decision.

On one matter, she was adamant: No healing!

"I'm not going to put in place the apparatus for a healing show so it shouldn't even be a concern. If you get in a jam I'll radio to you what to say. And you just say it! You are my ventriloquist's dummy. Yes?"

"Yes, ma'am."

I accepted the folder with the same enormity that one might come into possession of, say, the Colonel's secret recipe of eleven herbs and spices.

Isabella let out a long breath. She was getting her second wind. She was goddamn strong. "We just need to get through it."

From the screenplay to *The Wrong Way Son* (H.E.L.R. Prod., 2007)

```
INT. PSYCH SERVICES - FCI OTISVILLE - DAY

Alex and Laura lie sweaty and spent on the floor
behind a desk in Laura's office. Covered only by
her coat, they are out of breath, blissfully
content.

                    ALEX
          Doctor, I think I'm dehydrated.
          I need fluids.
                    LAURA
          Nurse, an IV, stat.

They laugh, cuddle closer.

                    LAURA (CONT'D)
          Oh, this is just wonderful,
          Alexander. Our own little world.

Alex stiffens.

                    LAURA (CONT'D)
          What's the matter?
                    ALEX
          I'm in pain.
                    LAURA
          I think I have a little rug
          burn, too.
```

ALEX
No. I'm serious. Here.

Alex massages Laura's hand and places it over his heart.

LAURA
That's called guilt.

ALEX
It's killing me.

LAURA
Well you can't change the past.

ALEX
Thanks for the bad news.

LAURA
But the good news is, you can change the future.

TWENTY-NINE

The next morning a practically mythological heat met the Holden Ministry faithful upon exiting the air-conditioned haven of the Gold Spur Ranch and Spa and, at 110 degrees, it fatigued the alabastrine pilgrims who crawled into rented vans and wedged their bodies beside each other, the bench seats neither allowing polite distance between neighbors nor affording comfort. Devotion alone had brought them this far but there was just so much the human body could take, and these were Christians who had already glutted themselves on yet another free breakfast buffet, as if the ratio between piety and bad cholesterol was directly proportional. They traveled ten miles outside of California City, to a part of the desert designated Our Lady of The Barrens, the location where a miracle was going to happen.

The heat, I could see it shimmering inches over the rutted dirt lane that passed for a road, the bounce of the sunlight off of the cracked earth causing me to squint behind sunglasses, as I rode shotgun in Laura's Mercedes with Jelly contorted into the tiny backseat where only yesterday she choked back sobs with pastel Derrick on our trip to the hospital. I hadn't realized just how dangerous the heat index was for August 13. True there was a tent already assembled in the desert (Holden had been so pumped up about this wacked piece of nostalgia, a tribute to his exploited youth on the revival circuit) and the tent came equipped with air conditioning, ice-filled coolers brimming with bottles of water, tubs of sunblock, umbrellas, hats and sunglasses, but it was still the Mojave Desert we're talking about, so that even the devout who made this trip monthly admitted to a drop off in attendance during the summer, and with good reason. Today, I doubted any group could match our contingency, head for pasty head.

So, 110 degrees. And the thing was, Mary didn't show up for at least another hour. What would it be then? 115? 120? I couldn't overstate it, *the heat*. Through it all, our crew was jonesing to see the mother of God. I'll give them that. It was clear in their bloated, wet faces and in the way they addressed each other that they were on the verge of having their faith validated. They knew it would be an ordeal. Such things didn't come easily. They were also looking forward to remembering the experience after-the-fact while pampering themselves on their last day at the all-inclusive resort.

The turnoff was an easy spot to miss, all this scabby desert land looking the same, and we were headed for an area that you couldn't punch into the dashboard GPS. We bounced along the dirt path for a while, as I studied the script that Salvador had delivered before dawn. He almost scared me to death looming bedside in the dark. "Mrs. Holden wanted you to have this," he said, putting the pages on the night table and leaving.

The service took the heat into account and, with me helming it, Isabella further trimmed it. But I wasn't ready to call it my own yet. The important thing I needed to remember was that I would be judged in reverse. Rather than rating me on how close I came to a Holden-style performance, I would be scored on how far from catastrophe I steered us. We believed the pilgrims would overlook whatever required overlooking, if it meant restoring them to livable conditions. What we weren't asking aloud, however (and I couldn't have been the only one thinking it), was what would happen should the heat cripple their patience and induce a fevered rage that they vented on me? For all my talk of their lacking the guts to call me out, I worried that my predictions were rooted in wishful thinking.

A white wooden shack, with a statue of Mary surrounded by flowers inside, materialized off the side of the road. A white wooden fence circled the shack and people were lined up near it. Because the site was predominantly associated with Catholics, our consort looked out of place. Just look at the people who were already there, setting up beach chairs and umbrellas and little tents of their own.

"A lot of Mexicans," I said.

"It's a good thing Rachel didn't hear you say that," Jelly chimed from the backseat. "I mean, how do you know they're Mexicans? Call them Latinos or don't call them anything."

"She's right," said the doctor.

"I am?" Jelly said, surprised by her salient point. "Well, yeah, like, no kidding I'm right. Alex, you just can't lump all the people here—"

"I get it. Look at all the Latinos."

There were vehicles parked in a makeshift, semi-organized lot: cars, vans, pickups, and one RV with its side door open, from where a group of women dressed as nuns (unless they were real nuns) floated down its steps, their white habits so bright against the day that they themselves resembled apparitions. Within seconds of filing out of the camper, their hems were covered in a fine patina of desert filth.

"They're so beautiful," Jelly said. She took a few photos of them with her phone. "When I was little I wanted to be a nun so bad. But then I found out that we were Presbyterian—I mean, like we used to be Presbyterian, then we were in this ministry, and I don't know what we are now. Anyway, that was that, no nun for this chick."

"I wanted to be a nun, too," Laura said, finding more common ground with un-nun-like Jill. "My family didn't like the subjugation of women in the Church and I was discouraged."

We drove past the wooden shack to our tent, a huge, circus-like construction that looked as if a mountain snowcap had been transplanted to sea level, strategically located a quarter of a mile away from the big show. It hadn't been Holden's intent to compete with them, but to funnel off some of the business, to get his name down avenues it didn't often travel, to record a fantastic new podcast, and, I suppose, to reward his wealthiest followers with an experience they wouldn't forget. Even in absentia, he had a very good shot of accomplishing most of his goals.

Isabella and her entourage were inside. My family was supposed to be here, but a text message from my mother informed me that Rachel slept poorly and greeted the morning in pain. It took forever, my mother's message said, getting her out of bed and cleaned up. *Not to worry. We'll be there in time :)*. I smiled because I was surprised she knew how to make a smiley face.

Ministry staff met the arriving vans and helped the members who stumbled out with hands shielding their eyes, or holding battery-powered fans whirling pitifully around their heads. They came into the tent nearly blind and spent a few minutes cooling down with water and slathering themselves in sunblock. The staff started handing out Polaroid cameras. Here was where Holden again demonstrated his genius. He gave away the cameras but collected offerings for the film, as only specially "blessed" film could record Mary's image.

"I'm going to say a few words to welcome them and then bring them over," Isabella said. She, with Salvador at her back, led the group out of the tent.

"You think they're screwing?" Laura said.

"It never occurred to me."

"I can't believe I'm about to get a pic of Mary!" Jelly said. She was bouncing on the balls of her feet, her well-formed, tanned calves flexing. With everything that had happened over the past few days, I forgot that she was religious. As much as she was here because of Rachel and me, she was also into the bigger cause.

Laura pulled me near the coolers. "Looks like we have a couple of minutes of downtime. I want to talk to you," she said, her eyes braziers of intent.

"Talk," I said.

"While you were with Rachel yesterday, I did a little investigating. I talked to Derrick and Jill. They told me about the accident."

As Laura rambled on, I dipped my hand into the cooler and tossed a few ice chips into my mouth, crunching loudly.

She said, "Then I talked to the paramedic, Joseph, very nice man, seventeen years on the job, because something didn't sit right with me. He said in this kind of accident, it's best for the driver to get tossed off. You don't want to get pinned underneath. You want to be thrown free, as long as you're wearing a helmet, like you're riding a mechanical bull. That's what happened to Rachel."

It was no surprise she would poke around. That she might have come to a conclusion consistent with the truth got my attention, however. I grabbed a bottle of water. "Thirsty?" I said, trying to veer her off course.

"No, thanks."

"What about you, Jelly? Want something to drink?" I yelled across the tent, holding up the bottle.

"I'm good. Trying not to pee out here. This girl I know was at the Grand Canyon and she popped a squat outside and a gecko or something jumped up her b-hole. So gross."

"Is she your girlfriend, by the way?" Laura said.

"Stop it."

"She's pretty, but her age is quite problematic."

"I said, stop it," I said.

"You don't expect me to believe Rachel is really in a body cast."

"Okay, I'm listening."

"I'd like to know what's going on."

I fell back on my instincts, my reflexive dismissal of her. "Why do you think you're entitled to anything?"

"I'm in on this," she said.

"In on what?"

"I'm an accomplice."

I laughed in her face. She had it coming. "An accomplice to what?"

"To whatever you're scheming."

She figured out what I did, not why, but she would have that shortly also. Soon everyone would know that Holden wasn't here. Laura didn't seem interested in busting me, though. I didn't know what she wanted, but whatever it was, it looked as if I was going to have to trust her, the author of *White Boy Bandito*. Talk about acts of faith.

"It isn't exactly the crime of the century," I said.

"Is it unethical?"

"Not more than usual."

"It's all right if you don't want to tell me. Just know I'm here to help because I like you."

I was afraid to ask how she wanted to help. "I'm pretty sure you don't like me."

"You know how sometimes you meet someone and he seems like a good guy, but over time you learn he's kind of a dick and his niceness is a front? You're the opposite of that."

It sounded as honest a compliment as she ever paid me, right down to her circuitous phrasing. I thanked her.

"Don't mention it. I'm your accomplice after all."

"Let's go see Mary, shall we?" I said, rushing out of the tent, leaving her and Jelly in my wake.

We wound our way along the dirt road where the other group had set up shop. The heat from the ground penetrated the rubber soles of my sneakers, and I realized I should have been wearing formal footwear. This, of all things, struck me as amateurish. I hustled to the front of our pack in time to see Isabella conferencing with one of the nun-looking women. She must have been important because Isabella had on her reverend's-wife face, that deferential palate of vacuity. She held both the woman's hands. Then they hugged. Isabella returned to us.

"Good morning, brothers and sisters. The moment is nearly upon us, but before then Sister Maria will be leading us in prayer. She's a very holy woman, with much to offer. Seek her out, should you desire, and listen to her heartfelt story."

The pilgrims resumed their sluggish shuffle, raising ankle-high dirt clouds, moving into position to hear this Maria woman. Compared to the other "nuns," Maria was the smallest. She was a brittle, old woman, her face sunken in its habit, but continually smiling. She might have been the genuine article were it not for her perfect teeth, a giveaway that she had skipped the vow of poverty.

Isabella hung back where I was standing. "She started this whole thing out here in '91, so you've got to give her credit for longevity."

"What's her game?"

"Same as the rest of us. I can't tell how much she believes, which means she's pretty good. But she never expanded outside of this dump. That says something also. The Catholic Church denies anything goes on out here. What does that tell you?"

"They don't like competition?"

"Really, I don't know what to make of her."

I was slick through the back of my shirt and a tributary of perspiration was running the length of my ass crack to form a gravity-defying pool under my scrotum. Who could argue that these visions in the sky were anything more than hallucinations induced by sunstroke, dehydration, and snake bites? "She doesn't care we're stepping on her toes?"

"That's another thing. She acts like she's happy we're here, but swears she's never heard of Warren."

"It's the west coast. Maybe she's doesn't know him."

Isabella gave me a look suggesting that if she considered me marginally more functional than a mongoloid, it had to do chiefly with my table manners. "Everyone who does what she does has heard of Warren."

"Is she coming to my service?"

"*My* service now, is it? I doubt it. It's a million degrees and my makeup is melting off my face, so I need to get back to the tent. Just tell me you're ready."

"You know it," I said.

She squinted up at the sun. "Miracles in the fucking sky. That's everything you need to know about Warren. The real miracle is if we get through this today." She left me.

I remained on the outskirts of our group, catching glimpses of Maria through gaps in the umbrellas and other improvised shades, her voice warbling out of a PA system so distorted I couldn't tell if she was speaking Spanish, Latin, or heavily accented English. Holden's people were courteous, some doing their best to pray along, even as I watched an attitude surface among many of them, a condescension born out of their entitlement.

One man whispered to his wife, "If English was good enough for Jesus Christ, it's good enough for me. And it should be good enough for her."

His wife rubbed his shoulder, supportive of, or placating, him. At any rate, she didn't disagree. I wished to tell them that if they were in fact better, it was only because they had a higher class of conman siphoning off their savings.

Maria made the sign of the cross in four directions and that was it. We disbanded in search of an unobstructed view of the sky, cameras poised, trigger fingers itching. Expectations had reached critical mass. Holden's pilgrims and Maria's followers began imprisoning the sky on Polaroid film, some staring idiotically at the sun itself, as if in worship of another deity altogether. The cameras belched out the square photographs, thus commencing the unbearable wait for the images to develop. Going against the method prescribed by the manufacturer, they hastened the process by shaking the photos, waving them around as if shooing an invisible fly.

Next they scrutinized the unalloyed likeness of that blue ceiling for a supernatural being and, of course, they found one. Jelly threw herself in my way. "Do you see? Do you see her, Alex? Do you see her?"

"I think so," I said, not having the heart to tell her the truth.

"She's right there." And so she must have been. Jelly described the picture as if I were blind. Mary was a beautiful young woman (who showed no wear and tear from what was unavoidably poor prenatal care,) appearing in form fitting robes of white, her arms slightly open at her sides in a gentle, inviting pose. "Look at her, look at her," encouraged Jelly. I massaged the back of my neck, where I could feel a sunburn starting.

Similar scenes popped up around us, a show-and-tell session, a claiming of bragging right. Who had the best photo? The clearest representation of Mary? Were those angels alighting on the sharp rays of sunlight? If so, I hoped they didn't snare their wings. Embarrassed as I am to admit it, I felt something like envy for the blob of overexposed color passing itself off as Jesus' mom. As much as anyone had ever liked me, unconditional love really took a beating when it bumped up against human imperfection. That was where Mary and her son had it made. Too bad for the living. Oh, well. *No hay remedio*, as Maria might have put it. Time had arrived to get ready for the service. Jelly hardly glanced up from the viewfinder when I said I was going.

In the tent I cooled off with two bottles of water. The stage was backed with Holden's customary thick blue curtains and behind these the production team was assembled. There was a makeshift dressing room in which I changed into a suit. No dress shoes—it really bothered me to step onstage with dust covered Nikes anchoring my ensemble. The air conditioning kept fogging up the dressing room mirror. I wiped off the condensation with my sleeve. My reflection showed an average looking white guy, maybe a notch below average without the suit. Sweaty hair slick on my forehead, pink half-moon stains under my eyes, I looked like someone who rejected your car loan application, not a receptacle of God's grace. I frowned at my face, knowing it wasn't good enough.

There was a knock on the accordion door. Dolores stuck her head in.

"There you are," she said.

"What if I wasn't decent?"

"You've got nothing I haven't seen before."

"You're a minx, Dolores. Who knew?"

"Keep it in your pants."

"Fair enough. What can I do for you?"

"Mrs. Holden wanted me to make sure you were here." She had the earpiece for me. She closed the accordion door behind her, arranged herself on a stool.

I fussed with my tie knot. A noise rose up from the front of the tent, on the other side of the blue curtains, a complaining human noise. "Sounds like everyone's back."

She fitted me with my earpiece through which Isabella would help me get past any hiccups in the service. "How are you feeling?"

"I don't know," I said.

"Do your best. That's all you can do." She left.

I listened to the commotion of other people taking their positions outside the dressing room and I knew I still had a few minutes until everyone and everything was in place. I enjoyed this time in a state of homespun meditation, fixing myself mentally, or attempting to, because while I'd watched Holden do this before I couldn't come close to approaching his lifelong expertise. If I understood his shtick in any way, it was on an intellectual, not kinesthetic, level, and great performances required a genius manipulation of the physical environment. The way he made the ten-thousand-seat arena feel like a living room was more or less unteachable. I repeated the advice, or maybe it wasn't advice but a statement of fact, that Isabella gave me in her room the night before: "You just need to get through it." Actually, I believe she said it in the plural, lumping us together, "*We* just need to get through it." Or maybe I confused her choice of preposition and what she really said was that we needed to get *over* it, as if she was suggesting an acceptance of some kind, the fifth Stage of Grief. I didn't know anymore what she said and my rumination was, in any event, at an end because it was quiet outside the dressing room. Another knock on the accordion door. It was time.

I stood at the bottom of three stairs at the back of the stage, gripping the two-by-four railing on either side. My pulse drummed in my ears, my throat, my fingertips, my toes. The Holden Ministry Orchestra launched without warning into its opening number, its familiar barrage of sound. Heroic and insistent, the music did for me what I was unable to do for myself, namely to put my adrenaline to good use. Holden's theme song pounded out of the speakers and, appropriating it as my own, I pushed up the stairs and through the opening in the curtains and came, for the second time in my life, face-to-face with his followers. Last time I was a bit player. Now I *was* Holden.

With the Klieg lights above and the dense carpet under my sneakered feet, the tent packed with bodies before me, Isabella and the production crew, unseen, behind me, indeed I felt an immediate rush, my senses elevated to redline levels, and the effect opened up a gap in my identity between who I was a minute earlier and who I was now, and the old me was scrambling fast to catch up to the newer version. Holden had a controlled intensity on stage, a slow burn, even when he jogged around and flew with outstretched arms. I was a yearling, lurching and halting as I tried to keep my legs under me, unleashing a power I had yet to govern. I didn't know what to do, so I did a little bit of everything: I strutted, pointed and marched, my head in wild oscillation, as if I couldn't find a spot to focus on. I spun around, I shadowboxed, I stripped off my suit jacket and helicoptered it over my head, then released it and kept moving, not watching where it landed. Sometimes I looked possessed by the Spirit; other times I looked like a shit-faced uncle dancing inappropriately at your wedding.

As the music faded and I located my place behind the pulpit, I noticed a considerable murmur from the audience. No doubt the confusion of seeing me, not their trusted reverend, was a disappointment akin to sitting in very expensive Broadway seats minutes before curtain and hearing a voice announce, "Tonight, the part of Hamlet will be played by Pauly Shore." This was not what they paid for.

The same people who had no problem seeing a holy image in a Polaroid strained to give me the benefit of the doubt, and maybe it was a mistake not to make the understudy announcement and warn them of a last-minute change in the program. No one guessed that Holden was, for all we knew, still holed up at Jackpot Joe's. Now they stared at me, as though through inspection alone they could solve the riddle of what I was doing there. *Aha!*, it came to them. I was the opening act. The warm-up band. *Of course.* They knew me. *The gun guy. The plant guy. With the sister who got hurt. Okay*, their revised look told me, *let's hear him out.*

I realized that when I tossed my jacket into the seats, my script, every word I was expected to say, went with it, folded up in the pocket. I scanned the shelf on the inside of the pulpit for a duplicate and, when I didn't see one, I searched the first few rows hoping to locate where my jacket had landed.

Isabella rang in over the earpiece, "Say something."

Her voice startled me, and I flinched as if snuck up upon, reflexively saying aloud, or what passed for aloud as my throat constricted in alarm, "What?", inadvertently beginning the service. My missing script was no longer of consequence because I had to continue without it. After all, I was wearing a tie and standing where someone more important usually stood.

"What," I repeated, "A. Day. What a day!" I slapped the podium for good measure and I'm not sure it conveyed the folksy charm I wanted. "What a day, indeed. What a special, holy, solemn, important . . . reverential . . . spiritual . . ." I was quickly running out of adjectives, "ah . . . holy—did I already say holy?—day! Miraculous day. That's what today is, am I right? I mean, how many of us witnessed a miracle today? I want to see hands."

The group participation trick worked. Hands shot up, many gripping the little miracle photographs as proof.

"That's wonderful," I said, my arm straight up in the air, a sweat stain flowering from my armpit, because I too was a miracle witness.

Isabella said to me, "What do you think you are doing?"

I answered her by way of communicating to everyone, "I am feeling the Spirit today, *unscripted!*"

Over the earpiece I heard a clatter and then a defeated, "Oh, no."

I walked away from the pulpit trying to find a cool spot to stand under and to decide how to proceed. If I hadn't memorized the script, I'd absorbed the gist of it. Perhaps a decent amount of it nestled into my subconscious, a wish not much different from a college student who sleeps with his text books under his pillow in the belief that he might sop up the curriculum through osmosis.

"So why are we here today?" I was paraphrasing the top of the second page because if I remembered correctly, the first page was a greeting and introduction and we were past that point. I started understanding the importance of transitions. They were essential in sustaining momentum, and insuring that everyone followed you as you covered many miles of thought. A deft transition could link illogical ideas. I was failing in this respect but, so far, my herky-jerky non sequiturs didn't seem to be leaving many in the dust. It was still early though.

"Are we here because we need a suntan?" I said, verbatim from the script. Holden would have killed with this line, but I nailed the delivery and they loosened up. "No, it's not because we need a little sun. Judging by what I see, most of us got quite a lot out there. We are here today to forge a deeper relationship with our Lord, and Savior, Jesus Christ, say Amen."

When they said Amen, Isabella came back on, "A rocky start, but we're moving now. If you need a line or help just say, 'Praise God.' Say 'Amen' again if you understand."

"Amen," I said again and the congregation gave it back to me. "You know, we've had a lot of fun these last few days. It's been a time to rejoice and say thanks. It's been a time to reconnect with our families, to slow down and reflect on our fast paced lives. But it hasn't been a vacation. Through Reverend Holden's stewardship we have been mindful of our faith."

The pilgrims assented with nods and smiles. I kept going. "Our true purpose here in the desert is to spread His word."

Isabella fed me the next line, "For as it is written in the Book of Matthew, 'Go, and make disciples of all nations, baptizing them in the name of the Father and of the Son and of the Holy Spirit, teaching them to observe all things which I commanded you.'"

When I quoted Scripture my voice started fading in and out of a gravelly and boisterous affectation, a caricature of a Confederate general. I don't know why this happened, I didn't do it deliberately, but I couldn't control it either.

"Excuse me, Foghorn Leghorn, you can stop that right now," Isabella said.

If she was aware of it, other people were aware of it. I tried talking in my normal voice and sounded as though I was pronouncing a language I didn't understand. "Lord God has commanded us to spread His word and, like the good Christians we are, that is exactly what we are doing."

"Okay, we're going to skip ahead to the sermon. Just try to talk like a human being. Less is more. Get to the pulpit," Isabella said.

I danced over to where she wanted me, a conga line of one.

"Repeat after me," she said. "Chapter 33, verse 14, in Exodus says,"

I parroted her, "My presence will go with you and I will give you rest."

It was a continuation of the theme that, as pilgrims, we were to be God's PR team, deliver his talking points and, for this work, He would reward us. It was the same old story, over and over, the single narrative of the Holden Ministry: serve the Lord and he'll give you all the loony crap you could dream up, but you have to go through the ministry—we're brokering this deal after all—because you have to be vetted first and we're the clearing-house on that end. They were conditioned to hearing it and it didn't matter if I or Holden told them. Provided someone rang the bell reminding them they were the beneficiaries of God's fortune, they would, Pavlovian Christians, drool for it. In my sermon I remind them once more that they could have it all—money, health, love, happiness (but mostly money)—and they were reassured and prayed with me.

I thought I was getting the hang of it. Isabella agreed. "I think you're getting the hang of it. Let's bring it in for a landing."

Here our plans diverged. At the back of the tent I saw my parents, each with a hand on the wheelchair, push Rachel closer.

Rachel! How sweaty and uncomfortable in those casts. I really wished I could have fixed her broken wrist. She'd learned her lesson, wouldn't be climbing atop motorized toys with a few drinks under her belt in the foreseeable future. She'd been as scared as anyone, more so probably, as it was her first brush with the unfair truth that she wouldn't live forever. The feeling was sure to dissipate and in no time she should find her immortality right back where it always was, until she was older, my age for example, a lousy example because I was still only slightly convinced that I could die.

Now I ran around, building up anticipation for the big reveal, pumping up the crowd, duck walking like an old Japanese man doing his Eastern calisthenics, jumping in the air, fists flying, recycling every bit of rock star choreography I could remember. I said, nearly out of breath, "And now, what you've been waiting for, the moment of truth. Are there sufferers out there? Anyone in pain? Jesus gonna make the pain go bye-bye."

Isabella cursed me with furious and inventive slurs, broke objects in the background. I pulled out the earpiece. She had to hold out hope that Warren would return in a day or two and get back to business, and if some dipshit started healing people then maybe the Holden Ministry wasn't the gatekeeper to the Lord's vast treasures. Maybe you could get there on your own. I worried she would kill the lights, claim technical difficulties, shut down the show before I got started, but maybe she felt like a swimmer in the riptide, finding herself worse off the harder she fought it. More likely, she assumed I was going to fail in a big way and further illustrate Holden's great power in the process.

A rabble of unaffiliated pilgrims had been milling around outside, drawn by the music and cheering. When they heard about the healing, a bum's rush erupted at the mouth of the tent. They poured in, finding room wherever they could.

"Brothers and sisters. All are welcome. Please step forward," I said. I'm positive I didn't say, "Shove your way to the front," but that was what they did. "Be gentle to one another," I urged, my voice again straining, ragged.

On the whole, the service itself had turned ragged. Holden was a brutally efficient ringleader. If things ever seemed out of control, it was because he wanted them to look that way. This service I helmed wasn't sham shambolic; it was a genuine fucking mess. It stunk, literally, I now noticed, our body odor rising to the tent ceiling where it was trapped, and then drifted back down again, a cascading funk returning to its restless source.

"Last night I was beside myself," I said. "As many have heard, my sister was maimed in an ATV accident. I know y'all," (Author's note: y'all?), "prayed for her and, my family and I, we thank you for that. Last night I was so worried about her and I worried that her accident came about because I wasn't a good enough man and that my sins had somehow brought a punishment down upon her. Well, what could I do? I'll tell you, I got down on my knees," I said, and I kneeled to show them. "I beseeched the Lord to stamp out my wickedness and help me onto the righteous path. For hours, I was on my knees, deep in prayer. Right before dawn, He came to me. Jesus said that Reverend Holden was needed by people less fortunate than ourselves, the Kawaiisu Tribe of Tejon Indian Reservation. The Lord told me that in the reverend's stead would go I. Then I heard Reverend Holden's voice. 'Son,' he said, 'today, you do the healing.' I was dumbstruck. How could I, a sinner, work miracles like our Reverend? But he told me to put my faith in the Lord. So that's what I'm going to do. Who has pain?"

A small unkempt man close to the stage motioned for my attention. I waved him to me. It was a gamble. I had to cure without prior intel, without Isabella feeding me the disorders. What if he wanted me to bring his wife back from the dead? The schlub joined me on stage and I found out what was bothering him. In short order I cured him of the pain brought on by ingrown toenails. The ushers had been instructed that there was no healing today, so they weren't onstage when I forced the issue and, running from ten feet away, dropped the toenail guy with a forearm to his jaw, screaming, "I heal thee!" (thee was a nice touch, I thought). The man crashed to the floor.

Next I handled a woman's chronic dry mouth with a karate chop to the center of her head, using the part in her hair as a landing strip (once healed, she kept drooling like a rabid dog). I eradicated another woman's tennis elbow, which she aggravated by excessive play at the ranch (talk about having your cake and eating it), by kicking her in the chest. In my penultimate act as lordly physician, I erased a knot of scar tissue and vacuumed up the bone spurs in some guy's ankle (something about falling down stairs at work).

Rachel and my parents looked for a clear path to the stage, while the guy with the bone spurs started shaking his leg for everyone to take a gander at his improved ankle.

"Thank you. Thank you, Reverend Holden," he said.

I was tempted to shove him off the stage. I was no substitute teacher puppeting the lesson left by the ailing instructor. This was all me, baby! I was healing in conditions a hell of a lot tougher than the Arena. I turned away from this ingrate and couldn't wait for his pain to reappear, returning, I hoped, when he was buckled into his seat on the flight home with nowhere to stretch his legs for six hours. "Good riddance," I said, as he hopped off the stage, and then, waiting a beat, added, "to the demon bone spurs and scar tissue. Be gone! Satan, be gone!"

I strutted some more to demonstrate my disrespect for all things Satanic, inciting my flock to carry on cries of "Be gone, Satan!" There was a connection to be made between this sort of mob mentality and the kind prone to prison riots. Given more time I might have parsed it out, but I had my masterpiece waiting for me. I needed Rachel on stage immediately, my window to glory closing around me. I brought myself under control. I said, "Dear Lord, please give me the strength for one more. Please heal my sister." I commanded the sweat-laden pilgrims to move aside.

They parted wordlessly so that I heard the squeak of the wheelchair's rubber wheels against the wooden plank running up the aisle. Rachel was made up and wearing a dress of local thrift store provenance, her legs splayed in stirrups, pink casts on her four appendages, right arm in a sling. I faltered for an instant because she looked very much like I had imagined when I first heard she was in the hospital. I'd brought my fears to life.

Two pilgrims helped my father lift the chair onstage. I asked Rachel, off-mic, if she was ready. Her eyes acquiesced and I leapt up and pivoted to the back of the chair, shoved her recklessly across the stage, forcing sudden turns that put her on one wheel, a holy-roller coaster. She screamed for me to stop and I yelled, "Stop your pain? Stop your suffering? Is that what you want?"

Rachel and I puttered to a stop at center stage, as if we had run out of gas. I said I needed them to help me through this. "With your help, brothers and sister, I'm going to mend these broken bones."

Total goddamn pandemonium. Shouting in the holiness, hysterical hollering, tears rolling down faces, clapping to no end. Standing room only in the big tent.

I fell to one knee, hand outstretched, palm up, and my father sprang into action, handing me a hacksaw (as if by luck he just so happened to have one. What were the odds?), presenting it to me like he was Unferth and I Beowulf. I'd wanted one of those electric cast cutters that doctors use, but this was a better substitute actually, sawing through the casts was grander theater. I brandished the hacksaw and said to Rachel, "My sister, do you give your life to our Savior?"

She was crying real tears and sniffled, "Yes."

"I'm sorry, but that's not enough. Do you pledge your life to Him."

"Of course I do," Rachel cried.

I got to work. My sweat-slick hands hardly kept hold of the saw and her cast was unyielding. The blade eventually found purchase and I cut a divot, working it back and forth, breaking through to the gauzy wrap.

Rachel's tears dried. She was terrified I was going to saw into her. "Careful," she begged.

I took it easy to avoid cutting her. When I was through, I held the cast in both hands and cracked it in half against my knee. I tore at it until I could yank the narrowest part over her hand, the section nearest her elbow being wide enough to slide off. I ordered her to raise her castless arm. "How does it feel?"

"Amazing," she said on cue.

Turning my attention to her legs, I worked frantically with the hacksaw. I realized early on that getting those off her would take more time than I had, so I sawed them into separate pieces at the knee. I gave her joints. "Are you ready to walk again?"

"Yes," she said.

I laid my hands on her head and ordered her to "Heal!" I walked to the back of the wheel chair and yanked it away. She wobbled, found her balance, stood firm, wobbled again. I took her hand and, with my help, she staggered along the length of the stage. The hundreds of people before us had yet to reconcile what they were seeing when the ushers set upon them with the offering buckets.

March, 2008

This is my final dispatch from behind bars. I have just over eighteen days until my release (Hallelujah!), where I'll be taking with me the skills I've acquired as a guest of our government—how to wash dishes, how to mop floors, how to build a tattoo gun out of a gel pen, the motor of a CD player, the spring from a stapler, and a toothbrush. Thus armed for life as a law-abiding citizen, I'll make a quick pit stop at Wolf Manor to charge my batteries, and then, with a little luck (alright, a lot of luck), on to bigger and better.

I know I don't have much going for me, but I'm optimistic. Is it strange that I feel this way? It feels strange to me. I'm accustomed to its opposite and sometimes I don't think I have the make up to support such an emotion for the long run. I need to build up my stamina in this department. I expect you guys are already there, doing sanguine interval training, hopeful plyometrics. When I was sentenced, Martin Skolnick told me that prison would suck but the crisis was over. I could begin making preparations for a new life. It was hard to listen to him at the time because I hadn't even started my bid. It just seemed impossible. Anyway, knowing myself the way I do, I probably won't say this to you face-to-face, so let me write it now. Thank you for letting me come home, for taking me back. It might just be the euphoria of knowing that in less than 3 weeks I'll have the privacy to masturbate freely, but I'm starting to think that maybe Martin was right after all and I'm not doomed. I hope he was right. More than that though, I think WE are going to be fine. I'm looking forward to seeing you and putting these problems I've caused behind us forever. A normal, peaceful, boring life sounds great right about now.

Love,

Alex

THIRTY

Holden called the day after Thanksgiving. I picked up. What can I say? Curiosity won out.

"Season's greetings," I said.

"Luke 1:23."

"Whatever that means."

"It means get over here."

"Where? 123 Luke Ave.?" I said.

"'And it came to pass that as soon as the days of his ministration were accomplished, he departed to his own house,'" he said.

"When did you get back?"

"As if you don't know," and he hung up.

It was true that, while the last time I saw him was in the desert, I knew he was back. I hadn't quit his world cold turkey and I'd snuck peeks at holdenministry.org. He was gone a total of three days and now, months later, the event had entered into ministry lore as though he planned it that way all along. It helped that Isabella and her staff issued a statement, confirming my onstage story that Holden had been called away on a mission of immeasurable importance (they edited out the part, where I said he went to help the Kawaiisu Tribe, possibly because it could be verified,) and we should be grateful that he possessed such a surplus of God's love that he was able to loan some of it to me. The commenters on the message boards were hypervigilant reporting rumors, gossip, and conspiracy theories regarding the mission. A few did mention the Tejon Indian Reservation, but were roundly rebuffed. The prevailing hypothesis involved Edwards Air Force Base. Depending on one's brand of paranoia, either Holden was brought in to consult on an unexplainable celestial event purportedly witnessed by two pilots, or that he was questioned by federal officials at the behest of our tyrannical government in a highly organized, albeit Top Secret, campaign to intimidate the great man from persevering in his vital work. That I disappeared from the ministry immediately after the service fueled speculation over the latter.

Why did I go visit Holden? There was no easy answer. Maybe I wanted to prove that the concept of closure is a joke. Maybe I wanted to ask him about healing the snotty little girl. Maybe I was looking for the only critique of my performance that mattered. Or maybe because it was Black Friday and I've never been much of a shopper and I had some time to kill. Whatever my reasons, I drove to his house. As always with him, I was unsure of the situation I was entering.

Isabella greeted me on the front step in a manner far different from the one in which she last said goodbye. She seemed glad to see me and acted as if I hadn't done anything to make her hate me.

"Alex," she said. She placed her hands on my shoulders and fixed her eyes on mine. "How have you been?"

"About the same."

"I'm so sorry to hear that." She kissed me on the cheek. "Warren's out by the lake. You know the way?"

There was a breeze off of the mountains and, though Holden stood under clear skies, it was overcast in the long distance. On a crisp late-fall day like today, the view was so out of proportion to the rest of my life that by staring at it long enough, it was easy to forget the things Holden had done to attain it. I joined him at the edge of the water.

"There you are," he said, like he'd been searching for me. "Did you see Isabella? She was happy when I told her you were coming."

"I don't think she likes me."

"Why do you think that?" he said.

"At the airport in Mojave she said, 'I don't like you.'"

This took place on the tarmac. She shook my hand, told me she didn't like me and that I'd turned her life's work into pro-wrestling. She forked over my cut of the money from the service and my severance, stacked neatly in a leather cash bag with a thick metal zipper, and boarded the jet. As furious as I'd made her, she had the presence of mind to approve the severance deal, the terms of which prevented me from striking out on my own as a preacher. I was out of the ministry, forever. She couldn't have known that nothing made me happier.

"She likes you just fine," Holden said. "I'm the one you should have worried about. When I was flying back here, all I was thinking about was how I was going to kill you."

"I'm flattered."

"The method of your execution kept me going for a while, but there were other considerations. How was I going to dispose of your body? Would I have to kill Isabella for letting you betray me? Was I prepared to be a single father? All these thoughts. Then I saw the video of the service. What a joke."

In a way I was glad he was still a complete fucking lunatic. I didn't know how I would have reacted to a different man wearing his clothes.

"What made you change your mind?" I said.

"About killing you?"

"About coming home."

A pilgrim succeeded where Isabella's security team failed. Holden told me that on his third day of desertion, he was recognized at Jackpot Joe's by a drunk and suicidal man who recently finished losing to the casino everything he hadn't tithed to the ministry. The man trusted that Holden was there to save him and that his grand series of mistakes wasn't his final ruin. At the casino bar, the man ordered a pair of bloody Marys, the vaguely religious connotation of the cocktail the kind of deference to Holden a drunken man would make. I pictured Holden sipping the drink and thinking it revolting, as he preferred his vodka without mixers. The pilgrim said he saw me heal Rachel.

"That was the first time I heard what you did. And if I'm being honest with you, Alex, it was the first time it occurred to me that my ministry was anything more than an appendage of my willpower, able to exist without me. This stumblebum said he saw the whole thing and was once again baffled and humbled by everything in the universe he didn't understand. After hearing him out, so was I."

Holden chartered a jet that day. He and the pilgrim flew east, both on a mission to reclaim their lives.

His story sounded true enough. "You've got to admit it was pretty clever," I said.

He laughed out loud. In profile his eyes looked closed but I knew they were just those scary little slits and he could see perfectly from them. "Nothing to build a career on. Anyway, do you know why I wanted to see you?"

"If it wasn't to kill me then I'm not sure."

"First I want to know what you've been doing with yourself."

"As if you don't know."

"That's my line," he said. "But, yes, I've heard things. I want to hear it from you."

"I went to L.A. with Laura Sullivan. We made a few appearances together."

I didn't tell him that this was the bargain I made with her in exchange for editorial supervision on her sequel.

"Then what?" Holden said.

"We played house for a few weeks and plotted my ascension to guru-like status in the life-coaching business."

I had no real feelings for her, but I arrived at her home without a fight so there must have been something natural about the arrangement that prevented me from thinking too hard about it. In other words, I was blinded by steady sex and the fact that I wasn't sleeping in my childhood bedroom.

"And now I'm home," I said.

"I feel like that's not the whole story," he said.

He was right. I didn't tell him that one night while Laura was unloading the dishwasher, I found on her computer the book proposal she was working on.

> *Bestselling author, Dr. Laura Sullivan, PhD., is back with a follow up to her unforgettable debut,* White Boy Bandito. *In* The Preacher Con, *she takes a fascinating Where-Are-They-Now look at one of America's most memorable criminals, Alexander Wolf. Upon his release from prison for arms smuggling, Wolf, still furious at the system that put him behind bars, sets in motion a diabolical scheme that threatens to corrupt his family, ruin a religious institution, and destroy the life of an influential reverend, all while making himself a fortune.*

A chapter outline followed. None of it resembled the story she and I brainstormed. So much for my accomplice. The worst part of finding it was that it caught me off guard when I should have known better. I sat at her desk for a few minutes, feeling as if I was coming down with a cold. My mouth went dry and my body was achy. Laura was stacking salad bowls when I highlighted the document and pushed delete before hitting Command-S and walking away from her West Hollywood house.

"You know how it is," I said. "These things don't always work out."

"And the Crown of Thorns?"

"The economy just collapsed. What did you expect?"

"Did you and your family bail out?"

"Pretty much."

My payout from Isabella yielded us enough profit to further pay down our debts, close to breaking even. But when cell phone videos of the healing went viral, sales exploded. For the first time in years, my family had savings. I had to imagine it didn't hurt the Holden Ministry's coffers either. That was the thing Isabella would never confess: It was easy to make a clean split with me because the service had been a triumph. The pilgrims had a selective and forgiving memory, dismissing my flubs and gaffes and remembering only my healing of Rachel. By the end of September, however, our entire business fell apart. With the stock market cleaved in half, the Holy Houseplant showed its obsolescence.

"What's your next move?" Holden squatted and flicked stones into the water.

"I'm not sure. Maybe I'll write a book."

"Memoir: the last refuge of the narcissist. Even I never stooped that low."

"You have a better idea?"

"I'll never understand why you ask such stupid questions."

He was investing in new ventures, ones straddling the faith-based and secular worlds. "It's a veritable infestation of new prospects," he declared. These uncertain times were lousy with opportunities. "I've tunneled as deep into this thing as I can," he said. "Time to turn the machinery outward."

By outward he meant pop culture—movie and music and television and video game production.

"If this recession gets as bad as I think it will, people will be looking for distractions from their problems even more than usual. Entertainment. They will also be looking for someone to answer their prayers. I am going to do both. Are you with me?"

"Your wife banned me from the ministry."

"Rightly so."

"That settles it," I said.

"Since when do you decide that things are settled? I want you to head up the new company. I'm talking executive status."

He must have already known that, following the service in the desert, a slew of offers came my way. The radio show was in a local market not far from the site of my miracle, with no chance of syndication, and I turned it down, along with sundry endorsement deals tossed my way for bottom-feeding Christian products and festivals. A chance to star in a direct-to-DVD movie about a futuristic society in which leaders in the fields of science and technology have finally succeeded in passing an amendment to the Constitution outlawing Christianity, thus hastening the start of End Times? Well, thank you but no thank you. No, I understand I would play the part of the underground renegade who would rather die than publicly denounce his faith, but all the same, I'm going to have to pass.

Fun fact: there are agents who specialize in booking Christian entertainers. I hesitate to mention that they, like most other kinds of agents, are Jewish.

Of course, none of the people who contacted me was the Reverend Warren Holden, none had launched my product for me, none had acted as a boss and an advisor and a cautionary tale. None had the preternatural magnetism of the man standing in front of me, bouncing on the balls of his feet and breathing audibly through his nose, so that I believed his throbbing energy was somehow generating the wind that blew his hair straight back and that, at any moment, he could rechannel it in whichever direction he wanted.

Still, I turned him down and it had nothing to do with being afraid of him shifting that wind on me. "I don't think that's a good idea," I said.

"I'd be concerned if you thought it was a wonderful idea. Your instincts are a little fucked, if you don't mind me saying."

"At any rate, I'm out."

"Perhaps you don't understand what I'm proposing."

Without hearing the details, I understood exactly what he was proposing. There was no other way to interpret his offer. He saw my ethical fluidity as a quality to hone. Rather than a source of shame or the cause of all of my problems, it was what set me apart. The interesting thing was that I wasn't ready to say he was wrong. People don't get to pick their talents and I believed it was important to develop what you were given because it was all you had. What seemed wrong was my thoughtless deferral to that side of me, as if it was better simply because it came easiest.

"Warren, I'm not going to say thank you for everything you've done for me, but I realize it wouldn't have happened without you."

Holden made no plea to keep me from leaving, didn't even berate me for old time's sake. The interesting thing was that I was a little disappointed.

Home, my parents were huddled together at the oak dining room table, coffee mugs and a laptop between them.

"Hi, Alex," my mother said.

"Hey," I said. "What are you guys working on?"

"Work. What else?" said my father, but not like it was his punishment. He had that look he sometimes got, like when he first told me about his OBESE PEOPLE Post-it note, when his eyes grew wide because his mind was working fast enough to process more visual stimuli than usual. It was probably the same look he had in the last few seconds before a horse race.

As soon as we returned from the desert, my parents embarked on their riskiest partnership since their wedding day. They began providing nurse staffing services and distributing a line of home accoutrements to ease the process of protracted death. Ours was an aging society and its eldest members were achieving disturbing longevity. As seniors' health declined and their standard of living became harder to maintain, they required supplementary products and amenities to survive. That was where my parents came in. Mortality, it turned out, was a recession-proof industry. It was a venture that suited both their personalities. My mother pivoted facilely from the poor to the old and she coupled her vast knowledge of professional good-doing with my father's ability to sell. Although their business was still in its infancy, and our economy stood helplessly shell-shocked, my parents were just starting to eke out a niche for themselves.

"How was he?" my mother said.

"Holden? The same, I guess."

"What did he want?"

"Just to say hi. Season's greetings and all that."

"Are you sure that's all?"

"It's okay, Mom, you don't have to worry."

"I'm your mother. I always have to worry."

"Really, you don't have to worry about me anymore."

She was right, though. Whether or not I needed or deserved it, she was going to continue worrying about me. So would my father. And I would worry about them. It wasn't a bad thing to know and keep tucked away, something to pull out and use when necessary, because knowing that their concern was never going away was both happy and sad making, like being strong and weak at once, and could counteract the effects of the world spinning me too far in any one direction.

I let them get back to work. I heated a plate of leftover Thanksgiving food and took it with a beer up to my room. It looked like it was going to remain my room for the time being. Down the hall, Rachel and Jelly were laughing and screaming and maybe dancing, as the floors shook under their stomping. Good for them. They deserved to relax. Rachel applied for early decision to a private East Coast university once attended by the son of an assassinated president and her verdict was imminent. The personal essay that accompanied her application documented the upheaval wrought by my coming home after prison, proving that Laura Sullivan wasn't the only one willing to sacrifice our privacy upon the altar of literature (or something less pretentious), though Rachel's motives were also defensive, a method of explaining away potential question marks that might have attached themselves to her name.

Jelly didn't need Rachel to tell her that the healing was staged, all of them prearranged, and that Holden wasn't a great man, but only a man. Then, after losing her role model, her parents split up, which was the real reason they quit the ministry. Holden had counseled them to stay together. Perhaps he understood that the expense of a divorce would cut into their offerings and seed gifts. On the upside, Jelly found a boyfriend her own age and therefore decided that I was just her best friend's creepy older brother. But on the occasions our paths crossed, we still shared a sarcastic, telepathic accord.

Eight months ago I left Otisville for a more confining environment. It would be nice for me to say that things worked out all right, but to do so would mean ignoring the frantic daily scramble that almost undid us. It would gloss over how very bad our situation was and how close we came to failing. When I let the undiluted facts settle over me, they hurt me in small places. Yes, we bailed out. But that was luck. Luck! What else could I call it? We were lucky.

I still had that vision of personal greatness, where my importance developed into a full-time vocation of its own. I was youngish and willing. *Able* had always been and remained unresolved. As for the specifics of my next move, I hadn't decided, though I'd reached the point where maybe it was no longer best to think of my life as a series of moves, as in gambits. But in the event I was too hardheaded to give up on ploys altogether, I hoped I could finally see my most advantageous tactic was to stop treating each sunrise as a fresh opportunity to manipulate and maneuver my way to a lusher sunset. If I'd learned anything, it was that I needed to balance the desire to follow my impulses with the desire to stay out of trouble.

Then there was a third desire: not to disgrace myself any longer. A modest aspiration, I thought, but the one capable of saving me.

About the Author

Photo by Shannon Aubourg

Aaron Jacobs' short stories have appeared in a number of literary journals including Alaska Quarterly Review, JMWW, The MacGuffin, and Atticus Review. He lives with his girlfriend and dog in Brooklyn and the Catskills. *The Abundant Life* is his first novel.

www.ingramcontent.com/pod-product-compliance
Lightning Source LLC
Chambersburg PA
CBHW030430010526
44118CB00011B/575